THE NEW MEDITERRANEAN DEMOCRACIES: REGIME TRANSITION IN SPAIN, GREECE AND PORTUGAL

THE NEW MEDITERRANEAN DEMOCRACIES: REGIME TRANSITION IN SPAIN, GREECE AND PORTUGAL

Edited by
Geoffrey Pridham

FRANK CASS

First published in 1984 in Great Britain by
FRANK CASS AND COMPANY LIMITED
Gainsborough House, 11 Gainsborough Road,
London, E11 1RS

and in the United States of America by
FRANK CASS AND COMPANY LIMITED
c/o Biblio Distribution Centre
81 Adams Drive, P.O. Box 327, Totowa, NJ 07511

British Library Cataloguing in Publication Data

The New Mediterranean democracies.
  1. Spain—History—1975—   2. Portugal
  —History—1974—   3. Greece—History
  —1974—
  I. Pridham, Geoffrey
  946.083   DP272

ISBN 0-7146-3244-9

This group of studies first appeared in a Special Issue on 'The New Mediterranean Democracies: Regime Transition in Spain, Greece and Portugal' of *West European Politics*, Vol. 7, No. 2, published by Frank Cass and Co. Ltd.

Printing by Adlard & Son Ltd, Dorking, Surrey

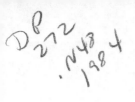

Contents

List of Tables and Figures

Notes on the Contributors

Thomas C. Bruneau is Professor of Political Science at McGill University in Montreal. In 1983 he was the Senior Program Associate at the Latin American Program of the Woodrow Wilson International Center for Scholars, Washington, D.C. He has been researching in Portugal since 1973 and has published a dozen scholarly articles and co-authored one book. His *Politics and Nationhood: Post-Revolutionary Portugal* was published by Praeger in January 1984. With Alex Macleod, he is currently conducting a large research project on politics in Portugal ten years after the revolution on 25 April 1974.

Mario Caciagli is Professor of Political Sociology at the Faculty of Political Sciences, University of Catania. He has authored and edited many publications in the area of parties and elections in Italy, West Germany and Spain, such as *Democrazia cristiana e potere nel Mezzogiorno* (1977) *Il voto di chi non vota* (with P. Scaramozzino) (1983) and *Elezioni e partiti nella Spagna postfranchista* (forthcoming).

P. Nikiforos Diamandouros is Staff Associate responsible for Western Europe and the Near and Middle East at the Social Science Research Council (USA). His most recent publications include 'La transición del autoritarismo a la democracia en Grecia,' in Julian Santamaria (ed.) *La transición a la democracia en el sur de Europa y América Latina* (Madrid: CIS, 1982); *Southern Europe: An Introductory Bibliographical Essay,* (Glasgow: Centre for the Study of Public Policy, University of Strathclyde, 1980); and 'Greek Political Culture: Historical Origins, Evolution, Current Trends,' in Richard Clogg (ed.), *Greece in the 1980s,* (London: Macmillan, 1983).

Salvador Giner is Reader in Sociology and Head of the Sociology Department, Brunel University, London. His interest in social theory is reflected in a number of books (such as *Mass Society,* 1975) and general essays on corporatism, inequality and the history of social thought. His empirical work concentrates on the comparative study of European social structures, with special attention to southern Europe. He is the co-editor and co-author of two companion volumes on *Contemporary Europe* (1971 and 1979), one short book on *The Social Structure of Catalonia* (second, revised edition 1984), a comparative study of the political economy of southern Europe (1980, and various later revisions), and several studies on the social structure and politics of contemporary Spain.

James R. Lewis is Lecturer in Geography at Durham University. His research interests are in the area of development and uneven regional development, and he has fieldwork experience in southern Europe, eastern Africa and Indonesia. He has co-edited with Ray Hudson the following books: *Regions in Crisis* (1980), *Regional Planning in Europe* (1982) and *Accumulation, Class and the State in Southern Europe* (1984).

Christos Lyrintzis has been a postgraduate student at the London School of Economics. The title of his Ph.D. thesis is: 'Between Socialism and Populism: the rise of the Panhellenic Socialist Movement'.

Kenneth Medhurst is Professor of Political Studies at the University of Stirling. His publications include *Government in Spain* (1973), *The Basques and Catalans*, report for the Minority Rights Group (1977) and *The Catholic Church and Labour in Colombia* (1984). He is also preparing books on *Contemporary Spanish Politics*, *The Catholic Church and Politics in Latin America* and *The Church and Politics in a Secular Age* (with George Moyser).

Giuseppe Di Palma is professor and chairman, Department of Political Science, University of California, Berkeley. In the last few years he has been working on regime changes and the problem of regime performance in post-dictatorial democracies. References to relevant publications are found in his contribution to this issue.

Geoffrey Pridham is Reader in European Politics at Bristol University. His works include *Christian Democracy in Western Germany* (1977), *Transnational Party Cooperation and European Integration* (1981) and *The Nature of the Italian Party System: a regional case-study* (1981). He is currently doing comparative work on coalitional behaviour in western Europe, and is writing a book on *Political Parties and Coalitional Behaviour in Italy: an interpretative study.*

Alfred Tovias has been a Lecturer in International Relations, both at the Hebrew University in Jerusalem since 1979 and at Tel Aviv University since 1981. Born in Barcelona, Spain, he studied at the University there before transfering to the University of Geneva. He obtained his doctorate at Geneva and later was appointed Lecturer in Economics. Dr Tovias is the author of *Théorie et Pratique des Accords Commerciaux Préférentiels* (1974), *Tariff Preferences in Mediterranean Diplomacy* (1977) and co-author with R. Arad and S. Hirsch of *The Economics of Peace-Making* (1983). He has contributed numerous articles to different academic journals, among others on the Second EEC Enlargement.

Allan M. Williams is Lecturer in Geography at Exeter University. His research interests are in the area of uneven urban and regional development in southern Europe, and he has undertaken extensive fieldwork in Portugal. He is editor of *Southern Europe Transformed* (1984), and co-author with David R. Phillips of *Rural Britain: A Social Geography* (1984) and of *Rural Housing and the Public Sector* (1983).

Comparative Perspectives on the New Mediterranean Democracies: A Model of Regime Transition?

Geoffrey Pridham

STUDYING NEW REGIMES: THE HISTORICAL DIMENSION

Both the obvious similarity of their respective regime transitions from authoritarianism to democracy and the mere contemporaneousness of this process in Spain, Greece and Portugal during 1974–5 invite comparison. One might add – again, to state the obvious – that the common situation of these countries in the Mediterranean area considerably reinforces the argument for treating them together as a compact case-study of regime transition.

History and geography have therefore combined to present the kind of classic example of what Dankwart Rustow no doubt had in mind, when he introduced a theory of transition to democracy before these particular national instances arose: 'A model or ideal type of the transition may be derived from a close examination of two or three empirical cases and tested by application to the rest'.[1] Not surprisingly, academic interest in the study of regime transition has been attracted and enhanced by recent political developments in these three countries, although so far little real comparative work on them has been done.[2] One such study opened with this compelling statement:

> The truth is that it is not easy to find such an accumulation of changes of régime within a relatively homogeneous cultural area, and in so short an historical period. And, in the same way, the opportunity rarely occurs for studying in such a living way that central theme of political science which is political change.[3]

Indeed, the argument is strong for considering these similar and contemporaneous versions of transition to democracy as constituting a Mediterranean case-study. This is facilitated by the disciplinary relationship between area studies and comparative politics with its explanatory advantages. In a note on this subject, Macridis and Cox pointed out that 'one approach to the study of comparative politics is the more systematic and precise use of the area concept'. They meant that the concept of area had previously been employed somewhat indiscriminately, associating it with geographical, historical, economic and cultural similarities, either separately or in combination. For them, such similarities did not constitute '*prima facie* evidence of the existence of similar political characteristics'; hence, 'if the concept of an area is to be operationally meaningful for the purpose of comparison, it should correspond to some uniform political patterns against which differences may be studied comparatively and explained'.[4] Implicitly, therefore, since western Europe as a whole is normally viewed as one of the 'world areas', this reasoning holds even more firmly for any sub-area such as Mediterranean Europe.

There are even those who view the homogeneity of this sub-area as having deeper historical roots than suggested so far. In a bibliographical essay on modern southern Europe, Nikiforos Diamandouros commented:

> The states and societies of Southern Europe ... present sufficient similarities in the evolution of their respective political systems, the patterns of structural societal change, and the dynamics of economic development in the nineteenth and twentieth centuries to warrant systematic study as a unit.[5]

However, as Diamandouros himself notes, systematic comparative literature on southern Europe overall has been very slim, not least because of the relative novelty of the concept of Mediterranean Europe as a sub-area in its own right,[6] but it is beginning to grow. The focus of this volume is, however, on an historical period that is both short and current. So how can one acquire an adequate perspective to interpret these events?

This study is based on the view that in fact sufficient time has elapsed since the end of their authoritarian regimes occurred – in Portugal officially with the revolution of April 1974, in Greece with the *coup* against the colonels in July 1974 and in Spain from the death of Franco in November 1975 – to make a comparative study viable. Since then, in the period of roughly a decade much has indeed happened; events have moved fast in all three cases, and it would seem that their respective phases of democratic transition (though not necessarily of democratic consolidation) have probably passed. But it may well be argued on the contrary: when does a period of transition actually end? Moreover, how does one distinguish between transition and consolidation? Since the latter phase has not advanced significantly in any of the three cases, how can one make any useful judgements? Even though time-boundness – or rather as considered here, *brevity* of time – always poses certain problems for political scientists, these have been somewhat greater than usual in this analysis of the Spanish, Greek and Portuguese transitions to democracy. Certainly, looking back only a few years, even some of the best academic work on this subject has suffered noticeably from the difficulty of events swiftly overtaking what at the time seemed to be reasonable assessments.[7] The approach of this particular volume does not allow for longer-term historical treatment, although individual chapters provide concise background material where necessary. Nevertheless, to quote Rustow again, 'the study of democratic transitions will take the political scientist deeper into history than he has commonly been willing to go',[8] for there are various advantages in referring to the historical dimension. Let us examine them briefly.

Firstly, there is the inevitable question of hard evidence. It is a persistent belief of traditional historians that political science lacks a certain credibility as an academic discipline because, concentrating as it habitually does on contemporary developments for its material, it is said to face an unavoidable shortage of reliable (especially documentary) sources, not to mention the presumed difficulties of 'objectivity' in utilising what evidence is available. This assumption has always been questionable, and it is therefore surprising it has not been challenged more often. In an imaginative essay justifying the writing of contemporary history, Alan Bullock made a variety of points which are worth mentioning because they have a bearing on the study of new regimes like those under review here.[9] Finding the distinction between 'history' and 'politics' artificial, Bullock commented (1) that what counted most was the actual quality of material accessible being subjected to the scepticism embedded in the historical method; (2) that students of contemporary or recent events had the advantage of a multiplicity of sources, some of them richer than for previous periods (e.g. oral evidence from participant witnesses, public opinion surveys); (3) that it should also not be forgotten that earlier historical periods such as the Middle Ages also suffered from incomplete and sometimes unreliable source material. As to the problem of acquiring a suitable perspective, Bullock rightly denied the possibility of complete objectivity and noted that, as a matter of fact, contemporary historians had the particular advantage of being able 'more easily to enter into the atmosphere of events and the climate of opinion than the historian can in the more remote past'. He did, of course, indicate that the main disadvantage under which the student of contemporary events labours is that 'of not knowing what happened next', because this may well affect perspective.

Now, comparative studies do after all need a solid empirical basis to be valid, so how does this look with regard to the new Mediterranean democracies? Several political scientists, writing in a different and earlier context, have bemoaned the absence of hard evidence, particularly data, in such cases. Drawing on his experience in working on regime transitions, Rustow emphasised that 'even reliable statistics are harder to come by early in any democratic experiment',[10] while Philip Converse drew attention in an article on the importance of the time factor in establishing new regimes to a similar difficulty encountered in Almond and Verba's classic work, *The Civic Culture:* 'Certain known defects of the Almond-Verba data become more intense in the countries that are less developed and hence are "newer" democracies'.[11] Essentially, this problem is the same when looking at Spain, Greece and Portugal since 1974–5, and this is illustrated by the so far underdeveloped state of the political science profession in these countries.

But, on the other hand, democracies being relatively more open systems than others, it follows that – certainly with time – evidence will become increasingly available. Already, for historians, archival material is gradually being opened on earlier contemporary periods; the Spanish government has recently released official documentation on the Civil War which had remained firmly closed until after Franco's death, so that along with newly attainable private papers it has become 'possible to study subjects considered off limits in the past'.[12] Because the regime transitions in the new Mediterranean democracies occurred less abruptly or dramatically than, say, with the collapse of Nazi Germany in 1945 – with perhaps the partial exception of Portugal – there has been less in the way of archival windfalls.[13] So far as more political science material on the current post-dictatorial periods is concerned, opinion survey projects, for instance, are beginning to develop, like those conducted over the past decade on Portugal by Mario Bacalhau and Thomas Bruneau.[14] More generally, some aspects of the transition process in these new democracies have been more 'open' (and hence more reported on) than others, especially the role of political parties and elections (on which there has been for some years a fast growing literature), but that is also true for other more established democracies.

Secondly, turning to interpretative problems, whereas historians conventionally tend to dwell on the uniqueness or diversity of national political development, political scientists more often look for comparative perspectives – whether bilaterally, or as part of a grander thematic schema – and seek to draw general lessons from their national case-studies. Admittedly, there is an obvious particularity about individual countries' histories, and this largely explains differences in national traditions and cultures. For instance, there are salient political patterns in all three new Mediterranean democracies that can only really be explained by their historical roots: regionalism in Spain (which reappeared with renewed vigour after almost four decades of Franco's rule), not to mention the profound effects of the Civil War experience in that country (without which one cannot understand the consensual urge towards moderate political positions, evident in this new democracy); the recent colonial past in Portugal as the clinching factor in the undoing of the Salazar-Caetano regime and which provided a key element in the ideological drive behind the 1974 revolution; and long traditions of hostility and tension with Turkey in the case of Greece, which similarly provided the final stimulus for the collapse of the authoritarian regime there in 1974 (with the dispute over Cyprus).

Furthermore, it becomes clear that the two different orientations of historians and political scientists mentioned above are not necessarily in conflict; in fact, such a suggestion could be turned around by arguing that alongside the similarities and contemporaneousness of the three transitions to democracy, some diversity of historical experience only enriches a comparative analysis. As Diamandouros points out, 'the obvious and significant differences existing between the models of transition followed by each regime in crisis constitute a rich field for both theoretical and empirical analyses',[15] in reference to particular features marking the inauguration of these transitions. He comes to the view that the factor of time 'in the concrete form of regime longevity inevitably becomes a variable that cannot easily be ignored, when one tries to study systematically authoritarian regimes'.[16] Gianfranco Pasquino expressed the same thought in an early comparative essay on the Greek and Portuguese transitions to democracy: 'The fundamental difference between the two authoritarian systems consisted essentially in the effects deriving from their different duration',[17] and he went on to examine some of these effects with regard to the experience and outlook of political elites, the nature of social structures and various aspects of the transition process in the two countries.

In other words, the diversity identified by historical studies with their long-term focus on national political development is indispensable in explaining the political cultures of individual countries. This question is undoubtedly basic to the stabilisation of the new democracies, for as José Maravall underlines in his book on the Spanish transition:

If it is accepted that cultural and ideological elements play an important part in consolidating a democracy, the experience of the transition to democracy in Spain must be taken as a quasi-experimental case . . . as these new institutions have become established in Spain during a relatively short transition period, and not as a result of a war or a confrontation leading to a sudden radical change, the political culture of the people becomes an even more crucial problem for political analysis. Political stability will depend to a very great extent on the support given by society to the institutions, practices and principles of democracy.[18]

It is therefore significant that one of the major gaps so far in research on the new Mediterranean democracies concerns their political cultures, for presumably it is still too soon to recognise any new patterns and where they might be leading. The little survey work carried out so far, like that of Bruneau on Portugal, makes one sceptical about any substantial change in mass-level political attitudes having taken place up till now, for in that country – which saw a more abrupt inauguration of its transition than Spain – such attitudes have continued to reveal a strong nostalgia for Salazar's *Estado Novo*.[19]

Thirdly, the historical dimension is particularly useful because it raises the key question of the degree or form of 'newness' about the Mediterranean democracies, and with it the inevitable problem of continuity or otherwise in their processes of transition. Not surprisingly, historians specialising in the one country or the other have been tempted to extend their interest to the post-dictatorial periods;[20] but this involvement in research bridging both periods before and after the end of the different dictatorships had also attracted political scientists.[21]

It is of course necessary to try to establish exactly what 'newness' is before embarking on a review of three Mediterranean democracies. There can be no absolute 'newness' about any fresh democratic regimes, let alone ones which are 're-born' for they have some precedent of democratic experience (even if presumably unsuccessful). Not even the collapse of the Nazi state in Germany and the subsequent launching of the Federal Republic – historically a more vivid occurrence than the three transitions that commenced in the mid 1970s – could be seen as representing an absolute state of 'newness', despite contemporary judgements about Germany having reached 'point zero'. Germany in 1945 is certainly the closest that any western European country has come in recent times to a complete moment of truth in regime transition, but all the same there was continuity in some respects (e.g. not all elites were dissolved, pre-Nazi party-political traditions reasserted themselves after the war, while the 're-making' of German political culture eventually happened during the course of the Federal Republic and not at its outset).[22] On the question of this relative meaning of 'newness' and possible turning-points, Almond and Mundt have from another angle emphasised that a *potential* for crisis is universal in political systems and that there are no 'final solutions', only more or less stable adjustments to more or less stable environments.[23] Whether such a potential transforms itself into an actual crisis and leads to regime collapse and transition depends on a variety of key determinants of change, relating particularly to the internal dynamics of the political system as well as to socio-economic change.[24]

Having said this, the discussion requires some tighter definition of what constitutes continuity. Leonardo Morlino distinguishes between 'continuity' in a process of transition as involving change taking place with the agreement of laws and procedures established by the previous regime with a view to (limited) adaptation; while 'discontinuity' is seen in the abandonment of such norms and procedures.[25] While generally valid, this definition is too institutional in its focus, so there is still a need for a more specific and all-inclusive basis for identifying the degree and form of continuity or otherwise. Juan Linz has offered a useful distinction between 'cultural' and 'organis-ational' continuity, though he was referring explicitly to party development, namely the distinction between ideological traditions and actual party structures.[26] In fact, the little empirical work that has been done by political scientists on the matter of continuity in the new democracies has concentrated on party systems and electoral behaviour,[27] because these areas do of course provide more ample evidence than any other. The crucial question of continuity will be resumed in the final section below in the more general context of theories of transition to democracy.

Since probing questions are being raised by the historical dimension, it might well be asked: why concentrate just on these three particular cases of transition to democracy? Some other studies on this theme have gone further in including Italy and also Turkey, not to mention in the drawing of parallels with the problem of democratic transition in the Third World.[28] It might also be pointed out that – at first sight at least – Greece stands in some contrast with the Iberian states because her military regime lasted only seven years and not over a full generation. The reasons for the selection of examples in this volume are several and support the argument for a compact case-study of regime transition: the contemporaneousness of all three processes; the striking similarities between them, not only because of the common time factor, but also because of the common geographical (and cultural) setting and the common international and economic environment; and, in the case of Greece, the fact that the political system established after the fall of the colonels was qualitatively different from the one previous to their rise to power in 1967, as will be shown by the two chapters on Greece in this study. The three chapters on the national processes of transition by Medhurst, Diamandouros and Bruneau pay attention to the effects of the various authoritarian regimes on the nature of the new democracies, and hence touch on the question of continuity. Given therefore the particular comparative framework of this study, as explained at the beginning of this chapter, the cases of Italy and Turkey have not been included because in the former case the contempor-aneous argument does not apply,[29] while in the latter case both this same point and the more frequent regime transitions – to democracy, but also back again to military rule – are seen as debarring Turkey.

In conclusion, it is evident from looking at the historical dimension that one should differentiate between the establishment of the political-institutional structure and the formation of the political culture when assessing the transition to a new democracy. If the first has essentially occurred in Spain, Greece and Portugal, with some potential for the second developing with time, then a comparative study on the subject is justified. Such a study therefore must discuss not only the structural nature of the political system and its performance and stability, but also consider the dynamics of social and economic development, for these are usually fundamental in some way as to how new regimes develop. However, the subject of political change is not only central to political studies, it is also intrinsically complex; and since the examples under review are of fairly recent occurrence, it follows that the historical method alone cannot suffice. While helpful in revealing necessary approaches to the subject, it cannot provide the all-inclusive and comparative basis for the study of regime transition.

COMPARATIVE PERSPECTIVES: A 'MEDITERRANEAN MODEL' OF LIBERAL DEMOCRACY?

As indicated at the start of the previous section, there is a compelling and compact basis for comparison when looking at recent developments in the Mediterranean sub-area of western Europe, not only because of its homogeneity but furthermore because of parallel and similar development in this respect – always an enticing comparative argument. This theme of comparability will therefore be taken up again and examined more closely before turning to the more particular question of theories of regime transition and their applicability to this sub-area. Indeed, can one go so far as to talk of the existence of a 'Mediterranean model' of liberal democracy?

In answering this question, we have to see how far the comparative method provides the necessary framework which, as just noted, the historical method cannot in assessing a complex subject of recent origin. This seems particularly worthwhile since general comparative political studies have not yet begun to incorporate much material on the new Mediterranean democracies, even though they do seem to offer interesting variations of this type of system. Admittedly, the comparative method has its own limitations – notably, the equivalence of hard information between different countries, other method-ological problems in conducting systematic cross-national surveys involving a wide range of background variables, the constraints imposed by specialism when looking at more than a handful of countries in any depth, and the usual dangers of over-simplification – but it is very arguable that all these difficulties are reduced by the very compactness of a sub-area case-study.

Seeing that the three countries under review present at least additional variations or possibly even alternative models of liberal democracy, and in sympathy with Rustow's comment quoted at the beginning of this chapter, one could go further and ask what contribution any enquiry into these new democracies may make to comparative studies. To quote Diamandouros: 'Indeed, viewing Southern Europe as a conceptual category worthy of scholarly attention in and of itself can promote the interests of comparative and interdisciplinary analysis in a variety of ways.[30] He continues by specifying that:

> the introduction of the notion of Southern Europe as separate and distinct from its western and eastern counterparts could help transcend the conceptual straitjacket which this long-established polarity has imposed upon the study of European history. In addition to allowing for

much richer intra-European comparisons, detaching Southern Europe from its illustrious northern sister and according it separate attention can make inter-regional analysis more fruitful and suggestive.[31]

Furthermore, comparative analysis of Southern Europe may 'open up numerous vistas for conceptualising, and even for modest theorising' on such features as corporatism, clientilism and authoritarianism; and in view of many parallels between Latin America and Southern Europe, 'the very diversity of the social and political experience of these societies makes them a veritable goldmine for comparative social and political analysis'. As Diamandouros puts it, 'alternatively, Southern Europe can be looked upon as either the most developed part of the Third World, or, conversely, as the least advanced part of the First'.[32]

This distinctiveness of the Mediterranean sub-area of western Europe has in the past and even until recently led to the exclusion of countries like Spain, Greece and Portugal from comparative studies. In the introduction to his book *Political Parties in Western Democracies*, published in 1967, Leon Epstein explained this exclusion on the following grounds:

> Portugal and Spain are excluded, obviously because they are nondemocratic as well as unadvanced; Greece and Turkey are also excluded, because of their limited economic development and their unstable democratic experience.[33]

Obviously, this omission of these three countries – and certainly of the two Iberian states – from comparative work had much to do with their authoritarian regimes and the fact that West European studies have perforce entailed the comparison of liberal democracies. But there seem to be broader reasons going back beyond these countries' experiences of authoritarianism. According to Howard Wiarda, who in a study on Spain and Portugal makes a plea for the inclusion now of these countries in comparative studies,

> Spain and Portugal have long been considered a part of Europe, and yet apart from it. This is true not only in a geographic sense . . . but in a social, political, economic, psychological, even moral sense as well. . . . At least from the time of Charlemagne and Roland, there has existed a certain European prejudice towards Iberia, and a certain vague hostility. This historic prejudice undoubtedly has complex racial, social, cultural, religious and political roots. At the same time, the sense of both distance and rejection which the nations of Iberia feel has bred in them a sense of separateness, a certain national inferiority complex and, frequently, a desire to 'go it alone' regardless of the wishes of Northern Europe. . . .
>
> During the long Franco and Salazar eras this sense of isolation, distance and rejection continued – of course at least as much for the nature of these regimes as for any historic prejudices. Spain and Portugal remained outcasts of the European community, a position that often strengthened their own resolve to maintain the distance and distinctiveness of their socio-political structures. But the long-standing authoritarian regimes of these two nations have by now been relegated to the past. . . . In their place have come the new institutional structures

of 'democracy', including democracy's various accoutrements: a gamut of political parties, a fully-fledged party system, elections and 'party' government. This transition has been accompanied by a new opening toward Europe on the part of the Iberian nations, a sense that they are no longer outcasts but part of the Western democratic community, as well as a new acceptability and legitimacy for Spain and Portugal in European liberal and social-democratic circles.[34]

On the question of institutional structures, not only do the three new Mediterranean democracies include many features very recognisable elsewhere in western Europe, but in some respects the former have attempted to transplant institutional mechanisms from the latter – if one recalls the influence on Karamanlis of the French Gaullist constitution as a model for the Greek presidency, or more specifically the provision in the Spanish constitution for a constructive vote of no-confidence, as a direct borrowing from the West German Basic Law. The Portuguese institutional structure (before its reform in 1982) was somewhat deviant from the norm of parliamentary states, notably in the policy-making role granted the military which reflected the revolutionary outcome of 1974, although here the powers of the presidency and the dual executive again present an obvious parallel with the Gaullist constitution. In all three countries, the political parties are indentifiable in relation to the different ideological movements in western Europe accepting that, as elsewhere, their individual ideologies reflect particular national concerns, although on the political right some of their labels differ, e.g. the Greek conservative New Democracy. Morevoer, there has been a marked similarity in the basic economic problems faced by southern Europe together with the rest of western Europe, if one looks back over the past decade (on this, see the chapter by Alfred Tovias). Salvador Giner has explained this similarity succinctly and eloquently:

The uncertainties of the Western world are now the uncertainties of Southern Europe. . . . In the same way as the 'dual' economy soon ceased to exist, at the national level the European (North and South) 'dual society' has ceased to exist through supranational and international integration and mutual dependence. Now, there are vast economic interests of Northern Europe involved in the South, from the simple ownership of houses to large industrial investment. And the weight of the South is not limited to supplying a work force for the North, as appeared to happen during the decades of the 1950s and 1960s: its political and economic force is beginning to be felt beyond the confines of the European Parliament. The hard facts of interdependence mean that we have all ceased to be islands, if we were once that.

The problem, then, is not one of economic underdevelopment and of 'setting about the day' – even if one must not forget the question, more urgent than ever, of regional disequilibrium between North and South, East and West – but rather the larger question of liberty. The question is to know how to overcome in this Europe of today the limits imposed on growth by the economic crisis, the limits on opposition imposed by an excessive politics of consensus and some distant agencies of negotiation

situated over and above us, the limits on personal liberty produced by
class barriers and bureaucratic control, the limits on well-being created
by some inflationary health services, pollution and dangers from
technology.[35]

So, if the similarities between Mediterranean and the rest of western Europe
and the awareness of these have grown in recent times, what about the
'Mediterranean model' of political development set in the context of
European comparative studies? The discussion so far of the possibility of such
a model has been either descriptive (recognising common features of these
new democracies, e.g. the background of authoritarianism and corporatist
tendencies) or somewhat assumptive (that the occurrence of parallel and
similar development leads to equivalent regimes), but we need now to examine
this possibility more systematically. Themes of particular importance to the
development of the new Mediterranean democracies – that is, a certain
uniqueness of southern European socialism, the influence of the international
environment and the question of government performance and its
relationship with system legitimacy – are examined in some depth and detail in
the comparative chapters in this volume. The intention here is to identify
useful comparative approaches.

References so far in the literature to comparative perspectives have
suggested there is something intrinsically different about these southern
European polities (Italy is usually included too), despite points of convergence
with other West European democracies, like those mentioned above in
relation to contemporary politics, institutional arrangements and economic
interdependence. One of the most commonly used phrases is 'difficult
democracies', referring especially to the inefficiency of political and
bureaucratic structures, the extreme government 'overload' in the face of basic
problems of socio-economic backwardness and the underlying theme of
instability and possible threats to the continued existence of these
democracies (another phrase used about them is 'vigilant democracies'). It is,
of course, precisely on these same grounds that the 'Nordic model' is
traditionally contrasted with such a 'Mediterranean model'; although the
essential differences between the various sub-areas of western Europe may
well have become more relative than absolute, if one takes Giner's view quoted
above that all West European democracies have become that much more
difficult to govern. However, in an early comparative essay on these new
democracies, Juan Linz drew attention to international concern for these new
systems' stability – 'both the hope and the fear for democratic political
stability in Mediterranean Europe have turned the attention of the world to
this strategic area'[36] – together with the fact that these regime transitions were
taking place against the backdrop of considerable and sometimes rapid
economic and social change. On a more specific level, Peter Merkl has noted
'many possibilities for comparative perspectives' when looking at these three
countries, e.g. post-dictatorial systems, 'the parties and party systems cry out
for systematic comparison', and also the differing paths of transition as
offering a fruitful area for investigation. Commenting with some surprise on
the absence so far of such systematic comparison, Merkl argues that
'comparison helps to place all of these "new" political systems more firmly

into our present cognitive map than they have been so far'.[37]

Given the existence of the kind of 'uniform political patterns' desired by Macridis and Cox, what does all this add up to? If we are talking about a possible 'Mediterranean model', inevitably the term 'model' has to be clarified. Here, the compactness of the sub-area form of case-study helps, as when countering the scepticism that has in recent times surfaced about model-making. For instance, Blondel has criticised the over-abstractness of earlier political science models, for they were 'so general that they did not solve the real problems to which political scientists (and indeed the politically involved public) addressed themselves; they were like superstructures built before the infrastructure'.[38] He argues in favour of 'middle-range' analyses, where models do indeed satisfy certain needs such as that of looking 'at the practice and not merely at the rules and at the procedures':[39] hence the value of the sub-area study, since such 'middle-range' models are postulated on the basis of sufficient similarities in the evolution of the given political systems, patterns of social-structural change and dynamics of economic development.

Clearly, our interpretation will also be assisted by clarifying the nature of a liberal democracy. One fairly comprehensive definition offered is the following:

> Liberal democracies are characterised by a high and open level of competition for power within a stable framework of institutions. The liberal-democratic system is highly inclusive, with numerous and varied channels – parties, elections, interest groups and mass media – for the articulation of popular interests and preferences. Broadly attuned to predominant mass preferences, liberal democracies have developed a moderately reformist, welfare orientation since the extension of citizenship to the lower strata.[40]

The new Mediterranean democracies examined in the light of this definition reveal some features relevant to the fashioning of any 'Mediterranean model'. They cannot be described (yet) as 'stable', as noted previously. Again, doubts about the existence of articulated mass preferences have to be raised in view of the de-politicisation that occurred under the dictatorships, especially the Iberian ones. However, the formation of an institutional framework for political competition – together with the emergence of competitive agents such as parties – has happened at an impressive pace. All three countries have undergone several if not numerous experiences of elections (if regional and local elections are included as well as various referenda). Only the weakness of interest groups in some cases and voiced mistrust of the media (notably in Portugal since the revolution) require this point to be qualified. In short, the record of Spain, Greece and Portugal in so brief a period is on balance positive.

Although applying the above general definition does provide some leads, there is still a need for a more specific angle linked to the cases of new democracies. The main lesson to be drawn from examining the historical dimension concerns the distinction between establishing the political-institutional structure and the formation of the (system-supportive) political culture. This may be raised into a more principled categorisation between parliamentary states and liberal democracies, whereby the former is really the state structure characterised by 'limited' and responsible government, while a liberal democracy is characterised in addition by popular participation, the articulation of pluralism and, above all, by political parties performing a vital societal role (mobilisation, expression of demands). The latter being the wider entity does of course encompass the former; or, to put it crudely, it comprises the element of political culture as well as the political-institutional structure.

It has already been presumed that our three Mediterranean countries have successfully established their political-institutional structures, but not their system-supportive political cultures. Does this, therefore, make them parliamentary states (Portugal is really a semi-presidential state), but not to date fully-fledged liberal democracies? The deficiences identified in these three countries by the aforementioned definition of a liberal democracy suggest that. This is perhaps no surprise, for the time factor is inevitably a crucial determinant in the emergence of a 're-made' (i.e. pro-democratic) political culture. Changes in political culture may be speeded up by traumatic and mass-perceived experiences like war or by revolution, but all the same, since they involve some deep changes of conviction within popular attitudes, some evolutionary tendency is implied, which takes time.

But the growth of a system-supportive political culture is crucial to the eventual stabilisation of new democracies – in fact, this seems to provide the key to understanding the central problem of stability in looking at regime transition in Mediterranean Europe, as stated above by Maravall (see note 18). In a theoretical discussion of the subject, Philip Converse estimates that a state of democratic maturity is essentially approached after a period of more than two generations and assesses 'progress' towards stabilisation as occurring in crabwise fashion, with backward steps nearly as frequent as forward ones at many times and places.[41] However, he asserts:

> What is utterly predictable is that threats to the survival of a new institution will be very high in its infant stages. In the degree that it can outlast these first precarious periods, it will typically have put forth roots of sufficient strength so that challenges to its very being diminish in number and those that do occur are warded off with increasing ease. It becomes sanctified and protected by the 'weight of historical tradition'.[42]

Converse's further comment on the early stage of regime transition that 'in most such situations, there is initially a residuum of elite personnel, which either poorly understands the constraints of democratic values, or which is downright hostile to them',[43] seems ominously recognisable in the new Mediterranean democracies, most dramatically with the attempted Spanish coup in 1981 and also that in Portugal in 1975, not to mention other exposed plots or rumblings of discontent among the military in all three countries at different times.

This distinction between the political-institutional and political-cultural dimensions and, more broadly speaking, between parliamentary states and liberal democracies does therefore offer a useful analytical approach for a comparative assessment of the new democracies. But it does need some further conceptual honing before considering theories of regime transition.

Firstly, the term 'stability' is one that has surprisingly lacked definitional exactitude. However, it is crucial to understanding the new Mediterrean democracies, not least because it refers to both of the two dimensions (e.g. government stability, but also the stability of system-supportiveness among the public). In a recent article,[44] Dowding and Kimber attempt such a definition. Since the term is relative and not absolute it follows that this concept must not exclude all change, but for these authors 'the problem lies in the type of change that may be allowed for a system to be said to be the same system after the change as before'. The notion of forced change is seen as essential to the idea of instability, so that change that is accepted voluntarily by any political object is not proof of instability. Hence, 'stability' is defined as 'the state in which a political object exists, when it possesses the capacity to prevent contingencies from forcing its non-survival'. They conclude:

> Perhaps future research should focus more on particular threats, or combinations of threats, and their effects on the survival of political entities, rather than attempting to link some generalised and absolute notion of stability to various factors which may or may not be causal. The stability of any political object is conceptually related to the contingencies that threaten it, and its overall stability at any given time is related to the contingencies it faces at that time. Thus, it is not meaningful to make the bald assertion that a given system is stable. At best, we might assert that a particular system has a high probability of surviving for a given number of years, or that the system is stable in relation to the contingencies it is now facing and has a high probability of remaining stable in relation to the threats that it is likely to face in the future.[45]

This kind of differentiating and sceptical reasoning is useful and very applicable when looking at both the fall of the preceding authoritarian regimes as well as the establishment of the new democracies.

Secondly, a similar scepticism is in order when applying models of political systems, not least because the sub-area study requires a stricter analytical approach than broader comparative work. Take, for instance, Easton's well-known analysis of political systems, in which he speaks of the input-output balance as a vital mechanism in the life of a political system (i.e. the relationship between demands on the one side and decisions or policies on the other). As he puts it:

> Not all withdrawal of support from a government has consequences for the success or failure of a regime or community; but persistent inability of a government to produce satisfactory outputs for the members of a system may well lead to demands for changing of the regime or for dissolution of the political community.[46]

The three new Mediterranean democracies would seem to be likely candidates for Easton's scenario of regime collapse, bearing in mind the serious economic and social problems they all face and the extreme constraints on their scope for performance. But, as Giuseppe Di Palma argues in his chapter in this volume, other variables have to be taken into account when looking at these particular examples, such as the widespread desire for democratic stability, a basic consensus on the rules of the (new) democratic game as benefiting to some extent all participants and the fact that in the western Europe of the 1980s the authoritarian system as the main alternative is no longer legitimate.

Thirdly, the term 'party government' is rightly employed when discussing the actual operation of liberal democracies, since in such systems political parties are regarded as the 'gatekeepers', to use Easton's own phrase. That is, they are the vital linkages or channels of political communication between state and society; in short, they perform two crucial and complementary roles as both institutional (policy-deciding) and socio-political (mobilising) forces. An examination of their nature and role is therefore bound to say something about the quality and stability (one might also add 'depth') of the political systems as a whole. In both their key roles they have shown serious weaknesses up to now and, significantly, this has been the more evident in their role as socio-political forces. In the first decade since the end of the authoritarian regimes, there have emerged patterns of continuity in voting behaviour although these have been marked by strong volatility due, among other things, to the low level of party identification. At the activist level, participation has been relatively low compared with most other West European democracies – both in terms of party membership totals and in the degree of involvement within party structures. The strength of parties' organisational roots in society is naturally decisive in their stability and effectiveness as socio-political forces, but – apart from the communists – the various parties could only really organise themselves once the transitions began, and there has not been sufficient time for them to set down firm roots. In addition, their leaderships have generally been intent on working under pressure of time to establish the new democracies, and have paid much less attention to such matters as party structures and internal party democracy.

Accordingly, political parties in the first decade have given a distinct priority to their institutional over their socio-political roles, but even this has not meant that the three new democracies have developed clear cases of 'party government' within their state structures (i.e. the parties playing the central role in formulating and deciding policy). In Portugal, this obviously comes from the semi-presidential system whereby the president has enjoyed an important controlling function over the executive (i.e. party leaders), and until the constitutional revision of 1982 a key co-policy-making role via the Revolutionary Council (see the following chapter by Bruneau). More seriously, these three countries have not met the normal requirement of liberal democracies that the military are clearly subordinate to the civilian authorities and remain politically quiescent. In Portugal, the military or rather its radical left wing (Armed Forces Movement – MFA) as a result of its key role in the 1974 revolution was very influential politically in the years immediately afterwards. However, its constitutional status through the Revolutionary Council has now been abolished, and so it could be that Portugal after the first decade is beginning to evolve more in the direction of a normal liberal democracy. In Greece, the military's role in politics was discredited after the fall of the colonels, although its important role in that country is guaranteed by persistent tensions in the Aegean. It is in Spain that the role of the military in politics has been least regulated, no doubt reflecting the fact that that country's transition process has been the most clearly evolutionary, although a plan to subordinate the military to the democratic framework has been initiated by the socialist government (see the discussion of this problem in the following chapter by Medhurst).

In other words, there have been structural limitations on the scope for 'party government' in the state with the existence of other (rival) agencies of power, although in contrast with postwar Italy one other parallel and potentially influential institution, namely the Church, has been distant from the game of politics in the three new Mediterranean democracies. At a broader level, as Salvador Giner shows in his chapter on the role of the socialists, neo-corporatist environments acted as a fundamental constraint on partisan initiative in power, but this is not unique to these countries. Nevertheless, as he also points out, the full integration of the various socialist forces into the democratic framework is itself a significant achievement. Indeed, with the main obvious exception of the Portuguese communists, the principal political parties in the three new democracies have been very system-supportive.[47]

These various basic doubts about the scope and 'depth' of 'party government' in these countries might be resolved with time – a further decade could tell – and in which case the problem would be due largely to the very 'newness' of their party systems. This seems particularly to be the case with the Iberian states because of the longevity of their previous authoritarian regimes and 'interruption' of democracy although, as Christos Lyrintzis also shows in his chapter, the relatively short 'interruption' with the military regime of 1967–74 also allowed for 'new' elements to emerge in the Greek party system. Whether the three party systems suffer, however, from any inherent and possibly fatal weaknesses cannot yet be said. Their future also depends on what future challenges they face in line with the previously quoted thesis of Dowding and Kimber about stability.

Such a differentiating approach is necessary when assessing the existence or possibility of a 'Mediterranean model' of political development. Clearly, there can be no absolute examples, not least because of some important similarities between Spain, Greece and Portugal and other democracies in western Europe. There are, as we have discussed, various other problems which are unique to these three new democracies, notably the question of regime stability which is certainly a much stronger consideration than elsewhere. It might well be that in the course of time these three democracies become established in a manner similar to the rest, but what has distinguished them in their first decade is that they – unlike democracies born in the nineteenth century, or even in the uncertain interwar period of the 1920s and 1930s – came straight into a West European world dominated by modern democracies. Certainly, this international environment has – as Tovias shows – been an influential factor in easing the transition to democracy in the Mediterranean states, and helps to account for the relative speed with which this occurred. This is not to discount the chance factor and also individual national explanations of why their regime transitions were embarked on, but rather to note that there may be different versions of liberal democracy (itself a broad category of political system). In the relative sense, then, the

Mediterranean sub-area forms one such group of liberal democracies in western Europe. Certainly, the basis for a compact comparative study (always itself a relative exercise) of these new Mediterranean democracies still exists, and this will be explored further in the following section.

THEORIES OF DEMOCRATIC TRANSITION AND THEIR RELEVANCE FOR THE NEW MEDITERRANEAN DEMOCRACIES

In this final section, various theories of democratic or regime transition will be tested for their applicability to the three examples under review and for further approaches and insights they may offer.

Some questions pertinent to this have already been raised here, concerning the 'newness' of such democracies, the degree and form of continuity in the process of transition and the problem of locating the time boundaries of the transition period. It is a matter of choosing criteria, and this leads to the need for theoretical approaches. For instance, in trying to determine when exactly a given transition period ends, it is arguable that the periods of transition and of consolidation (conceptually neat, but in practice probably not fully distinguishable) overlap somewhere, but one cannot estimate at what point except by establishing the necessary yardsticks. Then, at the other end of the time-scale, one might also question when a process of transition actually starts. The conventional view could be argued that the processes of transition commenced with the Portuguese revolution of April 1974, the coup against the Greek colonels in July 1974 and the death of Franco in November 1975, but this is possibly too one-dimensional a focus on the formal or institutional aspects. In Spain, for example, the process of transition can be said to have started in an incubatory form well before the death of Franco eventually opened the way for liberalising (subsequently, democratising) initiatives at the elite level (i.e. in the form of pressures accumulating from social and economic change and popular political discontent – see the chapter by Medhurst), and a similar line of argument may be pursued when looking at the other two transitions.

The effect of this line of reasoning is to relativise the events of 1974–5 within the overall context of the regime transition process, though not necessarily to diminish their intrinsic importance, and to strengthen the need for an all-inclusive basis for comparison. This is also likely to contain the problem of what has been called 'the fallacy of retrospective determinism'.[48] Much has happened in the relatively brief time of the past decade, and making sense of its different and sometimes conflicting trends is not necessarily easy. In particular, there is an inevitable temptation to view these events in the light of the current situation. For instance, the outcome for a liberal democracy in Portugal now looks distinctly better in 1984 than it did only a few years ago, since the post-revolutionary turmoil has diminished. With regard to Spain, views were for long positive then, impressed by what seemed to be an almost classic model of evolutionary transition (marred only by terrorist violence); the attempted military coup of February 1981 abruptly shook confidence in the Spanish experiment, although after a time, and with the significant change of power to the socialists in 1982, interpretations have tended once again to be optimistic though more cautiously so than before.

In introducing the various theories, it should be noted that the trend of interpretation in this volume is sympathetic more to the genetic than the functionalist theories of transition to democracy. That is, the view that such a transition is not an inevitable process but one dependent on how and when it originates and on the outlooks, strategies and behaviour of different actors is preferred against the view that the outcome of this process is conditional on certain requirements or functional preconditions, usually of a socio-economic nature. The former approach, where causal relationships are seen more as open-ended, does more justice to the complexity of different interacting factors in this process in the new Mediterranean democracies, and also is more likely to sustain an analysis of fairly contemporary developments. Different theories will be grouped according to whether they focus on (1) political perspectives, (2) socio-economic perspectives and (3) both together, and they will be discussed in that order.

First, concerning political perspectives the problem of continuity is once again important as a leitmotiv of regime transition. Richard Merritt offers various categories of change (dysfunctional conservatism, vigorous conservatism, segmental change, cumulative change and revolution) involving a range of different degrees or qualities of regime transition, but for him the crucial distinction is between 'change' and 'transformation', or change within continuity (*'plus ça change, plus c'est la même chose'*) as against decisive change (namely, of something which is central to the definition of the system itself).[49] By emphasising the dynamics of systematic transformation, Merritt presents a more differentiated angle on this question than the blander approach of Morlino noted above in the first section. He draws attention to the degree of 're-bornness' of these systems (they did have some previous experience of democracy, though varying in quality and longevity) as well as to the nature of the means by which they overcame the recent authoritarian past (evolution, revolution, etc., but also where there were elements of both). For instance, the case of Greece is neither clearly in the evolutionary nor clearly in the revolutionary category, though as Diamandouros and Lyrintzis show in their chapters there were elements of transformation. In Spain, a striking case of evolution, there were nevertheless some 'revolutionary' outcomes (where discontinuity merged with continuity), for liberalising elites can rarely control fully the process of change they have initiated because of probable pressures 'from below' or from the environment, as in fact happened there (events moved faster than planned). In Portugal, typed as a revolutionary situation, there were features which conformed to that model – e.g. turmoil and disruption, experimentation with different 'extreme' solutions – but there were also other aspects which did not: the events of April 1974 were more similar to a straightforward coup than to a popular uprising, there was hardly any violence and the prospects for socio-economic modernisation were very limited, at least for the time being.

For Merritt, a key indicator of systematic transformation is the role of elites as instigators of change, specifically which elites they are and what their motives are. They may be minimisers set on preserving the essential structure as it is, though prepared for tactical or other short-term reasons to adopt bold initiatives, or they may be potential or actual maximisers ranging from open liberalisers setting out on uncharted political seas to radicals with definite transformative objectives. While, as just noted, the leadership in a transition process may well be subject to environmental or popular constraints, several general studies on regime transition have underlined the importance of political leadership in explaining significant transformations of political systems. According to Gabriel Almond, 'great leaders are great coalition makers' in their ability to gather together different groups in favour of change on a consensual basis.[50] They may be constrained, but

> in so far as preferences and resources are not fully fixed – as they are in games – leadership may have certain ranges of manoeuvre, oppor- tunities for affecting preferences and resources. Surely leadership implies an ability to sense latent preferences, reorder the priorities of followers, accentuate or reduce their intensities, and the like. Leadership also implies a capacity to impute relatively correct values to resources, sense the point at which and the extent to which the legitimacy of a regime is being built up or drained away, and to mobilise and bring to bear upon politics latent resources that other political actors may neglect or fail to appreciate.[51]

Pasquino has similarly stressed the concept of the 'swing man' in his essay on the Greek and Portuguese transitions, with particular reference to the crucial role in the former case of Karamanlis[52] (on which also see the following chapter by Diamandouros); while Samuel Huntington in his *Political Order in Changing Societies*[53] has discussed the concentration of authority in a single individual during a modernisation process such as a 'modernising monarch' (who builds a coalition from both modernising and traditional sources), a phrase that is tailor-made for King Juan Carlos's performance in the years immediately following Franco's death. As far as Portugal is concerned, the role of President Eanes (in office from 1976) may also be mentioned, although he has acted less as an innovator and more as a stabiliser in what has, however, been a more disorderly transition process.

A further variation on this theme of the role of key elites has been the attention received from consociational democracy theorists, who focus on consensual behaviour among elites for the sake of stability in divided or fragmented societies. This would seem at first sight a model for the Spanish situation, but as Huneeus notes in a study of this very case, such consociational theories have been formulated with respect to established democracies. They were not intended to cover the inauguration of such regimes and, as he points out, the political parties in Spain could not perform the necessary role as transmission agents for elite decisions because of their weak roots as socio-political forces.[54]Huneeus does, however, agree on the importance of 'founding coalitions', that 'the crucial moment of the transition to democracy' is when a constellation of political factors produces a collapse of the minimalist strategy and 'simultaneously there appears a coalition with the possibility of impelling political change based on collaboration between political and social actors'; and that the emergence of this coalition is important in helping to 'neutralise the danger of inversion in the process back towards an authoritarian restoration'.[55] Certainly, in Spain's case, the consensus between rival political elites was most marked during the constituent period of 1976–8, and temporarily again during highpoints of terrorism or just after the attempted coup of 1981, but a long-term consociational-style interpretation does not hold. Earlier observations about a 'Mediterranean solution' of grand coalitions including the 'radical' left along consociational democracy lines – and that in this respect the Mediterranean was becoming 'the political laboratory of Europe'[56] – have not measured up to later developments. So far as Spain is concerned, alternation in power (as in 1982) has replaced elite convergence, and this has also been true of Greece (in 1981) and even of relatively less stable Portugal (in 1979, and through coalitional change again in 1983). In this particular – and significant – respect, the three new Mediterranean democracies have been more 'normal' in their operation of democratic ground rules (with their element of political competition) than many other more established West European democracies, including the two postwar cases of new democracies, Italy and West Germany.

Secondly, the question of socio-economic perspectives in the transition to democracy has been dominated by views about the relationship between necessary levels of socio-economic development and the prospects for democracy. This has been controversial because, on the one side, the functionalist theorists have argued for a high level of the former as being an essential precondition for the latter, while on the other side advocates of the genetic school of interpretation have attacked this view as being too deterministic and rather one-dimensional. Among the latter, Dahl has written that ' the evidence simply does not sustain the hypothesis that a high level of socio-economic development is either a necessary or a sufficient condition for competitive politics, nor the converse hypothesis that competitive politics is either a necessary or a sufficient condition for a high level of socio-economic development'.[57] The functionalist viewpoint does of course exclude or underplay the importance of other factors – the political, those relating to chance and those intrinsic to a particular country – in addition to equating incorrectly the co-existence of advanced socio-economic development and democratic stabilisation with their mutual functionality. As Maravall notes in looking at the transition in Spain, it would be commonsensical to agree that democracy benefits from affluence (in producing general satisfaction), but this is not the same as a certain threshold of affluence being the cause of democratic institutions.[58]

The argument of Dahl's that the functionalist view here is simply not proven is underlined by the example of the three new Mediterranean democracies over the past decade. For despite their relatively backward state of socio-economic development, compared with other West European democracies, they have in that decade at least successfully established their democratic systems – and that during a period of recession (on this see the following chapter by Alfred Tovias). This is also broadly true for Portugal, the country with the most backward economy and arguably with the most fragile democracy of the three (excepting, perhaps, the potential threat from military circles in Spain). One study of the Portuguese economy since the 1974 revolution has more pessimistically commented that 'economic hardship, not improvement, followed closely on the heels of the rebirth of political freedom and civil liberties has been a severe disappointment and a source of continued controversy', and considered 'how long the Portuguese will be willing to tolerate this fall in their standard of living is problematic'.[59] But this relates to expectations about revolutionary aims, and it does not follow that such disappointment would automatically rebound on the democratic institutions themselves. Di Palma's essay in this volume on government performance and legitimacy provides a useful analytical antidote to such assumptive assessments.

On another level of argument, the question of political culture needs further mention in the more specific context of transition theories rather than in the broader framework of general comparative approaches alone. Maravall has, in his book on the Spanish transition, indicated a difficulty here by noting that it is not easy 'to account for the birth of political democracy solely from the point of view of political and civic culture; culture and political institutions together form a web in which it seems impossible to untangle a longitudinal or cross-cultural causal order'.[60] This is partly because the term 'political culture' is definitionally loose so that some more explicit conceptual slants are necessary.

Converse has provided a sceptical corrective to bland assumptions about the need for the (broadly-based) 're-making' of the political culture with his remark that 'the mass side of the picture is at least somewhat more perplexing, for there is a good deal of evidence that the more subtle and important of democratic values never have much more than an extremely limited absorption'.[61] The implication must be that this limited penetration of democratic values in society has more potential for political adversity in such inchoate cases as our new Mediterranean democracies. Pasquino has distinguished between 'horizontal' legitimation (i.e. at the institutional level) and 'vertical' legitimation involving popular approval of a new system.[62] The latter sounds like an alternative term for 'political culture'; however, this distinction has the virtue of pointing out that legitimation among elites can occur autonomously from that among the public. From our sparse knowledge so far of mass-level political attitudes in the three countries, this would appear to be a useful and relevant form of differentiation. Finally, an approach with a capacity for longer-term projection is the thesis of 'diffuse support' offered by Easton.[63] This proposes that stability might eventually develop despite occasional declines in system output, that a high level of performance can, over time, 'take on a life of its own' whereby a system may accumulate a 'reserve of goodwill', which can be drawn upon in times of crisis or low performance, though not indefinitely. This approach has, for instance, been applied pertinently to the case of West Germany, where it has been found more useful than a simple discussion of 'system affect' as such.[64] However, the very example of the Federal Republic, which in the 1950s proved to be a clear case of 'high performance', tends to underline that the same cannot be claimed for the new Mediterranean democracies. We have to remain satisfied at this stage with the assumption that time together with reasonable (or not disastrous) system performance may eventually consolidate the transition process at this deeper popular level.

Thirdly, of the more comprehensive theories three may be mentioned as relevant to the new Mediterranean democracies. Modernisation theories, although normally directed towards the Third World, are none the less applicable to those among the West European countries which are less developed, particularly when focusing on the collapse of the authoritarian regimes and the start of the transition process. Both Apter and Huntington have pointed to the serious political management problem produced by socio-economic modernisation, involving co-ordination and control in response to the need for change, and hence the need for the ruling political system to be sufficiently articulated to be able to respond effectively. This recalls Dowding and Kimber's concept of stability, whereby the ability of the respective authoritarian regimes to handle change may be seen as questionable – there was an element of 'forced change' about their strictly limited and belated 'liberalisation' measures. For instance, this is noted by Medhurst and Bruneau *à propos* the inertia of the Franco and Salazar systems, while in Greece's case, the shorter-lived military regime, in consequence of a less deeply-rooted authoritarian system, had less articulated means to cope with a serious crisis.

Apter has taken this reasoning further by arguing that highly industrialised societies, by virtue of the need for multiple sources of information, have a 'systems-tendency' towards some form of 'democracy'.[65] However, none of these countries could in the mid-1970s be classified as 'highly industrialised' although, as Medhurst points out, rapid economic change with industrialisation in Spain promoted major social conflicts and political change that began to threaten the regime in the decade before Franco's death. According to Huntington, this state of affairs had the makings of a revolutionary situation, for this is most likely to arise in societies which have experienced some social and economic development and where the processes of political modernisation and political development have lagged behind the processes of social and economic change.[66] This implies that the actual timing of Franco's death might well have been decisive in the avoidance of a revolutionary outcome (another five or so years of his rule might have made an evolutionary transition impossible), and this therefore confirms the widely-held belief that the sensitivity to the need for change on the part of the key (ex-Francoist) leaders was crucial in the transition that commenced in 1976. In Portugal, with a less developed and less rapidly changing economy, there were not the same social and political pressures 'from below'. The state of affairs there before the 1970s was therefore less approximate to Huntington's revolutionary situation than Spain, even though, as Bruneau shows, the Salazar system was a closed one with 'no structured access to political power by the general population'. The clinching factor was external, with Portugal's deteriorating colonial position in Africa, coupled with the fact that the only possible source for political change within the system was the military. In Greece, similarly, an external crisis provided the final reason for the fall of the authoritarian regime (the disaster in Cyprus), although that regime while repressive had not had time to institutionalise itself, so that internal political opposition was not impossible.

The example of Greece, particularly with the opprobrium earned by the colonels' regime in western Europe, reminds us of one basic variable in the process of regime transition that demarcates these three new Mediterranean democracies from the Third World experience. While there have been some obvious similarities, such as the traditional role of the military in politics, the relative state of socio-economic backwardness and a certain background of institutional instability (which have made modernisation theories precisely relevant to these three cases), the difference from the international environment of western Europe is stark. The close interdependence of economies together with the special integrative framework of the European Community, as well as the existence across western Europe of very or fairly stable liberal democracies are factors which have had an important influence on the transition to democracy in Spain, Greece and Portugal, in line with various theories that international factors may well play an important part in transitions to democracy.[67] In most areas of the Third World – generally in Africa, and in Latin America – the environment has hardly been conducive to liberal democracy. In fact, apart from indigenous institutional and political-cultural factors, it could be said that foreign intervention in these areas has more often than not favoured authoritarian over liberal-democratic systems. This is different, however, from the sense of identity with 'Third-Worldism' which is present in the Mediterranean democracies, especially on the political left. It is present in the ideology of the Greek Socialist Party, illustrated by the extensive coverage on Spanish television of developments in Hispanic America and it colours the foreign policies of these countries. In short, it is a historical and cultural phenomenon and involves political sympathy, but such sense of identity does not detract from West European influences on the transition to democracy in southern Europe. The only main exception to this generalisation must be the influence of liberation movement ideology on the thinking of the Portuguese military as a result of their African experiences, which was reflected in the left-wing outlook of the Armed Forces Movement which spearheaded the 1974 revolution.

A further all-inclusive theory of democratic transition is Kirchheimer's thesis about 'confining conditions' in explaining the interaction between political power and socio-economic determinants, with respect to revolutionary breakthroughs.[68] This may not have a literal applicability to our three Mediterranean democracies, but his discussion of the conditions (chiefly those of social structure) which have to be overcome if a new regime is to continue, therefore of the relationship between 'old' and 'new' elements in the transition process, is relevant. According to Kirchheimer, the social and economic frame of the particular society lays down a conditioning perimeter within which the original political choice has to be made and solutions have to be sought. Nevertheless, this situation does not have to be static for, as Kirchheimer asks, can the very exercise of the new regime's option change the social preconditions releasing new psychic energies? There may, for instance, occur an 'expansion of the perimeter', where the social structure or economic basis of society – or, more slowly, intellectual habits – alter. As a result, 'confining conditions' may then still be present though absorbed in a new context, and thereby deprived of their confining nature. The possibility for such a change exists in the twentieth century, he points out, all the more because of the greater capacity of the state for mass mobilisation.

The applicability of this theory to the Mediterranean democracies is clear. In revolutionary situations, according to Kirchheimer, the outcome in terms of politically-inspired radical change is said to be constrained by social and economic preconditions; and it is to be assumed that such preconditions operate all the more in situations of regime transition which are not essentially revolutionary and certainly where they are evolutionary. However, gradual change is possible, and it is perhaps indicative of the complexity of this process in the new Mediterranean democracies, that some eventual consequences could be seen as 'revolutionary' in comparison with the (static) nature of the preceding authoritarian system. It might also be added, with reference to our three cases, that socio-economic conditions – so far as they might have favoured these authoritarian systems rather than the new democracies – were in any case beginning to change before the transitions formally commenced during 1974-5, though to a varying degree in each case.

This theory does, of course, allow us to gauge the possibilities for or degree of real change once transition was embarked on, and to assess how far the outcome has in any way been 'revolutionary' or not. In both Greece and Spain, the first crucial years of transition saw these countries under conservative rule (the first seven years in Greece's case, the first six or more in Spain), the main domestic priorities of which centred around democratic stability as such rather than socio-economic change. This further provides a useful context for estimating the scope for change with alternations in power, such as occurred in these two countries in 1981 and 1982, but as Giner points out in his chapter the emphasis of the respective socialist parties including the Portuguese has been distinctly more on the moral reform of public life and civil modernisation than on socio-economic change. The Greek PASOK has been somewhat less typical of this trend, although its radical positions have usually been more rhetorical than actually programmatic in nature. Only in Portugal during the first decade of the transition has there been any overt attempt at revolutionary change, such as the radical policies of land reform carried out in the first flush of the post 1974 revolution period. Finally, it is worth noting that Kirchheimer's theory of 'confining conditions' has something in common with the earlier discussion of the relationship between the advent of democracy and the level of socio-economic development, again more differentiatedly than the functionalist theories, in that this relationship is viewed in a dynamic rather than static context.

An emphasis on the need for a dynamic model is also the keynote of Dankwart Rustow's theory of transition to democracy. In seeking to answer the question about what conditions make democracy possible and what conditions make it thrive, he argues that a model of transition does not 'need to maintain that democratic evolution is a steady process that is homogeneous over time', and criticises previous theories based on notions of temporal continuity and linear correlation.[69] This and his general view that there may be 'many roads to democracy' offer new insight into the central problem of continuity. There are a number of working hypotheses in his theory which strengthen its relevance to our case-study: that conflict is intrinsic to democracy and that this is likely 'to be compounded during the formative period when part of the quarrel must *ex hypothesi* be between democrats and non-democrats'; that 'a dynamic model of the transition must allow for the possibility that different groups – e.g. now the citizens and now the rulers, now the forces in favour of change and now those eager to preserve the past – may furnish the crucial impulse toward democracy'; that, concerning the assumption about the need first to foster democrats to promote democracy, 'instead, we should allow for the possibility that circumstances may force, trick, lure or cajole non-democrats into democratic behaviour, and that their beliefs may adjust in due course by some process of rationalisation or adaptation'; and that 'the "advent" of democracy must not, of course, be understood as occurring in a single year', and that 'since the emergence of new social groups and the formation of new habits are involved, one generation is probably the minimum period of transition'.

We are therefore back to the distinction between the political-institutional and political-cultural dimensions discussed in the second section. Indeed, Rustow's theory of democratic transition has the virtue not only of being comprehensive, but also of being more sophisticated than most other such theories. The distinction between what may be called 'functional democrats' (alternatively, 'pragmatic' ones) and 'cultural democrats' is particularly useful in covering Rustow's various hypotheses, although these may be seen as ideal or pure types if one pauses for a moment to reflect on the complexities of human psychology. Furthermore, Rustow's theory of transition is all the more applicable to the new Mediterranean democracies because it postulates that, taken in all its aspects, the establishment of a democracy is essentially an evolutionary process. His theory is discussed further in this volume by Giuseppe Di Palma in his chapter on the problem of government perfor- mance, in particular Rustow's thesis that democracies are really by nature born out of compromise and that this provides an inherent basis for their legitimacy.

The burden of Rustow's theory is that a transition to democracy passes through three phases from initiation through to consolidation. These phases are subject to the necessary precondition of national unity, whereby the physical identity of the country in question is not in doubt:

1. *Preparatory phase.* 'The dynamic process of democratisation itself is set off by a prolonged and inconclusive political struggle', usually involving rival or even antagonistic social and economic groups, for remembering that there are many separate paths to democracy, 'a country is likely to attain democracy not by copying the constitutional laws or parliamentary practices of some previous democracy, but rather by honestly facing up to its particular conflicts and by devising or adapting effective procedures for their accommodation'. Although polarisation rather than pluralism is the hallmark of this phase there are limitations on this struggle implicit in the precondition of national unity, so that a fine balance has to be struck between outright intransigence on the one hand and mild conflict falling short of required democratic solutions ('what infant democracy requires is not a lukewarm struggle, but a hot family feud'). Hence, this preparatory phase can be a delicate one, when many things may go wrong and an apparent evolution towards democracy may be deflected.

2. *Decision phase.* 'What concludes the preparatory phase is a deliberate

decision on the part of political leaders to accept the existence of diversity in unity and, to that end, to institutionalise some crucial aspect of democratic procedure'. Democracy is 'acquired by a process of conscious decision at least on the part of the top political leadership', and such decision 'results from the interplay of a number of forces', usually seen as ideological ones. Since democracy is likely to stem from a large variety of mixed motives, the decision phase may be considered 'an act of deliberate, explicit consensus', and 'in so far as it is a genuine compromise it will seem second-best to all major parties involved', but 'what matters at the decision stage is not what values the leaders hold dear in the abstract, but what concrete steps they are willing to take'.

3. *Habituation phase.* 'A distasteful decision, once made, is likely to seem more palatable as one is forced to live with it.' Democracy being by definition a competitive process, this competition 'gives an edge to those who can rationalise their commitment to it, and an even greater edge to those who sincerely believe in it'. In short, 'the very process of democracy institutes a double process or Darwinian selectivity in favour of convinced democrats: one among parties in general elections and the other among politicians vying for leadership within these parties', for what particularly distinguishes this phase is that the agreement worked out during the decision phase is now 'transmitted to the professional politicians and to the citizenry at large'. In other words, politicians and citizens learn from the successful resolution of some issues to place their faith in the new rules and to apply them to new issues, experience with democratic techniques and competitive recruitment confirms politicians in their democratic practices and beliefs, and the population at large becomes fitted into the new structure by the forging of effective links of party organisation that connect political elites with the mass electorate.

There are therefore several advantages of Rustow's theory of transition to democracy for this study of the new Mediterranean democracies. An additional one to those already outlined is that it answers the problem touched on before; of trying to determine when a process of transition ends and to disentangle this process from the period of consolidation. It has, in fact, been presumed that the transition and consolidation experiences overlap to some extent. The merit of Rustow's model is that, unlike the vaguer terms 'transition' and 'consolidation', his sequence of phases provides a tighter framework for assessing the establishment and early development of new democracies, which is precisely – in taking the first decade of this experience – the subject of this volume. It avoids the need to distinguish starkly between transition and consolidation because broadly speaking, the second is assumed hardly to have begun in the case of Spain, Greece and Portugal; moreover, arguably, if there is common ground between transition and consolidation it lies within the habituation phase.

One final question is bound to concern at what stage the new Mediterranean democracies find themselves, taking Rustow's sequence of phases. At this point, it is clear that differences between these three national examples will emerge. As to the preparatory phase, what is striking is that none of these countries underwent any prolonged struggle save for the inconclusive first couple of years in Portugal, when liberal democracy was implicitly or explicitly under challenge from Soviet and Third World models of 'democracy'. Evidently, the preceding distintegration and/or de-legitimation of the authoritarian regimes, together with the pervasion of the liberal democracy model in western Europe, meant that the political cards were heavily stacked in favour of liberal democracy in these countries. In effect, there was and has been no really credible alternative political model to liberal democracy, and this may continue for the foreseeable future. It may also be said that all three cases have passed through their decision phases, although again in Portugal's case this has been more painful in that the constitutional settlement of 1976 was subsequently contested and then revised in 1982; a cautious judgement might even warn against this phase being clearly over.

All three new democracies are therefore apparently at some point in the habituation phase, but it is difficult to estimate how far exactly they have progressed. The speed and relative ease with which they have passed through the first two phases may be a good omen for the future – or it may not, depending on one's point of view. For instance, poignant memories of the Civil War among other things created pressures for moderate positions on the part of the political elites in Spain, but this occurred somewhat at the cost of solving serious outstanding problems, notably the role of the military in political life. On the other hand, all three countries have already embarked on such features of habituation as regular elections, also with some signs (in the last year or two) that previously sceptical political elites (i.e. 'functional democrats') have become more converted to the new democratic game of politics. This may be that much more true of Greece than the other two cases, but then Greece's 'interruption' of democracy was much shorter-term. However, the Rustow model of democratic transition appears useful as a framework for assessing the further development of democracy in these countries, for undoubtedly many other studies of them will appear in years to come. As suggested by several of the theories quoted in this chapter, the process of consolidation takes a very long time.

In summary, this discussion of theories of democratic transition confirms the viability of a 'Mediterranean model' of liberal democracy, if used as a relative concept, and such a model certainly provides a useful framework for analysing the three new democracies of Spain, Greece and Portugal. Most clearly, it is the temporal factor in conjunction with the overriding question of stability that distinguishes them from other liberal democracies in western Europe. Whether time will solve this problem – which is conditional on reasonable system performance – remains to be seen, but meanwhile they must be viewed as democracies still moving towards consolidation rather than ones well established. Nevertheless, as new versions of parliamentary states (in Portugal a semi-presidential state) they began to operate quickly, and indeed the political-institutional structures of these new democracies are very similar to those elsewhere in western Europe. It is rather their political cultures, as yet not sufficiently 're-made' to consolidate these new democracies, combined with their relative socio-economic backwardness that differentiates them from the other European liberal democracies. Therefore, their simultaneous regime transitions and consequently their comparable stages of democratic development, together with similarities in their socio-economic conditions and political cultures, argue in favour of their being considered as a case-study in 'Mediterranean democracy'. But, as noted before, there are no 'final solutions' in how political systems develop. It may be that in the future the Spanish, Greek and Portuguese systems become 'ordinary' versions of liberal democracy but, as Rustow maintains, there are 'many roads to democracy', and these three examples have chosen both a contemporaneous and broadly similar path.

NOTES

1. Dankwart Rustow, 'Transitions to Democracy: towards a dynamic model' in *Comparative Politics* (April 1970), p. 347.
2. See Nikoforos Diamandouros, *Southern Europe: an introductory bibliographical essay*, Studies in Public Policy, University of Strathclyde, No. 56, 1980, for a detailed discussion of work on this area.
3. Julian Santamaria (ed.), *Transición a la Democracia en el Sur de Europa y America Latina* (Madrid: Centro de Investigaciones Sociologicas, 1982), p. 4.
4. R. C. Macridis and R. Cox, 'Area Study and Comparative Politics' in R. C. Macridis and B. Brown (eds), *Comparative Politics: Notes and Readings* (Homewood, IL: Dorsey Press, 1964), pp. 102–3.
5. Diamandouros, op. cit., p. 1.
6. Ibid., p. 2.
7   This is particularly evident in work on the various party systems, with major new developments only in recent years.
8. Rustow, op. cit., p. 347.
9. Alan Bullock, 'Is it possible to write contemporary history?' in M. Beloff (ed.), *On the Track of Tyranny* (London: Vallentine Mitchell, 1960), reprinted in *The Wiener Library Bulletin*, special issue, 1983, pp. 20–25.
10. Rustow, op. cit., p. 347.
11. Philip Converse, 'Of Time and Partisan Stability' in *Comparative Political Studies* (July 1969), p. 164.
12. James Cortada (ed.), *Historical Dictionary of the Spanish Civil War, 1936–1939* (Westport, Conn.: Greenwood Press, 1982), introduction, p. x.
13. One has in mind particularly the Nuremberg Documents on Nazi Germany which, for instance, Alan Bullock found so useful in his biography of Hitler, *Hitler: A Study in Tyranny* (Feltham: Odhams) first published in 1952. On none of the three authoritarian regimes in the Mediterranean has anything so extensive become available. In the case of Portugal, the archives of the secret police under Salazar survived intact and there have been various personal papers, but generally there has been a slowness in the release of material by the new democratic governments, presumably partly because inconvenient knowledge might be revealed about some politicians still active (information from Tom Gallagher, University of Bradford). In the case of Spain, some memoirs of insiders in the Franco régime have been published and some private papers have become available, but again generally material has not been released systematically.
14. See Thomas C. Bruneau, 'Patterns of Politics in Portugal since the April Revolution' in J. Braga de Macedo and S. Serfaty (eds), *Portugal since the Revolution: economic and political perspectives* (Boulder, Colorado: Westview Press, 1981), pp. 1–24; also, Thomas C. Bruneau, *Politics and Nationhood: Post-revolutionary Portugal* (New York: Praeger, 1984).
15. N. Diamandouros, 'La transición de 1974 de un régimen autoritario a un régimen democratico en Grecia', in Santamaria, op. cit., p. 199.
16. Ibid., p. 202.
17. G. Pasquino, 'L'instaurazione di regimi democratici in Grecia e Portogallo', in *Il Mulino* (March-April 1975), p. 218.

18. José Maravall, *The Transition to Democracy in Spain* (London: Croom Helm, 1982), p. 77.
19. See Bruneau in Braga de Macedo and Serfaty, op. cit.
20. In the English language, notably work by Paul Preston on Spain and Richard Clogg on Greece.
21. For instance, the various writings of Juan Linz on Spain, and work by Kenneth Medhurst on the same country. George Mavrogordatos, currently working on the post-1974 Greek party system, published a study of interwar politics in Greece in *Stillborn Republic* (Berkeley: University of California Press, 1983).
22. See David Conradt, 'Changing German Political Culture', in G. Almond and S. Verba, *The Civic Culture Revisited* (Boston, Ma: Little, Brown & Company, 1980), pp. 212–72.
23. G. Almond and R. Mundt, 'Crisis, Choice and Change: some tentative conclusions', in G. Almond, S. Flanagan and R. Mundt, *Crisis, Choice and Change: historical studies of political development* (Boston, Ma: Little, Brown & Company, 1973), p. 621.
24. Ibid., chapter by Almond and Mundt.
25. Leonardo Morlino, 'Del Fascismo a una democracia debil: el cambio de régimen en Italia, 1939–1948', in J. Santamaria, op. cit., p. 104.
26. See J. Linz, 'Il sistema partitico spagnolo', in *Rivista Italiana di Scienza Politica*, No. 3 (1978), pp. 363–414.
27. For instance, Juan Linz, 'The New Spanish Party System', in Richard Rose (ed.), *Electoral Participation: a comparative analysis* (London: Sage Publications, 1980), pp. 101–89; also, Maravall, op. cit., discusses this aspect *passim*.
28. See J. Santamaria, op. cit.
29. On Italy, see S. J. Woolf (ed.), *The Rebirth of Italy, 1943–1950* (Harlow: Longman, 1972).
30. N. Diamandouros, *Southern Europe: an introductory bibliographical essay*, p. 1.
31. Ibid., p. 1.
32. Ibid., pp. 1–2.
33. Leon Epstein, *Political Parties in Western Democracies* (London: Pall Mall Press, 1967), pp. 3–4.
34. H. Wiarda, 'Spain and Portugal', in Peter Merkl (ed.), *Western European Party Systems* (New York: The Free Press, 1980), pp. 298–9.
35. Salvador Giner, 'Economía política y legitimación cultural en los orígenes de la democracia parlamentaria: el caso de la Europa del Sur', in J. Santamaria, op. cit., pp. 57–8.
36. J. Linz, 'Europe's Southern Frontier: evolving trends toward what?' in *Daedalus* (1979), p. 175.
37. Peter Merkl, review in *West European Politics* (January 1984), pp. 141–3.
38. Jean Blondel, *The Discipline of Politics* (Borough Green: Butterworths, 1981), p. 194.
39. Ibid., p. 185.
40. R. Hague and M. Harrop, *Comparative Government* (London: Macmillan, 1982), p. 42.
41. P. Converse, op. cit., pp. 140, 167.
42. Ibid., p. 139.
43. Ibid., p. 141.
44. K. Dowding and R. Kimber, 'The Meaning and Use of "Political Stability" ', in *European Journal of Political Research* (September 1983), pp. 229–43.
45. Ibid., p. 242.
46. D. Easton, 'The Analysis of Political Systems', in Macridis and Brown, op. cit., p. 100.
47. For a fuller discussion of 'party government' in these new democracies, see Geoffrey Pridham, 'Party Government in the new Iberian democracies', in *The World Today* (January 1984), pp. 12–21.
48. See R. Bendix, *Nation-Building and Citizenship* (New York: John Wiley, 1964), p. 13.
49. R. Merritt, 'On the Transformation of Systems' in *International Political Science Review*, No. 1 (1980), pp. 13–22.
50. Almond, Flanagan and Mundt, op. cit., p. 32.
51. Ibid., p. 32.
52. Pasquino, op. cit.
53. Samuel P. Huntington, *Political Order in Changing Societies* (New Haven: Yale University Press, 1968), Chapter 3.
54. Carlos Huneeus, 'La transición a la democracia en España: dimensiones de una política consociacional', in J. Santamaria, op. cit., pp. 247–9.

55. Ibid., p. 253.
56. See Luigi Graziano and Sidney Tarrow (eds), *La Crisi Italiana*, Vol. 2 (Turin: Einaudi, 1979), pp. 720–21.
57. R. A. Dahl, *Polyarchy, Participation and Opposition* (New Haven: Yale University Press, 1971), p. 71.
58. Maravall, op. cit., p. 5.
59. R. Morrison, *Portugal: Revolutionary Change in an Open Economy* (Boston, Ma: Auburn House, 1981), pp. viii, 1.
60. Maravall, op. cit., p. 4.
61. Converse, op. cit., p. 141.
62. Pasquino, op. cit.
63. See D. Easton, *A Systems Analysis of Political Life* (New York: John Wiley, 1965).
64. See D. Conradt in Almond and Verba, op. cit.
65. D. Apter, *Some Conceptual Approaches to the Study of Modernisation* (Englewood Cliffs, NJ: Prentice-Hall, 1968), p.329.
66. S. Huntington, op. cit., p.265.
67. See Rustow, op. cit.; Chapter 10 in Almond, Flanagan and Mundt, op. cit.
68. Otto Kirchheimer, 'Confining Conditions and Revolutionary Breakthroughs', in *American Political Science Review* (1965), pp. 964–74.
69. Rustow, op. cit., p. 345.

Spain's Evolutionary Pathway from Dictatorship to Democracy

Kenneth Medhurst

Spain's recent transition from dictatorship to liberal democracy represents a process unique in modern European politics. By contrast with postwar Germany and Italy, the creation of liberal-democratic institutions was not the result of military defeat or the subsequent intervention of foreign powers. By contrast with the later Greek and Portuguese experiences, there was no question of the overthrow of a dictatorship at the hands of domestic and, above all, military opponents. Rather, it was a question of reformist elements, associated with the incumbent dictatorship, initiating processes of political change from within the established regime. Equally, it was a question of reformists seizing and, for some time, maintaining the initiative in the face of opposition both from their own backward-looking colleagues and from the dictatorship's opponents who were dedicated to a complete break with the old order.

FRANCO'S DICTATORSHIP: A GROWING CRISIS OF AUTHORITARIANISM

To understand this outcome, it first seems appropriate to characterise briefly the Franco dictatorship and the dilemmas it faced when critical decisions about its future became necessary. The regime was, of course, born out of the victory in a civil war (1936–9) of those 'Nationalist' forces which Franco had been chosen, by fellow generals, to lead.[1] This war was the culminating point in a process of political polarisation that left Franco at the head of a quite broadly-based coalition of right-wing or conservative groups ranging from fascists to liberal monarchists.[2] Most of these groups were upper-strata factions lacking solid mass bases. The chief exception was the fascist element (the Falangists), who formed the backbone of the only legally tolerated political organisation in 'the New Spain'. This 'Movement' was in practice, however, used by Franco and his conservative allies as a bureaucratic instrument of political control, and not as a vehicle for the mobilisation of mass political support. It was used, in the main, to foster a process of mass depoliticisation in the aftermath of the Civil War, when repression, economic privation and war weariness continued to render most potential adversaries acquiescent.[3] During the same period a significant measure of legitimacy was conferred upon the regime by the Roman Catholic Church, whilst the army provided a relatively united last line of defence.[4] For his part, Franco judiciously pursued a divide-and-rule policy that permitted each group within the ruling coalition a measure of satisfaction that always fell well short of total hegemony.

During the 1960s, this regime presided over an unprecedented period of economic growth. Elements within the dictatorship perceived this as a means of securing the maintenance of authoritarian rule. The aim was to lay the foundations of a mass consumer society, whose rewards would continue to divert attention from politics and would promote satisfaction with the status quo. The regime was to benefit from a Spanish variant of 'the end of ideology'.[5]

In practice, however, rapid economic change exacerbated or catalysed major conflicts in Spanish society and promoted cultural, social and political changes that placed the regime's viability in doubt.[6] Political arrangements, originally constructed in a primarily agrarian society in the aftermath of a debilitating Civil War, appeared anachronistic when confronted with the tensions of a rapidly changing industrialised society. Similarly, generational change worked to the regime's disadvantage, for amongst those who had not experienced the upheavals of the 1930s its claims to be a necessary bulwark against disorder steadily lost credibility and appeared to entail increasingly unacceptable political costs.

Such change was observable on four main fronts. First, industrialisation created an enlarged working class with expectations that were increasingly difficult to meet within existing institutions. Growing strike movements, during the 1960s, testified to demands for increased economic rewards and, in time, for political change. Similarly, the activities of unofficial unions under Catholic, Socialist and, above all, Communist auspices exposed the unrepresentative nature of the state's officially monopolistic unions and their inability to offer credible responses to working-class demands.

Second, growing student dissent indicated, during the same period, mounting alienation amongst a minority – but still a significant portion – of those middle and upper-middle class groups who had habitually supplied the dictatorship with its most reliable sympathizers. Likewise, industrialisation helped to create a more diversified and questioning middle class. Only minorities within this sector were radicalised, but for significant numbers the growing rewards of a consumer society were proving to be insufficient compensation for the dictatorship's political constraints. Not least, more traditional middle-class and peasant groups, upon whom the dictatorship particularly counted for steady support, found their relative importance much diminished within this changed environment.[7]

Third, the regime confronted a revival of strong regional-based opposition from Catalonia and, above all, the Basque provinces. Efforts to eliminate forcibly the cultural and political basis of distinctive regional identities were seen to have failed as, in response to repression and as a consequence of socio-economic developments, local nationalist movements reasserted themselves. In the Basque region, ETA's (Euskadi Ta Askatasuna – Basque Homeland and Freedom) urban guerrilla activities came, in fact, to present the regime with its biggest-ever security problem. Repressive state responses to such challenges not only served to alienate or even to radicalise large portions of Basque society, but also to underline the extent to which the dictatorship was being driven back towards force of post civil-war proportions, in defence of its prerogatives.[8]

Finally, the 1960s and 1970s saw a steady withdrawal of the Roman

Catholic Church's support. By the time of Franco's death, Church-state relationships were in a state of unprecedented crisis and the dictatorship was losing much of the legitimacy which had once been conferred by links with the Catholic community. Socio-economic, cultural and political changes in Spain together with changes after the Second Vatican Council combined to push the Roman Catholic Church towards acceptance of a pluralistic model of politics and towards an opposition posture. This had, at the least, potentially serious consequences for perceptions of the dictatorship, especially amongst significant portions of Spain's middle classes.[9]

The dictatorship's diminishing popular base was reflected in the narrowing basis of recruitment into its political elite. Ministers drawn from established right-wing groups had, by the end of Franco's life, used up their political capital and, in the absence of any effective pro-regime party, they could not readily be replaced. The result was to drive the state towards increased reliance upon civilian and military recruits co-opted from within the state bureaucracy. Franco's last 'cabinet' was, in fact, largely composed of functionaries. Its lack of a real base in the country clearly left it ill-fitted to preside over a succession crisis.[10]

All these problems had a significant international dimension. Tourism, large numbers of migrant Spanish workers and other links with the outside world opened the country up to foreign influences which called into question the dictatorship's relevance. Working-class, student, regional and Catholic opponents of the regime all in different ways received encouragement or inspiration from abroad. Equally, it became plain that Spanish integration into NATO or the EEC could only be achieved within the context of major political changes. In the case of the EEC this was especially important for by the end of Franco's life a consensus had emerged in political and business circles that tended to see EEC membership as a precondition of Spain's long-term economic health.[11]

THE SUCCESSION PROBLEM: THE QUESTION OF REGIME MAINTENANCE OR TRANSITION

Franco's solution to the succession problem was the transfer of governmental responsibility to a team led by his deputy and close ally, Admiral Carrero Blanco, with a monarch trained under the dictator's auspices ultimately succeeding him as head of state. The monarch was intended to legitimise the continuance of authoritarian rule and, by supplying an element of continuity, was meant to offer symbolic reassurance to the dictatorship's supporters. In practice, Carrero Blanco's assassination (1973) much reduced the scheme's already limited chances of success, for he was perhaps the only figure capable of successfully arbitrating between the discrepant elements associated with the dictatorship. Similarly, as things materialised, the new monarch, Juan Carlos, gained an unexpected freedom of manoeuvre that he was to use in unanticipated ways.[12]

When Juan Carlos did succeed in 1975, the monarchy in principle had three major options.[13] First, it could have sought to preserve the essence of the existing regime. This option was espoused for both self-interested and ideological reasons by small but influential groups close to Franco's family, some unrepentant Falangists, small but vociferous ultra-conservatives, some senior bureaucrats and, most substantially, significant portions (particularly at senior levels) of the armed forces and police. Collectively, these groups were referred to in contemporary journalistic jargon as 'the Bunker'.

Second, there was the possibility of initiating change from within the regime with a view to broadening its base, incorporating fresh participants and so generating the legitimacy or consent arguably necessary for long-term stability. Well before Franco's death, this was a strategy that had been espoused by 'reformist' elements within his regime who saw it as the surest defence against more radical change. Such reformists were, however, divided about the particular evolutionary pathway to follow, and they certainly did not all favour parliamentary democracy. For example, some advocated a re-generated Falangist Party, whilst others supported a single party embracing an institutionalised pluralism of groups, perhaps analogous to the Mexican Institutional Revolutionary Party (PRI). The absence of clear agreement amongst those concerned was to be a major factor in the success of an alternative reformist strategy.

Third, opposition groups or parties, clearly at odds with the dictatorship, advocated a 'democratic rupture' whereby the nature of the future political system would be left an open matter to be decided by a freely-elected constituent assembly, presided over by a provisional all-party government that did not guarantee places to pro-regime forces. This was the preferred strategy of the Socialist Party (PSOE) and Communist Party (PCE), as well as of regional parties, Christian Democratic, Social Democratic and Liberal groupings. It was a strategy that kept open the possibility of a republican form of government. It also implied a loss of political initiative on the part of the existing regime's beneficiaries, and so pointed to possible confrontations with some of the latter.

Spain's prime minister at the time of Franco's death, Carlos Arias Navarro, initially seemed to offer some possibility of a limited reformist strategy. It became apparent, however, that he lacked the necessary will and capacity. He was hemmed in by members of 'the Bunker', and was unable to mobilise the support needed to break free from the latter's constraining influence. The result was to drive his government back in the direction of the first or most defensive strategy, and so to deprive some of his ministers of their once apparently promising 'reformist' credentials.[14] This was particularly true, for example, of Manuel Fraga Iribarne, a former Francoist minister who, following a period out of government, had seemed likely to re-emerge as one of the chief architects of a new political order. The net result was a vacuum, close to the heart of the existing political system, that others subsequently filled.

In saying this, it is the view of this author that there was nothing inevitable about the final outcome. Different decisions or attitudes on the part of the major protagonists could have produced different and arguably more disastrous results. On the other hand, it seems that a more decisive leader than Arias Navarro would also have found it hard to provide long-term stability on the basis of his initiatives. Given the changed political environment, following

Franco's death, the viability of any apparently defensive strategy was bound to be open to question. Thus in opposition circles the dictator's departure had aroused great expectations, for it was widely sensed that the removal of the regime's lynchpin would create an unprecedented crisis of authority without obvious solutions. Nobody, it was assumed, could in the long run continue to mediate successfully between the regime's constituent groups. It was similarly assumed that the dictator's undoubted charismatic and legitimising authority could not be readily transmitted to his successors. Even the regime's adversaries acknowledged that Franco's unique historical role and his sheer durability had vested him with authority, *vis-à-vis* his own followers, that gave to his regime a degree of stability likely otherwise to be denied. Equally, there was some acknowledgement that within the wider society Franco had as an individual acquired a degree of respect that was not accorded to the political system as a whole. Even whilst he was alive that personal authority was something of a diminishing asset. Given the extent of the changes in Spanish society, it was clear that his departure was almost bound to create fresh uncertainty in governing circles and new hopes amongst the opposition.

Such expectations were speedily reflected in the surfacing of still technically illegal parties, and in the organisation of still technically illegal strikes. Not least, the government faced openly expressed regional-based dissent which, in the Basque country, continued to take violent forms. Confronted by such pressures the first post-Franco government's response was to retreat from a relatively conciliatory posture toward reliance upon customary forms of police repression. There were, however, significant elements in the regime's by now obviously divided political elite who appreciated that undue dependence upon such methods could deny the new monarchy a chance of acquiring a significant measure of legitimacy and hence the prospect of survival.

Juan Carlos himself responded, in July 1976, by replacing Arias Navarro with his own appointee, Adolfo Suárez.[15] Initially the latter's elevation was greeted by unsurprising dismay in both reformist and opposition circles. The king, after all, worked through the legal machinery bequeathed by Franco, and Suárez himself had pursued a successful career under the dictatorship in a series of politically sensitive posts. Nevertheless, it became apparent that Juan Carlos had used the machinery, designed to perpetuate authoritarian rule, to promote an ally who would co-operate with him as chief architect of a transition to liberal democracy.

It is not clear if Suárez came into office with a pre-determined strategy, or whether he responded in ad hoc fashion to unfolding events. The pattern of change that emerged suggests that the king and he were initially agreed on the need for a decisive shift toward constitutional government, whilst the exact nature and timing of change was, in significant measure, a matter of coping with pressures that arose en route from within the governing coalition and from the opposition. Moreover, there are indications that office holders were sometimes constrained, by dint of quickly changing circumstances, to move further and faster than initially envisaged. The legalisation of the Communist Party is a prime example.

THE TRANSITION STRATEGY OF ADOLF SUÁREZ: WORKING TOWARDS CONSENSUS

With hindsight, one can see that the very qualities that made Suárez seem an unlikely promoter of major evolutionary change were the very ones that qualified him for this task. He was almost the archetypal technocrat ('tecnico') of the sort that had characterised Franco's last government but, for that reason, he was of a pragmatic disposition and relatively unencumbered with inherited 'ideological baggage'. He was an outstanding member of the younger generation of officials who surfaced toward the end of Franco's life – officials who looked to the state as a source of patronage and career advancement. As such, they were generally conservative in outlook and unsympathetic to radical socio-economic change. Many of them acquired links with banking or industrial interests, and were correspondingly concerned to safeguard existing economic arrangements.[16] They were also concerned, as far as possible, to protect the state bureaucratic institutions that had provided them with their initial base. On the other hand, they were too young to have personally experienced the upheavals that led to the creation of Franco's regime, and so had a commitment to the dictatorship that tended to be provisional and prudential in character rather than deeply psychological or ideological. They also tended to be more cosmopolitan than their elders, and so more open to foreign influences. In particular, they came to see that the legitimacy likely to be conferred by liberal democracy might provide better long-term safeguards for their interests than a narrowly-based dictatorship. For many from such backgrounds, liberal democracy was, at the outset, pragmatically embraced as the political formula most likely to guarantee their preferred form of stability. It was by mobilising such elements inside the state apparatus that Suárez secured his initial base for the delicate task of re-writing Spain's political rules.

The task was obviously delicate because of continuing opposition from unrepentant Francoists within the regime and because of pressures, on the other flank, for 'a democratic rupture'. There always seemed the possibility that major changes could provoke such resistance from entrenched elements within the Movement's bureaucracy, portions of the civil service, the business community and the security forces that a military takeover would eventually be attempted. The price of the evolutionary pathway was the need to leave groups with a potential veto power temporarily undisturbed. It was this which obviously marked off the Spanish from the Portuguese and the Greek transition experience. There was clearly no question of colonial wars leading to the radicalisation of the military and so to the military's overthrow of dictatorial institutions. Equally, there was no question of an overtly military regime collapsing in the wake of a last desperate overseas venture. Rather, it was a matter of certain leaders, with some military allies, outflanking a military establishment that was indifferent or hostile to the liberalisation process.[17]

Paradoxically, Franco's lengthy dictatorship had succeeded in promoting a significant degree of depoliticisation within the military, and this perhaps left his successors with initial if limited freedom of manoeuvre. Nevertheless, Franco's deliberate refusal to promote military reform left it more resistant than any other major institution to processes of change in Spanish society. Thus, there was always the danger that opposition pressures could turn latent hostility into overt resistance. On the other hand, an insufficient response to the opposition's heightened expectations would mean a forfeiting of that trust and co-operation upon which a putative liberal democracy depended for legitimacy and stability. In such a situation, serious elements of risk were always present. Could therefore the negotiating skills of Spain's new leaders, and perhaps a necessary ambiguity on their part, suffice to contain such risk during the intitial transition period?

In confronting such difficulties Suárez, besides his supporters in the bureaucracy and some business sectors, had four significant assets. First, his career under Franco had provided him with an unusually good knowledge of the dictatorship's personnel and customary procedures. Equally, he had developed to an unusual extent the bargaining and other skills needed to manipulate successfully the bureaucratic machinery. This, ironically, was to be of importance in exploiting the existing political system's legal and political resources for the purposes of dismantling it.

Second, Suárez could count on continuing support from the king who played an unusually active role as the legitimator of change amongst those, particularly though not exclusively in the armed forces, who were at best ambivalent toward proposed reforms. In doing so, the monarch was drawing on more than one political tradition. As Franco's chosen heir he was perceived by conservative political groupings associated with the dictatorship as a symbol of continuity, whose claims to allegiance could be invoked in support of change as a necessary development of Francoist legality. The king, therefore, played a pivotal role in using Franco's legal framework to dismantle his regime. Equally, he helped to quieten the doubts and to undermine the bargaining position of those committed to Franco's own solution to the succession problem. On the other hand, Juan Carlos also clearly aligned himself with the liberal monarchical tradition whose roots are traceable back through the reign of his grandfather, Alfonso XIII, to the Restoration political settlement of the 1870s. His role in appointing Suárez, in subsequently supporting his refoming initiatives and in helping to draw opposition parties into the transition process all showed that he placed himself in this camp. The monarchy, in such circumstances, was to serve in some degree as the symbolic focus of a certain process of national reconciliation.[18]

Third, Suárez's control over the state apparatus, apart from initially leaving him with the political initiative, gave him control over sources of information denied to all his competitors. In particular, his capacity to monitor the state of public opinion was to prove especially significant when it came to out-manoeuvring opposition parties. His intelligence identified large bodies of moderate or conservative opinion desiring change, but not yet identified with established parties and ready for mobilisation in support of his programme. Equally, he realised that advocates of 'the democratic rupture' might be exaggerating their potential support.

Finally, Suárez was able to exploit the opposition's internal divisions.[19] Partly, this was a question of a plethora of newly-formed parties emerging under the leadership of 'notables' anxious for a place in any new political order. It was also a question of more deep-seated rivalries – rivalries sometimes cutting across the simple division of government and opposition. Christian Democratic groups, for example, emerged out of both camps. Not least, there were deep-rooted antagonisms, going back to Civil War days, that engendered friction between socialists and communists. In the period of manoeuvring prior to and immediately following Franco's death, this division was expressed in the adherence of these two parties to separate opposition alliances. It continued with differing responses to official initiatives. Thus, perhaps paradoxically, the PCE, concerned to rehabilitate itself following decades of anti-communist propaganda, was relatively more co-operative than its socialist counterpart. Such a division was perhaps especially advantageous for the government, given that these two parties were the only ones, with claims to national status, that had effective organisations and contact with actual or potential constituents.

The significance of these assets can be gauged by charting the process whereby the dictatorship was dismantled from within.[20] Thus, Suárez's knowledge and successful manipulation of existing institutions became apparent in the decision of Franco's quasi-legislative body, the Cortes, to vote itself out of existence.[21] That body, significantly enough, was largely composed of public officials vulnerable to governmental pressures. Under Franco, this had ensured that it remained a largely rubber-stamping body. Now it opened the way to the old order's legally-sanctioned demise. Similarly, in December 1976, the premier showed astute management of public opinion by successfully invoking a referendum in support of his proposed constitutional changes. In this referendum 77.4 per cent of the electorate voted; 94.2 per cent backing the government, and only 2.6 per cent recording their opposition. Overwhelming approval was consequently registered for the dismantling of 'the Movement', the legalisation of political parties and the holding of elections to a bicameral parliament to be charged with supporting a government and drawing up a constitution. The ground was thereby cut from under proponents of 'the democratic rupture', whose call for abstention in the referendum had been largely ignored. Rather, the incumbent government had, in significant measure, successfully established its claim to determine the timing and terms of the projected transition. It had clearly retained the political initiative both in face of opposition demands and in dealings with pro-regime advocates of continuing authoritarian rule. Though the latter remained entrenched in strategically located parts of the state apparatus, within the wider society they were seen to be isolated.

The net effect of such developments was, at least for the time being, the initiation of what may be described as a period of consensus politics. Opposition parties, having been out flanked over the matter of the refer- endum, became drawn into a process of collaboration which enabled the government to implement its proposals. Such an opposition response was not inevitable, for the leaders of opposition parties might have heeded their more intransigent adherents and continued to espouse a 'maximalist' position. As it was, the opposition's leaders chose to moderate their demands for the sake of stabilising the new democracy. However, continuing violence in the Basque region combined with the army's traditional antipathy towards any challenge to the unitary conception of the state threatened to disrupt this emerging pattern of consensus, since government concessions could have been seen as made under duress.

Military opposition also underlay one particular crisis which could have jeopardised the process, namely the legalisation of the Communist Party. In right-wing and, above all, military circles decades of anti-communist propaganda had confirmed a fundamentally negative view of this political force. The Civil War, after all, was ostensibly an anti-Marxist 'Crusade', and the dictatorship had particularly justified itself as a bastion against the spread of communism. Thus, in some military circles, proposals to incorporate the PCE into a new political system represented an apparent sticking point. The democratic opposition, however, felt constrained to withhold co-operation from an experiment seeking to place such limitations upon the liberalisation process. This was partly an ideological matter, but it was also seen as an alternative to driving the communists into a potentially destabilising underground opposition. Initially Suárez tried to evade responsibility by appealing for a judicial ruling, but the judiciary's refusal to adjudicate in such an obviously political matter ultimately obliged him to cut the Gordian knot. Thus in April 1977 the PCE was legalised, but not without the generation of serious tensions inside the armed forces. On this occasion, the monarch's legitimising role proved particularly important in gaining grudging acceptance of change.

The way was eventually cleared for elections. In so far as the electoral process and its results are relevant for understanding the overall dynamics of the transition from dictatorship to democracy, a brief discussion seems in order,[22] especially with respect to Suárez's own 'Unión del Centro Democrático' (UCD), which emerged only weeks before the elections. Responding to initiatives first taken by moderate opposition and 'reformist' notables of monarchist loyalties, Suárez's lieutenants, operating from within the government, reached out to negotiate a merger. The result was a federation of Liberal, Social Democratic and Christian Democratic factions emanating from opposition ranks, together with Suárez's allies emanating from within the existing state apparatus. Within the new alliance key positions tended to pass into the hands of the premier's supporters, and he became the acknowledged leader. To that extent, he had confirmed his hold on the political initiative and, in the process, had forged a previously absent pro-government electoral machine.[23]

The UCD, which emerged from the June 1977 election as the largest single party, was to prove a transient phenomenon, but it did play a crucial role during critical stages of the transition to liberal democracy. It temporarily offered Suárez the base he needed to retain the political initiative during the final constitution-making process, and also served as the agency under whose auspices strategically-placed sectors of the post-Franco electorate were first politically mobilised, both in the 1977 elections and again in those of 1979. On both these occasions, many of the previously uncommitted were drawn to the UCD by Suárez's personal appeal as successfully projected by the still government-controlled media. Amidst a still fluid situation, they responded often in deferential fashion to the image of a leader. Not least, it appears,

Suárez benefited from his association with the monarch.[24] The latter eschewed overt involvement in electoral politics, but his known approval of Suárez worked to the premier's advantage amongst many of the more traditionally-orientated sectors of the previously uncommitted electorate. Such support was to prove unstable, but it did in the short run give Suárez the base needed to pursue his chosen strategy.

THE CONSTITUENT PROCESS, 1976-8

Having thus confirmed his hold on the political initiative, Suárez was subsequently able to retain a large degree of control over the detailed constitution-making process.[25] Much of the spade-work was done in sub-committees or, at most, committees of the two houses of parliament on which the UCD had majorities. Opposition parties other than the socialists were minimally represented on such bodies. This produced understandable complaints from affected groups, but generally it favoured simplified bargaining procedures. Party discipline was invoked usually with success, when agreements reached in committee became the subject of full-scale parliamentary debate. Such debate did involve the amending of detailed proposals, but the underlying principles were largely unaltered. In general, UCD leaders remained senior partners in a co-operative exercise involving major but restricted portions of the nation's political elite.

Periodically, contentious matters arose which endangered the consensus thus nurtured. The critically important co-operation of the UCD and the PSOE threatened to founder over such sensitive matters as Church-state relationships and related educational issues. Equally, the sharply conflicting priorities of the right-wing 'Alianza Popular' and of the Basque nationalists threatened to prevent a resolution of the regional question. In such cases, however, progress was maintained by resorting to informal meetings where handfuls of leaders negotiated 'treaties' without publicity or wider-ranging discussion. Such tactics were criticised as being unduly reminiscent of the 'backstage' politics of Franco's era. Certainly Suárez and his lieutenants seemed more at home with such manoeuvres than in deploying traditional parliamentary skills. It was, however, a modus operandi which most political groups were ultimately prepared to accept. To some extent defiant opposition gestures, especially in the PSOE's case, were designed more to appease party militants than seriously to obstruct the parliamentary bargaining process.

The national political elite's prevailing mood favoured constitutional consensus, but the price of this was a constitution shot through with ambiguity and unresolved contradictions.[26] This particularly seems to be the case where the constitution, following previous Spanish practice, included provisions of a relatively detailed socio-economic kind. The constitution, for example, underwrites the notion of a mixed economy, whilst being unclear about the balance between public and private sectors. The net result is to leave room for future freedom of manoeuvre, but also to create the possibility that somewhat routine political debates could become the subject of constitutional controversy. On the other hand, the present constitution, by contrast with all its Spanish predecessors, cannot be perceived as the 'private' property of particular sectional interests, ideological tendencies or political groupings. Spain's history of constitutional government had been one of changing regimes launched with ground rules established by the currently dominant coalition of interests, and effectively discriminating against their opponents. The republican constitution of 1931, for example, contained anti-clerical provisions liable to alienate large sections of conservative Catholic opinion. The present constitution's architects, by contrast, sought to avoid such an outcome. Therefore, despite its ambiguity, this document was arguably much more likely than its predecessors to provide a basis for widespread popular consent and hence legitimacy.

This outcome may be partly seen as a reflection of the more deep-seated socio-economic and cultural changes that had made the survival of Franco's dictatorship a doubtful proposition.[27] For example, the emergence of a larger and more variegated middle class discouraged the kind of sharply polarised and ideological conflicts that characterised the 1930s. Equally, secularising tendencies, coupled with changing Catholic values, have tended to defuse the clerical issue in Spanish politics. But alongside these significant factors, the outcome owed much to the leadership of the nation's political elite and its calculated response to this changing environment or its own experiences. To some degree, the latter may be a question of generational change. Certainly, the leadership of both the UCD and PSOE came into the hands of politicians with no experience of the 1930s but with shared experiences of the declining years of Franco's dictatorship while, equally, the passage of time had removed from the scene the doctrinaire republican parties and the mass anarchist movement of a previous era.

It may also be said that a 'learning process' was at work. On all sides, there was a determination to avoid the violence that had given rise to Franco's regime and the oppressive rigidity characteristic of his brand of stability. This was true, also, of the Communist Party, whose most senior leadership was relatively unaffected by generational change. Under Santiago Carrillo (who had been active in the 1930s), the PCE remained, if anything, more conciliatory than the Socialist Party. For example, communist parliamentarians voted during the constitution-making process for the monarchy's permanent restoration, whilst PSOE members abstained. Similarly, communists voted to accept a compromise provision that disestablished the Catholic Church whilst stipulating that the authorities 'will take into account the religious beliefs of Spanish society and will, therefore, maintain relations with the Catholic Church and other confessions'. PSOE members adhered more closely to their original concept of an unambiguously secular state by, once more, abstaining. The extent to which the shared experience of dictatorship had left its mark on the quest for consensus may possibly be gauged by the way in which the new constitution not only enshrined 'classic' liberal freedoms or rights, but also went out of its way to repudiate explicitly characteristic practices of the defunct dictatorship. For example, the final document effectively outlaws the death penalty and the use of military courts in dealing with civilians. In this important sense, the constitution, employing S. E. Finer's terminology, bore the distinctive imprint of an 'autobiographical' exercise.[28]

Parliament's final vote on the proposed constitution testified to the extent of the final agreement.[29] In the lower house, 325 'yes' votes were recorded as against 'no' votes from five 'Alianza Popular' members, one Catalan nationalist and one left-wing Basque nationalist. Eleven members abstained – most of these also being Basque nationalists. The upper house produced much the same result. Similarly, in the ensuing popular referendum, in December 1978, all the major national parties campaigned for acceptance. Rejection was favoured only by fascist groupings, some small 'New Left' groups, left-wing Basque nationalists and a minority faction of the 'Alianza Popular'. The 'mainstream' Basque nationalists (the PNV) were the chief advocates of abstention.

In the referendum itself, 67.7 per cent of eligible voters turned out, of whom 87.8 per cent approved the constitution and only 7.9 per cent voted 'no'. The net result was declared support for the new political system from 59.4 per cent of the possible electorate, as opposed to the 73.2 per cent who had voted positively in the earlier 1976 referendum. This decline in popular enthusiasm has a variety of explanations: disillusionment on the part of a politically inexperienced electorate that had attached unrealistic socio-economic expectations to the advent of a more open political system; particular groups objecting to specific constitutional provisions as, for example, in the case of some more traditional Catholics who felt the Church had been given insufficient guarantees; while finally, amongst the least politically aware it was simply a question of electoral participation losing its novelty. Nevertheless, the overall result still leads one to re-affirm that the vote represented a historically high level of popular support for a new constitutional experiment. Conversely, anti-system parties, with the possible exception of militant Basque nationalists, could acquire little comfort from the limited size or the generally thin spread of clearly expressed dissent.

The end result of the constitution-making process was, for the most part, a conventional parliamentary system, the details of which need not detain us long in the context of this discussion.[30] The chief emphasis, particularly reflecting the UCD's preoccupations, was upon the strengthening of the executive's hand *vis-à-vis* parliament in order to facilitate effective and stable government. The aim, in principle, was to minimise the parliamentary damage that could be inflicted on governments in the context of the sort of multi-party situation that prevailed during Spain's last liberal-democratic experiment. For example, the idea of a constructive vote of no confidence was consciously borrowed from the West German constitution. In similar vein, the election and composition of the two houses of parliament was geared so as to over-represent somewhat the more traditional, rural and thinly populated parts of Spain from which the UCD expected to derive much of its support. At the instigation of the socialists, a form of proportional representation was adapted which partially offset the consequences of this. Nevertheless, the net effect was deliberately to erect structural obstacles to electoral victory on the part of left-wing political forces. A significant role for the monarch in resolving possible governmental crises was part of the same attempt to maximise the elements of continuity and stability.

Provision for a Constitutional Court apparently subjected the executive to significant limitations, but the mode of appointment to the court meant that, even here, the new political system was liable, at least in the first instance, to operate with a generally conservative bias.

Probably the most distinctive feature of the system was constitutional provision for the creation of autonomous regions. Discussion of this gave rise to a particularly controversial debate, which reflected the exceptionally divisive nature of the issue. The result was a series of compromises between centralists, mainly associated with the former dictatorship, and those who to varying degrees favoured decentralisation. UCD concessions on this front illustrated well the general approach of that party's leaders to the constitution-making process over which they presided. Whilst generally stressing the creation of stable institutions less vulnerable to the kind of strains that had helped to destroy earlier Spanish experiments in liberal democracy, they also shared real willingness to compromise in order that the new political system could be launched with the widest possible measure of public support. In order to retain the short-run political initiative, Suárez and his lieutenants were constrained to yield ground to opponents with mass-based and hence substantial bargaining power.

DEVELOPMENTS SINCE 1978: LIBERAL DEMOCRACY ON TRIAL

Since 1978, Spain has passed through a period during which its new liberal democracy has been 'on trial'. In a literal sense, the fate of all liberal democracies may be regarded as perennially or ultimately hanging in the balance. There is often a constant underlying tension between dynamic factors working for stability or survival and those which may be working in contrary directions. Nevertheless, it seems appropriate to discriminate between relatively well-entrenched liberal democracies that have an apparently well developed or established capacity for containing potentially destabilising forces and those, like Spain, with an unproven capacity for managing conflict within the context of institutionalised political competition. Moreover, one can talk of 'virtuous' or 'vicious' circles tending respectively towards the consolidation of established arrangements or towards an accelerating destructive process.

Viewed from such a perspective, sheer durability may be one factor in making for further long-term stability. Freshly created liberal-democratic institutions, operating amidst uncertainty concerning the extent or depth of commitment to liberal-democratic practices, may need time in which to demonstrate their capacity to tackle pressing problems on the national political agenda. Such time may make it possible to confirm previously qualified support for the new arrangements or perhaps to transform largely instrumental commitments into commitments of a more affective nature. Equally, it may be possible to nurture a more widely and deeply shared sense of the legitimacy of the experiment and so create reserves of goodwill which can be drawn upon when future difficulties have to be faced. Much may depend on the extent to which political elites satisfy the changing expectations of their constituents and communicate to their followers a determination to abide by the liberal-democratic 'rules of the game'. There is an important question of denying actual or potential opponents of the system the incentives or opportunities to mobilise significant anti-system forces. If, as in Spain, there has been recent experience of authoritarian rule this question has a particularly pressing and obvious significance.[31]

Given the time-scale involved one may say that, in the case of Spain, such an initial testing period has yet to end, and that conclusions about long-term prospects must be of a correspondingly provisional character. In the language of Rustow, Spain's new liberal-democracy has yet to emerge from its period of 'habituation'.[32] Nevertheless, it seems possible to make interim judgements. Not least, it is possible to assess the performance of Spain's new polity in the light of those factors or processes deemed by Rustow to be characteristic of such an 'habituation' period.

For Rustow, the situation is typically one of politicians and citizens learning, through actual use of democratic institutions, 'to place their faith in the new rules and to apply them to new issues'. Such trust grows, it is further suggested, if at an early stage a wide variety of groups can gain access to political power, for then the incentives to abide by the rules seem likely, on all sides, to be increased. Not least, it is indicated, there is the whole question of integrating the mass of citizens into the new system through the medium of political parties and also (though Rustow himself does not mention this point) through the medium of previously non-existent or illegal interest group activity.

The task of generating and confirming trust in liberal-democratic procedures may be said, in Spain's case, to have been somewhat complicated by the extent to which the initial constitutional consensus was bought at the price of deferring potentially divisive issues – issues that have subsequently further forced themselves on the attention of political leaders. Spain's present constitution, by contrast with its predecessors, did not seek to embody relatively specific programmes of political action but, instead, established general principles perhaps liable in practice to mask potentially serious disagreements at the level of routine political conflict.

This was true, albeit to a limited extent, of Church-state relationships. The constitutional compromise over this matter disestablished the Church whilst continuing to acknowledge the institution's traditional social importance, but it left unresolved such potentially serious matters of dispute as the law on divorce or abortion and the Church's role in education. Even during the UCD's period in office, and still more during the present socialist government's tenure, such matters have given rise to inter-party and Church-state conflict. The latter may be of particular concern, given a possible need to mobilise reserves of support for the new regime from outside the conventional party-political arena and the Church's still quite significant standing within Spanish society. That institution was generally behind moves to open up the political system, but had reservations about some specific implications of change that could be perceived, at least by more traditional Catholics, as threatening to established doctrinal or moral positions. Thus, the Catholic Bishops' conference adopted an essentially neutral position *vis-à-vis* the new constitution, and a minority of its members were critical. This in its turn provoked angry reactions from socialist and other proponents of a more obviously secular society. The relative restraint characterising such disputes confirms, it must be stressed, that the issues involved have lost much of their once explosive quality. Nevertheless, conflicts of this type during the early stages of a liberal-democratic experiment, and taken in conjunction with arguably more salient issues, could adversely affect the regime's legitimacy amongst significant portions of Spain's still relatively numerous traditionally-orientated Roman Catholics.

Far more contentious, in practice, has been implementation of the constitution's provisions covering regional autonomy.[33] Above all, difficulties have arisen from the now diminished but continuing violence of militant Basque nationalists. Indeed, their activities seem still to present Spain's political institutions with their single most menacing and potentially destabilising challenge, for they represent in a particularly pronounced form a provocation to right-wing exponents of that centralist Spanish nationalism which has traditionally regarded decentralisation as a step toward the existing state's destruction. The new socialist government's inability to make a wholly fresh start on this front, which some had believed possible, simply underlines both the intractability of the problem, and the extent to which it gives the management of Spanish liberal democracy a problematic dimension without real parallels in other West European states that have recently moved from dictatorship to democracy. Convincing militant nationalists and dogmatic centralisers that fruitful accommodations can be reached within the framework of existing institutions remains a major unfinished task. Serious miscalculations on the part of those most concerned with the management of centre-periphery relationships could have correspondingly serious consequences for the future of the entire polity.

A less obviously pressing but, over the long term, fundamentally important problem is the continuing issue of the economy. In the long-term, popular perceptions of liberal democracy seem likely to be significantly affected by perceptions of economic performance and responses to governmental handling of economic problems. Dilemmas on this front are, of course, accentuated by the general international economic circumstances prevailing during the formative years of Spain's new political system. Just as the republic of the 1930s was established amidst troubled economic conditions, so the re-launching of liberal democracy has coincided with a period of international recession – recession that has ended the dramatic growth of Franco's last years, and exposed the extent to which earlier expansion depended on tourism, foreign investment and other factors ultimately lying beyond Spain's own control. The dependence on imported energy sources has further complicated the situation, and added to the general problems of costs, inflation and unemployment. The net result was a relatively unpropitious climate for the launching of new institutions, and one liable to diminish the freedom of manoeuvre of political leaders.

These environmental factors were almost inevitably compounded by the extent to which Franco's immediate successors became absorbed in constitution-making tasks, and so neglected underlying economic problems. On the other hand, it was the UCD's own internal divisions which, after the adoption of the 1978 constitution, stood in the way of effective management, and so led to a dramatic collapse of this party's electoral base.[34] Indeed, the socialists' recent electoral victory (1982) was, in part, expressive of popular protest against their predecessor's performance on this front. Consequently, the new government's performance in the same sphere, over the next one or two years, will not only affect its own electoral fate, but may also help to shape popular evaluations of liberal democracy itself. The PSOE capitalised upon a widespread sense that there was a big backlog of economic and social reforms that needed to be tackled before Spain could regard itself as a thoroughly 'modern' industrial society. A good deal depends on the socialists, in government, being able to make some significant progress in appropriate directions. Partly, this is a matter of the PSOE satisfying the expectations of its own party militants, but it is also a question of satisfying important segments of moderate liberal-minded opinion, for whom the PSOE now offers the most credible vehicle for gradual but significant reform. As already noted, the frustration of the perhaps more exaggerated expectations attached to liberal democracy's advent led to some disillusionment and some decrease in overtly expressed support for new procedures. In 1982, it appeared as if that tide had been at least temporarily stemmed. Political parties and trade unions rallied considerable bodies of support in the election of that year. At this still relatively early stage, it is possible that failure on the part of the socialist government to generate a significant sense of achievement could lead to increased disillusionment. This seems most likely, in the first instance, to manifest itself primarily in apathy, but there is always the longer-term possibility of mobilisation, on both the left and right, of anti-system forces.

Within Spain it is agreed, across the conventional political spectrum, that avoidance of such outcomes partially depends on the international context. Just as externally-generated pressures helped to call into question the viability of Franco's regime so, it is suggested, the stabilisation of liberal democracy partly depends on a supportive external environment. During the delicate period of transition, considerable benefit was derived from the external support available to political parties seeking to establish themselves. This was particularly true of German Social Democratic support for the PSOE. Now, there is a broad measure of inter-party agreement in the country that Spain's accession to the EEC, on appropriate terms, is needed to provide the new polity with a suitably stable economic framework. It could be that too much is being expected of EEC membership. On the other hand, entry given Spain's present political circumstances could have positive psychological effects on both political leaders and citizens, whilst a closed door might have the reverse consequences.

The international context also has a bearing on the Spanish polity's capacity to cope with another and more immediately obvious stumbling block that has to be negotiated during the current stage in Spain's political development, namely the problem posed by inherited state and, above all, military institutions. Thus, the integration of the country's armed forces into NATO and the playing of a positive professional role within that context may be one of the factors needed to move those forces away from their traditional position of self-appointed political arbiter. Throughout the original transition process the military wielded an ultimate power of veto. In particular, it remained a centre of opposition to decentralising tendencies and, above all, to the politically-inspired violence associated most obviously with the Basque country though also associated with the ostensibly ultra-left wing GRAPO. The extent of the problem was finally revealed by the abortive but serious coup attempt of February 1981.[35] Equally, legislation following the attempt, which sought to reduce the powers of autonomous regions underlined the extent to which the political elite felt it necessary tacitly to accommodate military demands. The present government, and its successors, are therefore left with the delicate task of reforming the military without provoking it into renewed action, or creating conditions that might invite further intervention.

The events of 1981 and afterwards suggest that the key to success lies, in the first instance, within the civilian political arena. Thus, the coup attempt unfolded against the background of the political crisis that heralded the governing UCD's internal dissolution and final collapse. By contrast the socialist government, with much electoral support and an overall parliamentary majority, has presided over a situation in which anti-system elements in the military have been put on the defensive. It seems significant, for example, that military conspirators have had initially light sentences revised in an upward and far more exemplary direction. Put another way, the chief medium-term danger to civilian institutions is likely to spring from an absence of coherent political leadership capable of generating significant and relatively broadly-based reserves of popular consent. Given such leadership, the long-term military reform programme upon which the socialist government has embarked may succeed in its objectives. The military may then be confined to a professional role, operating in the political arena as one more, albeit important, corporate interest group. In much less dramatic form the same could be true of programmes to reform the bureaucracy and judiciary.

Paradoxically, the nature and activities of the military may, in the long run, have indirectly contributed to the stabilisation of Spanish democracy.[36] It is to this arguably more positive side of the account that we finally turn. One major effect of the military's presence has been to contribute toward a certain process of deradicalisation on the Spanish left. This has manifested itself in various closely-linked ways and with various consequences.

First, the military's potential veto power was a factor in persuading the Communist Party to moderate its stance and espouse a reformist Eurocommunist position.[37] This was intended to make it more generally acceptable, but has had the actual effect of undermining its credibility as a radical force and of consequently playing into the hands of its socialist competitors.

Second, the reduction of communist competition made it easier for the PSOE, under Felipe Gonzalez's leadership, to make the transition from a Marxist to a more obviously pragmatic Social Democratic party. This transition was itself a major factor in broadening the PSOE's electoral appeal to the point where it was able to overcome convincingly the obstacles put in the way of its accession to power.

Third, the PSOE's peaceful assumption of power, in the face of deliberately erected obstacles, has probably made a particularly significant contribution to the consolidation of liberal democracy. It satisfied Rustow's criterion that a 'maturing' democracy should maximise opportunities for exercising governmental responsibility. More concretely, it represented a major and peaceful transfer of power from elements largely associated with the former regime to a party having absolutely no stake in the old order. By demonstrating that obstacles to a left-of-centre electoral victory could be overcome, it fulfilled the hope enshrined in the constitution that the new system need not be the sole property of limited interests. In that sense, much was done to accustom the Spanish electorate to liberal-democratic norms and, more specifically, to increase the legitimacy of the new system amongst more 'progressive' elements.

Fourth, the shift in the PSOE's position made it easier for its conservative opponents, and particularly those associated with the 'Alianza Popular', to accept its electoral victory and subsequently to play the role of a conventional liberal-democratic opposition. The move in 1982 of the UCD's more conservative supporters toward the Alianza Popular, and the latter's emergence as the major opposition force, seemed to herald a certain polarisation of the Spanish electorate that some see as potentially dangerous. At least in the medium term, however, it seems as if the PSOE's pragmatism has denied its opponents any incentives to step outside the rules of the liberal-democratic game. Rather, the intially doubtful liberal-democratic credentials of at least some associated with the Alianza Popular now seem to be in the process of becoming rather more firmly established. Certainly, the PSOE in government seems to have generally adopted a reassuring managerial style. It has expressed willingness to manage and plan the economy in concert with business as well as trade union interests, and has not embraced any sweeping nationalisation programme. The net effect seems likely to be some strengthening of the new institutions.

The extent of commitment to liberal democracy was perhaps indicated during the dramatic crisis of February 1981. On that occasion the entire parliamentary elite, including the Alianza Popular, publicly identified itself with the threatened political system. Equally, large public demonstrations manifested significant reserves of support for liberal democracy, and highlighted the very small popular civilian base upon which military rulers could rely. Some conservative politicians may of course be constrained by this latter piece of knowledge. Nevertheless, their responses to the crisis have helped to create the climate in which a serious reform of military institutions can now be contemplated. Similarly, the very important role played by the monarch in containing the crisis seems likely, on balance, to have had positive medium-term effects for Spanish liberal democracy. It is now clear that any dictatorial regime is likely to be denied the legitimacy which the monarchy can confer. Of perhaps greater importance, the monarch's role in the crisis seems likely to have increased the standing of the monarchical institution to the left of the conventional spectrum. To that extent, the institution's significance as a symbolic focus of consensus or cohesion has been increased.

A continuing measure of consensus at the popular level and of cohesion at the elite level seems necessary if liberal democracy is successfully to manage underlying economic problems, political violence, centre-periphery conflicts and still dubiously loyal military institutions. It is still possible, in principle, that a combination of such challenges could precipitate threatening degrees of polarisation. The evidence so far, however, suggests a post 1978 period of 'habituation' generally pointing in the direction of an increased stability. The prospect of renewed dictatorship has not been banished, but it is receding.

NOTES

1. There is, of course, a large literature on Franco's regime. The seminal attempt to characterise its possibly distinctive characteristics was made by Juan Linz 'An Authoritarian Regime: the Case of Spain', published in E. Allardt and Y. Littunen (eds.), *Cleavages, Ideologies and Party Systems* (Helsinki: Transactions of the Westermarck Society, 1964). The regime's institutions are examined in José Amodia, *Franco's Political Legacy* (London: Allen Lane, 1977) and Kenneth N. Medhurst, *Government in Spain* (Oxford: Pergamon Press, 1973).
   A general history of the regime is contained in Raymond Carr and Juan Pablo Fusi, *Spain: Dictatorship to Democracy* (London: Allen & Unwin, 1981). A sociological treatment is contained in Amando de Miguel, *Sociología del Franquismo* (Barcelona, 1975).
2. Biographies of Franco are: Brian Crozier, *Franco, a Biographical History* (London; Eyre & Spottiswoode, 1967); George Hills, *Franco, the Man and his Nation* (London: Robert Hale, 1967); and J.W.D. Trythall, *Franco* (London: Rupert Hart-Davis, 1970). Also cf. Francisco Franco Salgado, *Coversaciones Privadas con Franco* (Madrid, 1976).
   On the Spanish Civil War the standard work in English remains Hugh Thomas, *The Spanish Civil War*, new edition (Harmondsworth: Penguin Books, 1977).
   For contrasting views of the polarisation process, cf. Richard A. H. Robinson *The Origins of Franco's Spain. The Right, the Revolution and the Republic* (Newton Abbot: David & Charles, 1970); and Paul Preston, *Reform Reaction & Revolution in the Second Republic 1931–36* (London: Macmillan, 1978).
3. cf. Stanley G. Payne, *Falange, A History of Spanish Fascism* (Oxford: Oxford University Press, 1962); also, Herbert R. Southworth, *Anti-falange – Estudio Critico del Falange en la Guerra de España* (Paris: Ruedo Ibérico, 1967).
4. The Church is discussed in Juan Ruiz Rico, *El Papel Político de la Iglesia Católica en la España de Franco* (Madrid, 1967). Also, Norman B. Cooper, *Catholicism and the Franco Regime* (London: Sage Publications, 1975). The army is the subject of a study by Julio Busquets Bragulat, *El Militar de Carrera en España* (Barcelona, 1967); also Kenneth N. Medhurst, 'The Military and the Prospects for Spanish Democracy', in *West European Politics*, Vol. 1, No. 1 (February 1978), pp. 42–59.
5. The 'end of ideology' thesis is presented in Gonzalo Fernandez de la Mora, *El Crepúsculo de las Ideologías* (Madrid, 1961).
6. On the general subject of social and economic change, cf. José Felix Tezanos, *Estructura de Clases y Conflictos de Poder en la España Post-Franquista* (Madrid, 1978).
7. On the general subject of opposition to Franco's regime, cf. Juan Linz, 'Opposition in and under an authoritarian regime: The Case of Spain', in Robert Dahl (ed.), *Regimes and Oppositions* (Yale: Yale University Press, 1973).
   Trade unions are discussed in J. Amsden, *Collective Bargaining & Class Conflict in Spain* (London: Weidenfeld & Nicolson, 1972).
   On both working class and student dissent, cf. José Maravall, *Dictatorship and Political Dissent, Workers and Students in Franco's Spain* (London: Tavistock Publications, 1978).
8. On the general background to the Basque and Catalan question, cf. Juan Linz, 'Early state building and late peripheral nationalisms against the state: the Case of Spain', in S. N. Eisenstadt and S. Rokkan (eds.), *Building Nations and States* (Beverly Hills: Sage Publications, 1973); Stanley G. Payne, *Nacionalismo Vasco* (Barcelona, 1974); José Jimenez Blanco, *et al., La Conciencia Regional en España* (Madrid, 1977); Kenneth N. Medhurst, *The Basques and Catalans, A Report for the Minority Rights Group* (London, 1977), and the same author's 'Basques and Basque Nationalism', in Colin H. Williams (ed.), *National Separatism* (Cardiff: University of Wales Press, 1982), pp. 235–61.

9. cf. Juan Ruiz Rico and N. Cooper, op. cit.
10. cf. Felix Tezanos, op. cit. Chapter 11.
11. On Spain and the EEC, cf. Peter Holmes, 'Spain and the EEC', in David S. Bell, *Democratic Politics in Spain* (London: Frances Pinter, 1983), pp. 164–79.
12. For the official answer to the succession issue as discussed by a prominent associate of Opus Dei involved in the process, cf. Laureano López Rodó, *La Larga Marcha Hacia La Monarquia* (Barcelona, 1977).
13. For the general situation at the time of Franco's death, cf. Raymond Carr and Juan Pablo Fusi, op. cit. Chapters 9 and 10.
14. For an 'insider's' view of this government, cf. José Maria de Areilza. *Diario de un ministro de la monarquia* (Barcelona, 1977).
15. The transition process with Suárez's role in it is elaborated in John F. Coverdale, *The Political Transformation of Spain after Franco* (London: Praeger 1979), especially Chapters 3–5.
16. cf. J. Felix Tezanos, ibid.
17. On the post-Franco military, cf. Pedro Vilanova 'Spain: The Army and the Transition', in David S. Bell, op. cit., pp. 147–64.
18. On this whole theme, cf. Kenneth N. Medhurst, 'Spanish Conservative Politics', in Z. Layton-Henry, *Conservative Politics in Western Europe* (London: Macmillan, 1982), especially pp. 296–307. Also, cf. Xavier Tusell, *La Oposición Democrática al Franquismo, 1939–1962* (Barcelona, 1977).
19. cf. Jonathan Storey, 'Spanish Political Parties Before and After the Election' in *Government and Opposition*, Vol 12, No. 4 (Autumn 1977).
20. cf. John F. Coverdale, op. cit., Chapters 3 and 4.
21. Ibid., Chapter 2.
22. On the emergent party system, cf. Raul Morodo *et al., Los Partidos Políticos en España* (Madrid, 1979). Also, cf. relevant chapters in David S. Bell, op. cit.
23. cf. José Amodia, 'Union of the Democratic Centre', in David S. Bell, op. cit. pp. 1–28.
24. cf. Peter McDonough, Antonio López Pina and Samuel Barnes, 'The Spanish Public in Political Transition', in *British Journal of Political Science*, Vol. II, Part I (January 1981).
25. cf. John F. Coverdale, op. cit., Chapter 7.
26. cf. José Amodia, 'The Making of the New Spanish Constitution', unpublished paper presented to the Conference of the Political Studies Association, 1981. Cf. also B. de la Cuadra and S. Gallego-Diaz, *Del Consenso al desencanto* (Madrid, 1981).
27. For a general interpretation of factors underlying processes of change, cf. José Maravall, *The Transition to Democracy in Spain* (London: Croom Helm, 1982).
28. cf. the introduction to S. E. Finer (ed.), *Five Constitutions* (Harmondsworth: Penguin Books, 1979).
29. cf. John F. Coverdale, op. cit.
30. The constitution is briefly discussed by John F. Coverdale, ibid. For a lengthier treatment, cf. Alberto Predieri and E. Garcia de Enterria, *La Constitución Española de 1978* (Madrid, 1981). Also, Jorge de Esteban and Luis Lopez Guerra, *El Regimen Constitucional Español*, 2 Vols. (Madrid, 1982).
31. On such themes, cf. Juan J. Linz and Alfred Stepan (eds), *The Breakdown of Democratic Regimes*, Vol. 1, *Crisis, Breakdown and Re-equilibrium* (London: Johns Hopkins Unversity Press, 1978).
32. cf. D. Rustow, 'Transitions to Democracy: toward a dynamic model', *Comparative Politics*, No.2 (1969–70).
33. For difficulties in this sphere, cf. Chapters 4 and 5 of David S. Bell, op. cit.
34. cf. José Amodia, op. cit.
35. On this episode cf. Julio Busquets *et al., El Golpe, Anatomia y Claves del Asalto al Congreso* (Barcelona, 1981).
36. Some of my thoughts on this general theme were inspired by S. Giner and E. Sevilla 'Spain: From Corporatism to Corporatism', in A. M. Williams (ed.), *Southern Europe Transformed* (London: Harper & Row, 1984).
37. On this subject, cf. David S. Bell, 'The Spanish Communist Party in Transition', in David S. Bell, op. cit., pp. 67–77. Also, Eusebio Mujal-León, *Communism and Political Change in Spain* (Bloomington: Indiana University Press, 1983).

Transition to, and Consolidation of, Democratic Politics in Greece, 1974–1983: A Tentative Assessment

P. Nikiforos Diamandouros

FOCUSING ON REGIME CHANGE

The momentous social and political changes associated with decolonisation, and the heightened awareness among the international, and especially the Western, scholarly community that conceptual categories derived largely from Western historical experience were woefully inadequate analytical tools with which to understand and evaluate the significance of these developments are very relevant in any analysis of regime change. For they lie at the heart of the greatly increased scope of social and political analysis in the past two decades, and of its emphasis on comparative, interdisciplinary and diachronic as well as synchronic approaches to the dynamics of social and political change.

Within this broadened universe of social science concerns, the issue of regime change emerged with particular force in the 1970s, as social scientists and historians grappled with the emergent problems of regime instability and regime breakdown so prevalent among the newly-created states of Asia and Africa. The poverty of theory concerning the relations between state and society became the object of renewed focus by both Marxist and bourgeois scholars. This trend was greatly strengthened by developments in Latin America and southern Europe, where events of a sharply antithetical nature provided ample opportunity for observation and raw materials for theorising.

The breakdown of competitive politics in the southern-cone countries of Latin America, and its obverse, the breakdown of authoritarian regimes in southern Europe – both areas where, unlike Africa and Asia, modern states had been erected over a century ago – added a diachronic dimension to the study of regime transition, and made for richer and more theoretically informed analyses which moved in divergent directions. While the emergence of authoritarian regimes in the southern-cone countries prompted both cultural and structural interpretations ranging from Veliz's centralist tradition argument to O'Donnell's bureaucratic authoritarian-model, the southern European experience focused scholars' attention on the immensely complex and delicate task of re-establishing competitive politics, and on the specific constellation of forces this entailed.[1]

More recently, as *dictadura* gave way to *dictablanda* (weak dictatorship) in some of the southern-cone countries, and as these began, however hesitantly, to edge towards some form of *abertura* or 'opening', the focus of scholarly debate shifted subtly: the concern with the structural, long-term trends which so heavily influenced most theoretically informed attempts to account for the emergence of authoritarian regimes gradually gave way to a heightened sensitivity to the more immediately political aspects of the transitions. The intensely political dimension of the early phase of the transition to competitive politics, the need for compromise, the very dynamics of forging founding coalitions and the exigencies of institution-building mean that, at this particular moment, concern with the more clearly structural problems tends to recede to the background, and to give way to more directly political considerations affecting the management of the transition process.[2]

Finally, a still more recent development relating to the shift in focus just mentioned, but also reflecting an evolutionary tendency in the nature of theoretical concerns, has been the growing emphasis on regime consolidation, and especially on democratic consolidation as a particular phase of regime change, conceptually distinct from regime transition. Though temporally overlapping, and often hard to distinguish in practice, transition and consolidation should be conceived as analytically distinct. The former involves the installation of a new regime, and encompasses an initial phase in regime change marked, above all else, by a series of critical decisions and delicate political choices. These are designed to ensure the active co-operation of social and political actors crucial to the maintenance of the momentum sustaining the new regime, and directly contributing to its legitimation; the acquiescence of potentially hostile forces; and the delegitimation of the predecessor authoritarian regime among as broad a spectrum of the public as possible. In this sense, the transition phase involves both hard political decisions, affecting the distribution of power within the new political system, and equally crucial symbolic acts aimed at delineating the new regime's identity, in providing it with a distinct self-image, and in distinguishing it as clearly as possible from its predecessor.

Consolidation, on the other hand, refers to that phase in a new regime's life which is concerned more directly with the erection of that set of institutions and with the institutionalisation of that set of formal and quasi-formal arrangements and practices which are likely to maximise the chances of its persistence and smooth operation, thereby further strengthening its legitimacy, and minimising the probability of regression, of breakdown and of a relapse to non-competitive politics. While conjunctural factors may indeed affect its course, consolidation is more centrally concerned with longer-term, structural dimensions of regime change. Among the latter, the relative strength or weakness of industrial classes, of the party system and of the trade unions in a particular social formation seem to play a potentially decisive role in the trajectory of the consolidation process. Taken together with alternation in governmental incumbency, these factors constitute fundamental parameters of consolidation, the strength or weakness of which will ultimately depend on the particular manner in which they interact, and on the particular dynamics generated by such an interaction in each case.

Thus, while the weakness of most of these structures coupled with the inability for a smooth and uneventful alternation in power would render consolidation highly problematic, if not unfeasible, a strong consolidation would inversely imply their strong and institutionalised nature, and would constitute *prima facie* evidence of their ability to maintain the dynamic arising from their positive articulation and to minimise the chances of a reversal. A weak consolidation, finally, would involve a number of intermediate combinations, in which the specific articulation of these factors would determine the particular place of a given consolidation on the spectrum, would bring out the nature of its dynamic and would hint at the probability for the maintenance, increase or loss of its initial momentum.[3]

Borrowing from Otto Kirchheimer, I would further argue that these structures, whether separately or in a variety of combinations, act as confining conditions to a strong consolidation; conditions, that is, which have to be overcome if a specific process (in Kirchheimer's case, a revolutionary breakthrough, here a strong consolidation) is to be considered successfully complete. At the same time, and in the absence of a strong consolidation, the same structures will directly influence the particular character and dynamic of the consolidation process, and will provide a basis for understanding the nature of its weaknesses.[4]

Focusing on the dynamic implicit in the consolidation process brings out the multiple points in time in which structural and conjunctural levels interact. This, for example, is particularly the case in the early stages of consolidation, which inevitably overlap with the transition phase of regime change. Indeed, it would seem that the management of the transition, its symbolic content and associations, as well as its length can have a decisive bearing on the initial stages of the consolidation process, and may significantly affect its momentum and long-term evolution. During later stages, as well, particularly in the case of weak consolidations, conjunctural factors can easily affect the dynamic of the process, advancing it, stalling it or causing it to regress, as the case may be.

It is with these considerations in mind that I should like to examine the 1974 transition to competitive politics in Greece, focusing my attention on two major phases: the transition phase *stricto sensu*, which will assign greater emphasis on the politics of regime change and regime instauration, and to the consolidation phase, where macrolevel considerations will be accorded greater weight in an effort to assess both achievements as well as weaknesses in the evolution of the Greek democratic regime, so far.

The study of the Greek transition will also allow us to explore an issue which has increasingly attracted attention in the theoretical debate concerning the requisite conditions for a successful transition to competitive politics: namely the political colouration of the founding coalition. A number of recent studies addressing this question seem to suggest that transitions to competitive politics presided over by moderate, centre and centre-right coalitions stand a better chance of coping successfully with the Scyllas and Charybdises of the early transition phase, and hence, by minimising the chances of involution from the right or of unpredictable radicalisation from the left, constitute a more auspicious beginning for eventual regime consolidation.[5]

At the same time, there can be little doubt that this course, like any other alternative, has its drawbacks which become especially salient in the area of regime legitimation – a critical factor which is immensely and directly affected by the extent to which a new democratic regime manages successfully to solve the issue of continuity versus break with its authoritarian predecessor. To the extent that many of these issues, dilemmas and options were both present in the Greek case, and were apparently consciously addressed as such, it would seem that a systematic examination of this particular transition to competitive politics might be able to contribute to the ongoing theoretical debate centring around this topic.[6]

A final note on method: a concern with the dynamics of transition and of consolidation correspondingly influences the focus of analysis, placing greater emphasis on actors and conditions which played a major role in shaping actual outcomes, and inevitably assigning lesser significance to others which, though essential to the efficacy of the new political system, had a less central role to play in this particular instance. Thus, for example, the conditions of external crisis and threat of war under which regime change was effected in Greece, and the dynamic arising from these initial conditions, allowed Karamanlis to play a disproportionately dominant role in the whole process, while correspondingly curtailing that of the opposition, which, preoccupied as it was with internal problems of organisation and identity during this early, fluid period of open political activity, found it convenient to cede the initiative to the government and to play a more passive role in the whole process. These idiosyncratic characteristics of the Greek case will be reflected in the ensuing analysis.[7]

THE TRANSFER OF POWER IN 1974

If the November 1973 events at the Greek National Technical College (Polytechnic) constitute the substantive *terminus ad quem* of the colonels' authoritarian regime, the July 1974 Cyprus crisis marked the formal end of that regime, and the *terminus a quo* for its democratic successor. Indeed, the crisis represents the single most important factor directly and decisively influencing the actions of protagonists, limiting choices, imposing certain courses of action and precluding others both during the disintegration and dissolution phase of the authoritarian regime and during the crucial initial stages of its democratic successor. In the former instance, it acted as the catalytic agent which, within the short space of 72 hours starting with the Turkish invasion of Cyprus, on 20 July 1974, precipitated a series of crucial decisions by the regime's leadership that effectively signalled the end of authoritarian rule in Greece and opened the way for the surrender of power to the civilian leadership. Chief among these decisions were: (a) the order for a general mobilisation designed to serve as a warning signal for Turkey, but which instantly backfired as an alarming and hardly expected lack of military preparedness was laid bare; and as the open defiance shown by reservists towards career officers revealed the intensity of anti-regime sentiment among the civilian population, and pointed to the grave dangers implicit in any subsequent attempt merely to put the lid down on civil society; (b) the decision of the Joint Chiefs of Staff, on 21 July, the day following the mobilisation order, that the Greek armed forces were not ready for war, and that, in view of the situation and of the dangers it entailed, they would seek 'a political solution' to what was fast threatening to become a major domestic crisis as well.

The decision by the military leadership itself to reassert the hierarchical line of command having been approved by the President of the Republic, Lieutenant-General Phaedon Ghizikis, the power base which had sustained Brigadier-General Demetrios Ioannides in his role as the regime's strongman since November 1973 suddenly collapsed, and the small coterie of army ultras that had been acting in his name found itself without a powerful patron and was eclipsed. The dismissal of the regime's inconsequential civilian government on 23 July set the stage for the surrender of power to the civilian leadership.[8]

The condition of external crisis which served as the proximate cause for the Greek authoritarian regime's self-dissolution acted as an equally critical setting facilitating the instauration of the new democratic regime. The powerful wave of national solidarity, which the imminent possibility of war brought about, made possible the simultaneous repudiation of the colonels and the emergence of a pervasive climate of self-restraint among mass actors which immensely expanded the new civilian leadership's freedom of movement and, at the same time, provided it with a precious interregnum during which it could smoothly effect the transition and make critical decisions designed to ensure the new regime's consolidation.[9]

The transfer of power from the military to the civilian leadership involved two distinct but equally significant phases which occurred fourteen hours apart on 23 and 24 July. In the first, the military leadership met with selected civilian leaders to explore the specific format under which the transfer of power would take place. The eight civilian leaders invited to this meeting represented a spectrum of the country's political forces, which ranged from the pre-1967 Centre Union party on the left, to the staunchly pro-royalist Petros Garoufalias and Spyros Markezinis (the political conservative who had acted as George Papadopoulos''prime minister' in the failed liberalisation attempt of November 1973) on the right.

The internal composition of the group, which leaned decidedly more to the right than to the centre, the absence of any forces to the left of the moderate Centre Union and an initial proposal by Phaedon Ghizikis, who presided over the meeting, that the incumbents in the crucial ministries of National Defence, Public Order and Interior be retained, suggest that the outgoing regime's transition strategy (to the extent that one had been consciously fashioned) was to transfer power to that segment of the civilian leadership which could best be counted upon to combine a return to formal democratic politics with minimal substantive changes in the operation of the political system. Such a formula, if successful, would help salvage as much as possible of the eminent role the armed forces had been able to play in the postwar exclusivist political system, which ingeniously combined formal parliamentary rule with the severe exclusion from political participation of the vanquished side in the civil war of 1946–9. But the leaders of the two major parties, Centre Union and National Radical Union (ERE), resoundingly rejected the proposal for the retention of the incumbents in the 'sensitive' ministries, and there was an icy reaction to Markezinis's suggestion for a 'non-political' government headed by an ultra-conservative diplomat, Christianos Xanthopoulos-Palamas. This suggested the degree of opposition to this scenario by the country's largest political formations, and of their commitment to a return to some form of competitive politics, the specific nature of which remained unclear for the time being.[10]

The second phase of the transfer of power took place in the early morning hours of 24 July, and involved the swearing-in as prime minister of Constantine Karamanlis, the former leader of the conservative National Radical Union (ERE) who since 1963 had lived in self-imposed exile in Paris. The choice of Karamanlis was arrived at following intensive backstage manoeuvring between Evangelos Averoff-Tossizza, a staunch Karamanlis lieutenant who enjoyed the military's confidence, and the regime's leadership. It involved a last-minute abandonment of a formula forged earlier in the day, which would have placed the transition in the hands of the two major political parties, with Panagiotes Kanellopoulos, head of ERE as prime minister, and George Mavros, leader of the Centre Union, as deputy prime minister, and minister of foreign affairs.

The Karamanlis solution, originally brushed aside on the assumption that physical distance from Athens precluded his quick arrival, was considered the best by all participants in this decision. Leader of the anti-communist right during most of the 1950s, a powerful and charismatic personality who had dominated Greek politics until the early 1960s, he had then gone into self-imposed exile following a clash with the monarchy and defeat in the 1963 elections which brought the Centre Union to power. Karamanlis therefore, untarnished by direct involvement in the events which led to the demise of parliamentary politics in 1967, appeared to possess the ideal credentials for being entrusted with the delicate role of transition manager, and for overseeing the whole process of democratic restoration. Acceptable to the military on account of his past anti-communist track record, he could also command the support and confidence of the non-royalist right. He enjoyed an unquestioned appeal to a wide spectrum of the population, which perceived him as a *deus ex machina* that could save the country from its external crisis and steer it in the direction of an uneventful 'normalisation' of political life. This won him the support of large segments of the traditional centre, while to the royalist right opposed to the military regime he was clearly the lesser of two unenviable options.[11]

The unanimity of support with which he was enveloped reflected the widespread assumption that he would preside over some form of restoration of the postwar Greek political system shorn, however, of the abuses which had led to its demise in 1965–7. Implicit in this view was the additional assumption, held by large sectors of the traditional right, that such a change would not involve any fundamental restructuring of the system or of the power relationships which had characterised it. Although the future of the monarchy remained uncertain, there were many among traditional political circles who were envisaging, or hoping for, a mere, albeit significant, liberalisation of the postwar political system, and not for its democratisation, with all the changes in power relations and the opening up of the system that this implied.

This implicit assumption that Karamanlis was the best candidate to preside over an effort to construct a liberalised version of the postwar exclusivist system, which would manage to cope with the uncertainties generated by political mobilisation and radicalisation among major segments of the electorate in the previous decade, essentially explained the virtual *carte blanche* given him in the handling of the transition. It is, in turn, to this *carte blanche* context, which was symbolised in Karamanlis' being initially vested with sole political power and which best explains his subsequent transition and consolidation strategies, that we must now turn.

THE TRANSITION STRATEGY OF KARAMANLIS

As already mentioned, the two strategies were in practice hard to distinguish, and their line of demarcation difficult to define precisely, because of inevitable temporal and spatial overlap. Still, it would appear that the 17 November 1974 elections (held, not accidentally, on the first anniversary of the Polytechnic student uprising which marked the beginning of the end for the colonels' authoritarian regime) provided a turning-point in the move from transition to consolidation.

What, above all, characterises Karamanlis's strategy during the 116 days between 24 July, when he was sworn into office *gratia militarium*, and 17 November when his electoral triumph provided him with popularly-derived legitimacy and independence *vis-à-vis* earlier partners and supporters at the elite level, was his attempt to maximise the benefits arising from the *carte blanche* context of his coming to power. This he did through the minimisation of commitments to both collective and individual actors, the personalisation of crisis management and the maximisation of his freedom of movement. He accomplished this by adopting a deliberately gradualist course of action in which elements of continuity and change, as well as substantive and symbolic acts, were finely and delicately balanced in an effort to attain three distinct objectives: (a) the maintenance, for as long as possible, of the unity of the founding coalition, and of the momentum for national solidarity generated by the humiliation in the Cyprus crisis and exhilaration over the fall of the military; (b) the gradual distancing from, and eventual isolation of, the more recalcitrant and unreconstructed elements of the right, which had acquiesced in or even assented to his recall because of the extraordinary circumstances of the crisis, but which, as already indicated, envisaged a mere liberalisation of the postwar exclusivist system, thereby trusting in Karamanlis's strongly anti-communist track record to ensure that more radical political change would be averted; and (c) the need to reassure, and even to placate, that very significant part of public opinion and those emerging political forces which clearly favoured a radical democratisation of the postwar political system and a major change in the rules of the game.[12]

A deliberate mixture of continuity and change in Karamanlis's strategy was striking from the start. In addition to Karamanlis himself, the civilian cabinet sworn in on 25 and 26 July consisted of well-established political figures associated with the right and the centre-right in postwar years. Still, while the new cabinet (much like the initial body which had engineered Karamanlis's recall) totally excluded the centre-left forces identified with the Andreas Papandreou faction of the old Centre Union, as well as the traditional left, its inclusion of figures such as George Alexander Mangakis (hallowed by resistance activities against the colonels) and in general of men with impeccable anti-junta credentials was important on both symbolic and substantive grounds. It was the first oblique – and at the time unseen – indication of Karamanlis's design to break with the recalcitrant anti-communist right, and to strive for a different balance in the new political system, in which the centre of gravity would be located more towards the centre than the right.

The same balancing principle seems to have lain behind his decision to announce, on 1 August, the return to the 1952 constitution as the interim law of the land, while suspending the articles pertaining to the monarchy; to maintain General Ghizikis as interim head of state, while stating that the nature of the permanent head of state would be settled in the near future, either by popular referendum or by a constituent assembly; to opt finally for a constituent assembly as the appropriate organ for the preparation of a new constitution, while restricting its role to that of a *revisionary* body. Similarly, he decided to return to pre-junta legality by means of a series of constituent acts relating to the judiciary, the universities, the civil service and local government while, at the same time, freeing political prisoners, proclaiming a general amnesty for political crimes, declaring civil-war and related postwar restrictive legislation to be no longer in force. He also legalised all political parties, thereby making it possible for the Communist Party of Greece to operate in the open for the first time since the civil war and, more generally, for forces of the left to participate legally and formally in the political system.[13]

Karamanlis's gradualism was equally evident in the very careful timing of these measures, in the incremental approach adopted in the announcement of changes and, especially, in the deliberately slow pace at which the government proceeded in dealing with the most sensitive and explosive of popular demands: purges of the military, the state bureaucracy, the universities, and the security forces; and, above all, the prosecution of the protagonists in the 1967 coup, in the suppression of the Polytechnic uprising and in the torturing of prisoners during the seven-year authoritarian regime. Here, Karamanlis's attitude seems to have been largely determined by his justified fear of a military reaction in the event of a thorough purge, or even of one which was perceived as 'excessive' among military and civilian circles close to the fallen regime.

The gradualist component of Karamanlis's transition strategy included three further implicit assumptions: first, that these issues should not be directly addressed until after the first election, when the legitimacy of the new civilian government would place it in an immensely better position to face the pressures and uncertainties related to such a delicate enterprise; second, that, in advance of dealing with these intractable issues, measures had to be taken to ensure civilian control of a number of agencies and institutions (police, security services, intelligence agencies, chiefs of staff), whose loyalty would be a crucial precondition for the uneventful handling of these emotion-laden issues; and third, that in the application phase of the strategy, a line had to be drawn between retiring, and therefore isolating, officers implicated with the former regime and prosecuting them for various offences. This line he carefully observed until after the elections on 17 November.

In this connection, it is characteristic that the only criminal prosecution proceedings initiated against protagonists of the colonel's regime *prior* to the elections were the result of a *private* suit, and did not involve government initiative. Equally significant, the case was not tried until almost nine months later, long after an overwhelming electoral victory had provided Karamanlis with unquestioned legitimacy, with independence *vis-à-vis* other actors in the transition, and with a crushing parliamentary majority in excess of two-thirds of all seats. It was only after a foiled military coup in February 1975 that he was given the long-awaited opportunity to move decisively against adherents and sympathisers of the previous regime, and to eliminate a source of major potential resistance to further change without risking serious erosion of his political support.[14]

At this point in the transition, gradualism gave way to a policy of swift, decisive, credible, but also contained and circumscribed retribution. This was designed to enhance the legitimacy of the new regime, to further delegitimate its discredited predecessor and, at the same time, to appear equitable, to avoid the potentially negative repercussions from too protracted a public focus on the emotional traumas of the past, and to prevent excesses that might undermine the climate of national solidarity so crucial to the regime's long-term consolidation chances. Thus, in less than six months, the protagonists of the 1967 coup, the leaders of the February 1975 foiled coup, together with the major figures in the suppression of the Polytechnic uprising and in the torturing of prisoners during the seven-year regime, were brought to trial and received sentences ranging from life imprisonment for the major figures to lesser sentences for others. In line with the government's determination to avoid action of a possibly destabilising and potentially divisive nature, the death sentence handed down by the courts against the three leaders of the previous regime, George Papadopoulos, Stylianos Pattakos, and Nicholas Makarezos, were immediately commuted to life imprisonment. The government's announcement of clemency significantly stated that 'in the fair state, the work of justice is completed by the final procedure . . . which permits the reduction of sentences; in this final phase, a high sense of political responsibility must prevail'.[15]

By the end of 1975, therefore, and despite opposition accusations that it had exercised excessive restraint, and that commutation of the death sentences 'smacked of a deal', the new Greek democratic regime had effectively dealt with what Herz has recently referred to as the 'legacy problem' crucial to the definition of a successor democratic regime's self-image, and for the demystification of its predecessor.[16]

If the conclusion of the various trials marks the natural end of the new government's policy for dealing with the 'legacy problem', a series of actions taken early in the transition attest to the significance attached to this issue: the immediate banning of the authoritarian regime's symbols, including the universally loathed and ridiculed 'phoenix'; the prohibition of all references to the 'revolution' as a term to describe the 1967 coup in all school textbooks; the appointment of men with known anti-junta and even leftist sentiments in key positions of the sensitive Ministry of Education; the early dismissal of junta appointees from the university system; and numerous official and unofficial utterances concerning the freedom of the press. All these constituted symbolic acts designed to serve the dual goal of demonstrating the new regime's unequivocal condemnation of its predecessor and, equally important, to signal its determination to proceed with the democratisation of the political system and to work for the consolidation of democratic politics in Greece.

If a judicious mixture of continuity and change, as well as deliberate gradualism in dealing with potentially divisive issues, were readily identifiable elements in Karamanlis's transition strategy, a less obvious but equally important component focused on the need to maximise the benefits which the circumstances of the transfer of power gave to the centre and centre-right forces, and consequently to contain the opposition and neutralise the left. In pursuit of these objectives, Karamanlis exploited the *carte blanche* context of his accession to power, ran an issueless campaign, took advantage of the colourless and timid opposition provided by George Mavros's Centre Union and, above all, opted for elections sooner rather than later. He knew that an early election would allow his potentially more dangerous opposition, the recently surfaced Communist Party and the newly-formed PASOK, minimal time to mobilise and to articulate an effective electoral platform. It would also make it easier to give the whole event a plebiscitary flavour, to which the slogan 'Karamanlis or the tanks' would become the dominant theme that would ensure his success, and would enable him to proceed with the implementation of his consolidation strategy.[17]

THE CONSOLIDATION STRATEGY OF KARAMANLIS

As noted earlier, this strategy, which went beyond the minimalist expectations of the predominantly conservative forces that had engineered his recall, sought to ensure consolidation through a genuine democratisation of the political system designed to make it responsive to, and congruent with, the deep structural changes that had occurred in Greece over the previous quarter century. As such, it involved at least five distinct, though partly overlapping, major components: (a) national reconciliation and an end to the civil war divisions successfully perpetuated in the postwar exclusivist state; (b) radical redistribution of power among the major political actors that had dominated the postwar political system; (c) democratisation of the Greek right to render it capable of playing a central and positive role in the new scheme of things; (d) creation of the conditions that would allow the left, including new left-of-centre forces, to participate fully in the political system, in the process legitimating it further and contributing to its long-term consolidation; and (e) the establishment of new institutions capable of accommodating the full range of political forces in the country, and the creation of requisite rules of the game which would ensure the smooth operation and continuing viability of the new, inclusive political system.[18]

National reconciliation entailed, above all, the dismantling of the postwar legal and institutional nexus. By placing effective and decisive disabilities on political forces identified not merely with the left, but even with the liberal centre, this had involved a massive violation of the liberal 1952 constitution, had facilitated the erection of a 'paraconstitutional' order that divided Greeks into 'nationally minded' and 'suspects', and had preserved the benefits of the political system exclusively for the victors in the civil war.

Karamanlis accomplished this in two principal ways: First, prior to the elections, through legislative acts of his government which officially put an end to restrictive legislation originating in the civil war years. The 23 September 1974 act, which legalised the operation of all political parties, also specifically put an end to Law 509/1948, the last major piece of civil-war discriminatory legislation. This had been a potent symbol of the divisions of those years which had survived into the postwar period, and which the colonels had attempted to turn into the ultimate justification and the governing principle of their regime. Further measures contributed to the restitution of civil liberties and rights to those who had been denied them in the postwar period. In less tangible, but equally crucial ways, Karamanlis's numerous pronouncements and harangues both before and after the elections centred around the need to break loose from the nefarious practices of the past, and to use the lessons from recent history and the new sense of national solidarity which the experience with authoritarian rule had produced to build a new system open to all Greeks.[19]

If such a change clearly involved the entry of the left and of new political forces into the political system on a subtler but ultimately more crucial level, this break with the past required for its success a fundamental redistribution of power among the main political actors (armed forces, monarchy and the parliamentary right) which had dominated the postwar exclusivist system. Karamanlis's handling of the armed forces during the transition period has already been described in some detail. Following the election, and the opportunity afforded him by the foiled coup of February 1975 to place in key positions officers loyal to the civilian regime, his strategy for ensuring that the military would not be tempted to leave the barracks again consisted of two approaches. He engaged in constant verbal reminders about the ill effects of military involvement in politics, and the evils of authoritarian rule, and emphatically reiterated the principle of civilian supremacy in official and symbolic messages (New Year, Easter, national holidays, etc.), at the same time, he filled key civilian positions such as the Ministries of Defence and Public Order with faithful lieutenants like Averoff, who enjoyed the confidence of a wide spectrum within the officer corps, and Solon Ghikas, who was himself a retired general with an impeccable anti-communist past.

On the other hand, Karamanlis shied away from more drastic measures that would have tackled the intractable presence in the police, security, and intelligence forces of extensive networks with strong roots in the civil war and postwar periods and with a questionable commitment to democratic politics. He also chose not to close down the armed forces radio and television station, a lasting reminder of the institutional autonomy the military had acquired during and after the civil war.

In sum, this was a strategy banking simultaneously on Karamanlis's immense personal prestige and on the military's traumatic experience in government and especially with the Cyprus folly. It was designed to offer reassurance in return for strict observance of the new rules of the game supervised and guaranteed by a 'stern but benevolent' leader, slowly shedding his partisan identity and assuming, instead, the national one which the circumstances of his recall had brought about, and which he was certainly not unwilling to adopt.

The issue of monarchy versus republic was decisively settled in favour of the latter with an impressive 70 per cent vote against the monarchy in what, by all accounts, was the fairest and freest plebiscite in modern Greek history. The monarchy had played a pivotal and divisive role in twentieth-century Greek politics; it had constituted a critical element in the operation of the postwar anti-communist state and had, on numerous occasions, acted as a central channel through which foreign interference, so long an institutionalised part of the Greek political system, could be exercised. Its elimination, therefore, represented a major precondition for the successful democratisation of the political system, and made possible a major redistribution of power in favour of the civilian component of the system.[20]

In addition, the creation of an elective head of state, to be chosen by a vote of parliament, made it possible for Karamanlis (whose attempt in 1963 to reform the postwar system had led him to a head-on clash with King Paul I and had precipitated his break with the monarchy) to ensure the election of a candidate of his choice, and opened the way for his eventual assumption of that office, from which he could preside over the political system and oversee its smooth operation.

If the elimination of the monarchy and what one hoped was a permanent return of the military to the barracks meant that the net beneficiary of this redistribution of power was the parliamentary right, the long-term prospects for the success of Karamanlis's consolidation strategy hinged, to a great extent, on the ability of the right to modernise itself. Karamanlis's answer to this challenge was the creation of a new political formation, aptly named New Democracy, which he headed from 1974 until May 1980, when he was elected President of the Republic and had to step down as party leader. Throughout this period, he strove to attain the goal of modernisation by pursuing a three-tier strategy: on the ideological level, he sought to forge a new identity which foreswore the sterile anticommunism that had marked the right for nearly forty years, since the commencement of its virtually uninterrupted dominance of Greek politics in 1935, and which had been the foremost characteristic of the National Radical Union during the 1950s and 1960s. The new identity of the Greek right in the form of New Democracy was to be that of a liberal, right-of-centre formation, very much in the image of modern conservative parties in western Europe, and completely cut off from its extreme and unreconstructed former fringe, which now emerged as a separate entity.

On the organisational level, too, the birth of New Democracy was heralded as the beginning of a new era for the Greek right and for Greek politics, marked by the abandonment of the traditional party-of-notables structure so characteristic of bourgeois Greek parties, permeated as they were with clientelistic practices and their concomitant personalistic politics. New Democracy was to be a modern mass party, democratically structured and run, capable of responding to the new realities of Greek politics, and of attracting, at both the mass and the cadre level, the support of the new and dynamic strata created by rapid social and economic change over the previous quarter century.

Such a change in organisation was to be accompanied by an equally significant shift in the patterns of recruitment. As Karamanlis described it, the new party was to look for new blood from two main sources. Socially, it was to come from among the new strata just alluded to, which included many upwardly mobile young, better educated and more sophisticated professionals, who could infuse the right with a new sense of purpose and reinforce the new identity its leader was trying to forge for it. Politically, the search for new blood was to turn to two very different groups: within the right, to an increasing pool of young technocrats who had studied abroad and had significant organisational and managerial experience, very often in the private sector; outside the right, to established leaders of the old centre whose political space the new party hoped to occupy if it were indeed to become a modern, centre-right force.[21]

Under Karamanlis's watchful eye and undisputed dominance, this experiment in transformation from above seemed to edge in the intended direction. The party maintained its newfound liberal image; carefully and repeatedly dissociated itself from its erstwhile partners on the extreme fringe, and proceeded to adopt a democratic constitution, to set up its various organs and grass roots organisations, and eventually, hold its first congress in 1979. The succession contest for the leadership of the party, once Karamanlis became president in 1980, was resolved democratically by means of a vote of the parliamentary party. George Rallis, the leader of the liberal faction within the party, who squeezed to a narrow victory over the conservative candidate, Evangelos Averoff-Tossizza, was to lead his party into the 1981 elections in which New Democracy suffered a decisive defeat. This involved two developments of historical import: the effective displacement of the right from power, for the first time since the 1935 unsuccessful Venizelist coup tipped the political balance away from the liberal forces that had dominated the interwar period; and the advent to power, for the first time in Greek history, of a political formation identifying with clear left-of-centre positions, and containing radical leftist elements in its ranks.

Both developments unquestionably represent a major moment in the consolidation process of the new regime, and in the evolution of the open and fully competitive political system inaugurated in 1974. Indeed, these developments also constituted an integral part of Karamanlis's consolidation strategy which, aside from national reconciliation, redistribution of political power among major actors in the pre-1967 political system and modernisation of the right, envisaged creating the conditions that would: (a) make it possible for new political forces on the left to participate openly and fully in the political system; (b) anticipate the possibility of such forces coming to power; and (c) provide for the institutional network necessary to manage such a momentous change in Greek politics and to ensure its uneventful evolution. It is to these that we must now turn.

The single most important problem facing Karamanlis in his regime-founding and regime-consolidation strategy was how to bring about the necessary democratisation of political structures that would render the Greek political system congruent with, and responsive to, major and long-term changes that had altered the profile of the electorate over the previous two decades. The product of rapid economic growth and of uneven development, these changes had produced a massive internal demographic shift away from the rural areas and had spawned new, upwardly mobile but highly transitional lower-middle class strata whose presence in Greek politics began to be felt during the political crisis of the mid-1960s that led to the breakdown of parliamentary politics in Greece. Already during this period of turmoil, the rising political significance of these new social strata was becoming apparent as the main force behind the left wing of the dominant Centre Union party headed and controlled by George Papandreou. It was George Papandreou's son, Andreas, who emerged as the leader of this new force, and who commenced to articulate some of its more radical criticisms of the postwar political system.[22]

While the 1967-74 authoritarian interlude placed the lid on the continuing political mobilisation of these forces, and unsuccessfully sought to resurrect fading civil-war cleavages in order to isolate them and to undermine their potential impact on Greek politics, the long-term social and economic changes behind these developments continued unabated. If anything, the authoritarian experience served to sensitise a much broader segment of the Greek electorate to the dangers inherent in such experiments, and effectively to shift the whole political spectrum somewhat to the left.

Even prior to the demise of the colonels' authoritarian regime, it became evident that a large part of the new social forces would look for leadership to Andreas Papandreou who, from his exile in Europe and later in Canada, co-ordinated the activities of the Panhellenic Liberation Movement (PAK) he had formed, and prepared for the moment when he would be able to exercise his leadership in post-authoritarian Greece. The creation of the Panhellenic Socialist Movement (PASOK) in early September 1974 represented the natural outcome of these developments, and gave organisational and ideological focus to these inchoate social forces, radicalised by earlier mobilisation and, more recently, by repression, and eager to support 'change' (*allaghi*) in Greece.[23]

With the benefit of hindsight, it is easier to see what was already becoming a discernible scenario in the summer and autumn of 1974: given the death of George Papandreou and the lacklustre personality of George Mavros who, in the interim, had emerged as the leader of the Centre Union; given the unquestionable charisma of both Andreas Papandreou and Karamanlis; and given, finally, the general demand at the mass level, and the recognition at the elite level, that the pre 1967 political structures would have to be superseded in the process of constructing a new and more open political system, it followed that the long-term future and very viability of the old centre was coming into question.

In fact, the threefold anticipation of a rapidly declining centre; of the increasing probability that the emerging political system would be dominated by a left-of-centre political force and by a hopefully modernised right; and the need to create the necessary institutional arrangements to regulate the new situation and to render it systemically functional, effectively found expression in the new rules of the game embodied in the 1975 constitution. This provided for a Gaullist-type elective head of state, with broad powers vested in the president, including the right to dissolve parliament, if he felt it was in discordance with public sentiment; to appeal directly to the electorate by means of a referendum which he alone could initiate; to declare martial law and rule by decree for thirty days without parliamentary approval; and to veto legislation, though such action could be overridden by a simple majority vote in parliament.[24]

In Karamanlis's veiw, these powers, to be invoked only if necessary, were congruent with 'Greek reality' – an elliptic reference to past troubles – and were introduced to ensure the stability and smooth operation of the new political system. In May 1980, following an uneventful five-year term as first President of the Republic by Constantine Tsatsos (chief architect of the new constitution, a prominent conservative intellectual and faithful Karamanlis lieutenant for two decades, and the latter's choice for the job) Karamanlis himself assumed this office which many had accused him of tailoring to himself.

From that position, he was to preside over and oversee the most delicate and crucial phase in the evolution of the new regime, marked by PASOK's electoral triumph in the 1981 elections, the obliteration of the centre, and the end of the right's 46-year long dominance of Greek politics. These developments were a central part of the major reordering of political structures in Greece and left their deep imprint on the new regime. Undoubtedly, the unquestionable personal charisma of Andreas Papandreou, the immense attraction of the electoral slogan of *allaghi,* and the widespread disappointment with New Democracy's performance over the preceding years did much to explain this historic phase. But beyond that, the apparent willingness of a near majority of the electorate (48 per cent) to vote, for the first time in modern Greek history, for a political formation which openly proclaimed its socialist identity owed a great deal to the reassurance felt by many voters that the architect of the new system now occupied the presidency of the republic and, thus, provided for an essential counterweight to the new government. Hence, this contributed to the maintenance of systemic balance, and allowed the Greeks to enjoy the combined fruits of a stable political system and a left-of-centre government of their choice.[25]

The two years that have now elapsed since PASOK's advent to power have notably confirmed these trends, marked above all by the smooth relationship between prime minister and president, the strict observance of the rules of the game on both sides, and their determination to ensure the long-term consolidation of the system. Karamanlis's performance to date has laid to rest early fears that he might seek to transform the presidency into an 'active' institution, thereby shifting the system's centre of gravity and rendering it more presidential than parliamentary. As a result, the original controversy surrounding the 'hidden powers' of his office has dissipated and, after eight and a half years of existence and two incumbents, a more 'withdrawn' type of presidency seems to be institutionalising itself. Finally, Papandreou's gradual distancing of himself from some of the more extreme and polemical positions he and his party had espoused before coming to power and his government's restrained behaviour in office have unquestionably favoured the regime's further consolidation. Karamanlis's rumoured intention, which allegedly enjoys Papandreou's approval, to seek a second term would certainly strengthen this tendency by further institutionalising the types of arrangements that have grown over the past few years, especially since 1981.

THE PROSPECTS FOR STRONG CONSOLIDATION AND THE PROBLEM OF 'CONFINING CONDITIONS'

In retrospect, then, it would seem that Karamanlis's transition and consolidation strategies have on the whole been remarkably successful. The former was based on a centre and centre-right founding coalition, and the latter on support from virtually the entire political spectrum. It was designed, through a complex combination of policies embodying continuity and change, to bring about the democratisation of the Greek political system, to break out of past patterns of political instability and the collapse of parliamentary politics and to ensure the system's long-term viability and persistence. At the same time, such a tentative conclusion raises the inevitable question as to whether these trends can be sustained and whether the dynamic so far generated by them can maintain its momentum. Put somewhat differently, and in the language of Kirchheimer's conceptualisation what, if any, are the confining conditions to the long-term consolidation of democratic politics in Greece, which could potentially and adversely affect the present regime? Three major such conditions seem to deserve attention in this context: (a) the greatly increased political importance of the petite bourgeoisie in Greek politics; (b) the continuing weakness of the Greek industrial classes, itself a reflection of the historical weakness of Greek capitalism; and (c) the apparent failure of the Greek right to modernise, despite Karamanlis's attempt at reform from above.

The growing significance of the petite bourgeoisie, and especially of its new upwardly mobile strata created over the last thirty years of rapid but sharply uneven economic development has already been alluded to. As I have argued elsewhere, what above all characterises these strata is their

> ... transitional nature ... ideological disorientation, ... loss of values, insecurity about what has been left behind ... but also about what lies ahead; a yearning for change, without any concrete notion of what change should bring about; a strong sense of malaise and of discontent, in part the result of [their] transitional character, in part a reflection of a lack of identity; and ... a vague, inchoate, almost manichean sense of class antagonism *vis-à-vis* the 'privileged' strata. In short, ... strat[a] without, as yet, a distinct class identity or ideology [exhibiting] a 'guild-type' mentality [marked by] ... insecurity, ... parochial attitudes, ... crass materialism, ... narrow concern with personal or professional issues, ... self-centredness ... an illiberal essence, and ... profound xenophobia.[26]

It is this nature, therefore, and the potential for political and ideological volatility that it imples, which introduces an imponderable element into the system and, as such, constitutes an obstacle to further consolidation. So far, these forces appear to have been harnessed by the charismatic appeal of

5

Papandreou's personality, and by their massive adherence to PASOK, whose populist image, subtly suggested in its self-definition as a 'movement' and not a party, has managed to provide ideological shelter for a wide variety of diverging tendencies and inchoate views. As such, their role in the regime consolidation process to date can be said to have been positive. It remains to be seen whether, as the exercise of power renders PASOK policies increasingly moderate, and the party moves closer to the centre of the political spectrum in search of critical swing voters, it will also be able to retain the continuing allegiance of these strata, thereby rendering this alliance more permanent; or whether, under some future and as yet unspecified conditions of crisis or of disillusionment, these same strata will swing in different directions that could pose a threat to continuing political stability and could erode the regime's consolidation momentum.

For the purposes of this analysis, the weakness of the Greek industrial classes, a phenomenon intimately related to the historical circumstances of Greek underdevelopment, implies a lack of significant experience with the type of social and political struggles and long-term mobilisation associated with the birth, institutionalisation and defence of competitive politics. Hence, it could be said there is a lack of a long-standing and intense commitment to this type of politics, and an absence of a strong and allegiant political culture which places a premium on them. Long burdened by state paternalism and overt or covert control from above, the industrial working class remains numerically small and organisationally weak in a social formation marked by the rapid expansion of petit bourgeois strata. PASOK's advent to power has brought little change in this picture, as the overriding concern with containing the Communist-controlled union organisations has effectively led to a continuation of past practices, and to renewed government dominance of the largely conservative General Confederation of Greek Workers (GSEE) and of other major non-Communist unions. Trapped between an ossified left and a strongly paternalist and partly authoritarian right, the Greek industrial working class cannot, so far, be said to have been schooled in a way which best prepares it for the sophisticated and delicate collective behaviour which participation in and, ultimately, defence of competitive politics implies.[27]

This lack of the requisite experience with competitive politics in an open political system is even more characteristic of the Greek bourgeoisie which, deeply traumatised by the massive challenge to its continuing dominance of the political system posed by the left during the years of the resistance to the Axis Powers (1941–4) and later, during the civil war (1946–9), allowed its more militant and unreconstructed wing to raise a sterile and uncompromising anti-communism to the level of ideology. This it utilised to erect and justify the exclusivist political system of the postwar years, of which it was one of the chief beneficiaries. In a very real sense, the history of the Greek right in the last thirty years is the history of the political coalition of this extreme and dominant wing of the Greek bourgeoisie in control of parliament, with the monarchy and the armed forces, a coalition which dominated Greek politics down to 1967 and which was irrevocably split as a result of the lapse to authoritarian rule that year.

This right was profoundly tainted by association with discriminatory and authoritarian practices, improperly schooled for a generation in a political culture based on the systematic denial of political opponents' civil liberties, and deeply mired in a morass of particularistic politics, clientelistic favours and blind adherence to the status quo. It was thus inadequately prepared for the type of behaviour, mentality and values needed for participation in open and competitive political systems. Yet Karamanlis, having apparently profited from the chance for contemplation and reappraisal offered by eleven years of self-imposed exile, sought to modernise it in the years after 1974, attempting to build upon the deep split that the authoritarian experience had produced between parliamentary and extra-parliamentary elements of the right, and endeavouring to transform the former into a modern right-of-centre mass party (New Democracy), capable of playing a central and constructive role in the new political system.

Developments since 1980, and especially since 1981, when New Democracy was resoundingly defeated at the polls, have amply demonstrated the limits inherent in any attempts at a major, as opposed to cosmetic, reform from above. Having dutifully followed Karamanlis's beckoning, and profited from his immense charisma during the years he served as its leader (1974–80), New Democracy proved unable to bear the combined burden of separation from its founder and, above all, electoral defeat. Clientelistic factionalism and ingrained past habits and mentalities pushed merely below the surface but hardly eliminated during the Karamanlis years became discernible once again following substantial electoral losses in 1977, and re-emerged with a vengeance in the aftermath of the 1981 defeat, precipitating a renewed swing back to more familiar but ultimately sterile ideological positions under the leadership of Averoff-Tossizza, the septuagenarian conservative who succeeded George Rallis at the helm of the party.

At present, although it has carefully kept its distance from the type of anti-communist excesses that characterised its predecessor (ERE) in the pre-1967 period, New Democracy, demoralised, faction-ridden and out of power, has drifted into a new ideological and political cul-de-sac, from which it seems unable to extricate itself. This retrogression, which robs this large political force of the ability to play the central role envisaged by both its founder and many others in the operation and, hence, legitimation and consolidation of the new political system, must clearly represent the greatest failure in Karamanlis's consolidation strategy, and inevitably acts as a confining condition impeding strong regime consolidation.[28]

While the persistence of these confining conditions points to some of the obstacles standing in the way of a strong democratic consolidation in Greece, it would be a grave mistake to ignore what has been achieved in that country since 1974 and to overlook the fact that, whatever its weaknesses, this is by far the most open, inclusive and democratic regime in modern Greek history. The foregoing analysis has sought to highlight the circumstances under which this has been achieved, and to suggest some of the reasons why the Greek case may be of interest to the comparative study of transition to, and consolidation of, democratic politics.

NOTES

1. On the heightened concern with the issue of regime change, see, among others, the special
    issue of the *International Political Science Review*, Vol. 1, No. 1, January 1980, and Julian
    Santamaria (ed.), *La Transición a la Democracia en el Sur de Europa y América Latina*
    (Madrid: Centro de Investigaciones Sociologicas, 1982), as well as the workshops on
    'Regime Change in Southern Europe', 'Late Redemocratization in Southern Europe', and
    'Prospects for Democracy: Transitions from Authoritarian Rule' sponsored respectively by
    the Social Science Research Council (Madrid, November 1981), the European Consortium
    for Political Research (Aarhus, March 1982), and the Woodrow Wilson International
    Center for Scholars (Queenstown, Maryland, September 1980). A selection of papers from
    the last workshop is scheduled to appear as a volume entitled *Transitions from
    Authoritarian Rule: the Prospects for Democracy in Latin America and Southern Europe*,
    edited by Philippe C. Schmitter and Guillermo O'Donnell. See also Dankwart A. Rustow,
    'Transitions to Democracy: Toward a Dynamic Model', *Comparative Politics*, Vol. 2, No. 3
    (April 1970), pp. 337–63.
       On the breakdown of competitive politics and the rise of authoritarianism in Latin
    America, see Juan J. Linz and Alfred Stepan (eds), *The Breakdown of Democratic Regimes*
    (Baltimore, MD: The Johns Hopkins University Press, 1978); Guillermo A. O'Donnell,
    Modernization and Bureaucratic-Authoritarianism: Studies in South American Politics
    (Berkeley, CA: University of California Press, 1979); David Collier (ed.), *The New
    Authoritarianism in Latin America* (Princeton, NJ: Princeton University Press, 1979); and
    Claudio Veliz, *The Centralist Tradition in Latin America* (Princeton, NJ: Princeton
    University Press, 1980).
2. Good examples of the increased sensitivity over the more political aspects of regime
    transition are the forthcoming volume by Schmitter and O'Donnell and the volume by
    David Collier, both cited above. For an earlier work, see Gabriel A. Almond, Scott C.
    Flanagan, and Robert J. Mundt (eds), *Crisis, Choice, and Change: Historical Studies of
    Political Development* (Boston: Little Brown, 1973). See also the more recent unpublished
    papers by Fernando Enrique Cardoso, 'Political Transition in Latin America?' (n.d.), and
    'Political Regime and Social Change (Some Reflections Concerning the Brazilian Case)'
    (October 1980).
3. On regime consolidation, see an earlier unpublished paper by Juan J. Linz, 'The
    Consolidation of Regimes: A Theoretical Problem Approach', presented at the VIII World
    Congress of Sociology, Toronto, 19 August 1974, as well as the more recent paper by
    Leonardo Morlino, 'Rules of Democratic Consolidation: Some Comparative Notes about
    Italy and Spain', presented at the Social Science Research Council workshop on regime
    change in Southern Europe, Madrid, 26–28 November 1981. See also Philippe C. Schmitter,
    'Historical Bloc Formation and Regime Consolidation in Post-Authoritarian Portugal',
    unpublished paper (1976), and John H. Herz, 'Introduction: Method and Boundaries', and
    'Conclusion', in John H. Herz (ed.), *From Dictatorship to Democracy: Coping with the
    Legacies of Authoritarianism and Totalitarianism* (Westport, CT: Greenwood Press, 1982),
    pp. 3–12 and 275–92 respectively.
4. For Kirchheimer's development of the concept of 'confining conditions', see Otto
    Kirchheimer, 'Confining Conditions and Revolutionary Breakthroughs', *American
    Political Science Review*, Vol. 59 (1965), pp. 964–74.
5. On the political complexion of founding coalitions as a factor in successful regime
    consolidation, see Giuseppe Di Palma, 'Italy: Is There a Legacy and Is It Fascist?', Edward
    Malefakis, 'Spain and its Francoist Heritage', and John H. Herz, 'Conclusion', in John H.
    Herz (ed.), *op. cit.*, pp. 107–34, 215–30, and 280 respectively.
6. The issue of democratic legitimation and of coping with the legacy of predecessor
    authoritarian regimes is one of the central concerns of the volume by Herz cited above.
7. The preoccupation with internal matters of organisation and identity was obvious in all
    three major opposition parties during this period. Thus, in the case of PASOK, by far the
    predominant concern was the definition of an image as a radical, left-of-centre party that
    stood distinctly apart from political formations to its right, and which represented the sole
    vehicle for substantive change in Greece. The Communist Party of Greece as well as the
    Communist Party of Greece-Interior, which represented the Eurocommunist tendency in

Greek politics, were both centrally concerned with adjusting to newly-found conditions of legal and overt operation, after more than 25 years in clandestinity. The old Centre Union, now 'reborn' under the name 'Centre Union–New Forces' in an attempt to underscore its adoption of some of the more radical demands for change identified with 'new' political forces emanating out of resistance to the colonels' authoritarian regime, was also involved in major attempts at self-redefinition. Its inability to convince the electorate about this change was to result in its electoral annihilation over the next seven years, reducing its share of the popular vote, which had been almost 53 per cent in 1964, to 1.5 per cent in 1981.

8. While the Cyprus crisis was the proximate cause for the demise of the Greek authoritarian regime, the November 1973 student uprising at the National Technical College, which cut short the regime's most serious liberalisation attempt, should be considered the deeper cause for the breakdown of authoritarian rule in Greece. For a fuller development of this argument, see P. Nikiforos Diamandouros, *The 1974 Transition from Authoritarian to Democratic Rule in Greece: Background and Interpretation from a Southern European Perspective* (Bologna: The Johns Hopkins University Bologna Center, Occasional Paper No. 37, 1981). For a theoretical treatment of the breakdown of authoritarian regimes and for an attempt to develop a typology for such change, see Philippe C. Schmitter, 'Speculations About the Prospective Demise of Authoritarian Regimes and Its Possible Consequences', paper presented at the workshop on 'Prospects for Democracy: Transitions from Authoritarian Rule', sponsored by the Woodrow Wilson International Center for Scholars, September 1980. See also M. Rainer Lepsius, 'Machtübernahme und Machtübergabe: Zur Strategie des Regimewechsels', in Hans Albert *et al.* (eds), *Sozialtheorie und Soziale Praxis: Homage to Eduard Baumgarten*, Mannheimer Sozialwissenschaftliche Studien, Vol. 3 (Meisenheim: Anton Hain, 1971), pp. 158–73. On the events surrounding the surrender of power to the Greek civilian leadership, the best available source is Stavros P. Psychares, *Ta Paraskenia tes allaghes* [The Change Viewed From Behind the Scenes] (Athens, 1975).

9. For an analysis of various aspects of the Greek authoritarian regime, see Richard Clogg and George Yannopoulos (eds), *Greece Under Military Rule* (New York: Basic Books, 1972); [Rodes Roufos], *La verité sur la Grèce* (Lausanne: La Cité, 1970); Nicos C. Alivizatos, *Les Institutions Politiques de la Grèce à travers les Crises, 1922–1974* (Paris: L.G.D.J., 1979); and the work by P. N. Diamandouros cited above.

10. On the political complexion of the civilian leadership with whom the military met to arrange for the surrender of power, see Stavros P. Psychares, op. cit., pp. 131–63. On the postwar exclusivist political system see Nicos P. Mouzelis, *Modern Greece: Facets of Under-development* (London: Macmillan, 1978), pp. 115–34; Roussos Koundouros, 'Law and the Obstruction of Social Change: A Case Study of Laws for the Security of the Apparently Prevailing Social Order in Greece', unpublished M.Phil. thesis, Brunel University, 1974; and Nicos C. Alivizatos, op. cit.

11. The best biographies of Karamanlis are Maurice Genevoix, *La Grèce de Caramanlis ou la Démocratie Difficile?* (Paris: Plon, 1972), and C. M. Woodhouse, *Karamanlis: Restorer of Greek Democracy* (Oxford: Oxford University Press, 1982). It is interesting to note that, his undeniably greater prestige aside, the choice of Karamanlis implied a preference for a transition manager with a weaker rather than a stronger partisan identity.

12. On the 1977 elections, the best source is Howard R. Penniman (ed.), *Greece at the Polls: The National Elections of 1974 and 1977* (Washington, DC: The American Enterprise Institute, 1981).

13. For a detailed listing of the various acts and decrees which provided the legal foundation for the instauration of the new regime, see Petros I. Pararas, 'To chronikon epanodou eis ten Demokratian' [The Chronicle of the Return to Democracy], *To Syntagma* [The Constitution], Vol. 1, No. 1 (January–February 1975), pp. 55–62.

14. On the February 1975 failed coup, see Richard Clogg, *A Short History of Modern Greece* (Cambridge: The University Press, 1979), pp. 207–9.

15. For the quotation, see *Facts on File*, 30 August 1975, p. 637. The decision not to proceed with the execution of the three leaders of the 1967 coup was motivated as much by a desire to prevent a possible military reaction as by the determination to avoid the type of profound and traumatic polarisation brought about by the execution of six conservative political leaders in the wake of the Greek defeat in Asia Minor in 1922. The so-called 'execution of the

Six' remained a haunting and lasting reference point in the interwar and postwar liberal/conservative cleavage in Greek politics.

16. On the legacy problem, see John H. Herz, op. cit., pp. 3–11 and 275–91.

17. For the best available analysis of the 1974 elections, see Howard R. Penniman, op. cit.

18. The various components of Karamanlis's consolidation strategy are not to be found, explicitly articulated, in any official statement or programmatic text. They can, however, be culled from his various utterances and even inferred from statements made by Karamanlis himself or by some of his closest lieutenants. See also the two biographies of Karamanlis cited in note 11. A more complex issue relates to Karamanlis's motives in devising such a strategy. While both hagiographical and conspiratorial interpretations abound, in the absence of concrete evidence it seems plausible to assert that his choice of strategy was the result of the pragmatic realisation that, unless political structures in Greece were radically modernised to become congruent with social and economic changes that had taken place over the preceding twenty to thirty years, the chances for political stability in that country would be greatly diminished.

19. On the various measures designed to put an end to restrictive legislation and to provide for an open system, see Pararas, op. cit., pp. 58–9.

20. On the role of the Greek monarchy in politics, see Jean Meynaud, *Les Forces Politiques en Grèce* (Lausanne: Etudes de Science Politique, No. 10, 1965); Richard Clogg, op. cit., pp. 166–99 for the postwar period; and Nicos P. Mouzelis, op. cit., pp. 105–33.

21. On the origins and early development of the New Democracy party, see John C. Loulis, 'New Democracy: The New Face of Conservatism', in Howard R. Penniman (ed.), op. cit., pp. 49–83.

22. On the long-term social and economic changes which so profoundly transformed Greek society in the postwar period and placed intolerable pressures on the exclusivist political system, eventually leading to the protracted 1965–7 crisis and to the breakdown of competitive politics, see Melina Serafetinidis, 'The Breakdown of Parliamentary Institutions in Greece', unpublished Ph.D. dissertation, London School of Economics, 1978; Michael J. Bucuvalas, 'The Breakdown of a Political System Experiencing Economic Development: Greece, 1950–1967', in Andrew W. Cordier (ed.), *Columbia Essays in International Affairs*, Vol. VII, *The Dean's Papers, 1971* (New York: Columbia University Press, 1972), pp. 131–48; John Campbell and Philip Sherrard, *Modern Greece* (London: Benn, 1968), pp. 247–321; and Nicos P. Mouzelis, op. cit., pp. 115–33.

23. For a study of PASOK's origins and evolution, see the unpublished doctoral dissertation by Christos Lyrintzis, 'Between Socialism and Populism: the Rise of the Panhellenic Socialist Movement', London School of Economics, 1983. For a more polemical evaluation, see Angelos Elephantis, 'PASOK and the Elections of 1977: The Rise of the Populist Movement', in Howard R. Penniman, op. cit., pp. 105–29.

24. On the declining fortunes of the centre, see Thanos Veremis, 'The Union of the Democratic Center', in Howard R. Penniman, op. cit., pp., 84–104. On the 1975 Greek constitution, see Antoine M. Pantélis, *Les Grands Problèmes de la Nouvelle Constitution Hellénique* (Paris: L.G.D.J., 1979); and Jean Catsiapis, 'La constitution de la Grèce du 9 juin 1975', *Revue du Droit Public et de la science Politique en France et à l'Etranger*, No. 6 (1975), pp. 1577–98.

25. The best available work in English on the 1981 elections is George Th. Mavrogordatos, *Rise of the Greek Sun: The Greek Election of 1981* (London: Centre for Contemporary Greek Studies, King's College, Occasional Paper 1, 1983).

26. P. Nikiforos Diamandouros, 'Greek Political Culture in Transition: Historical Origins, Evolution, Current Trends', in Richard Clogg (ed.), *Greece in the 1980s* (London: Macmillan, 1983), p. 59. On the significance of the petite bourgeoisie in Greek history, more generally, see, for the nineteenth century, Constantine Tsoucalas, *Koinonike Anaptyxe kai Kratos . . .* [Social Development and the State: The Establishment of the Public Sector in Greece] (Athens: Themelio, 1981), pp. 165–258, and especially 252–8; for the twentieth century, see George Th. Mavrogordatos, *Stillborn Republic: Social Coalitions and Party Strategies in Greece, 1922–1936* (Berkeley: University of California Press, 1983).

27. The most recent study of the Greek trade union movement in English is Theodore Katsanevas, 'Trade Unions in Greece: An Analysis of Factors Determining their Growth and Present Structure', unpublished Ph.D. dissertation, London School of Economics, 1980. For an earlier study, see Christos Jecchinis, *Greek Trade Unionism: A Study in Political Paternalism* (Chicago: Roosevelt University Press, 1967).

28. On the transfer of leadership from Rallis to Averoff-Tossizza, the sole available source to date is Rallis's own account: George I. Rallis, *Hores Euthynes* [Hours of Responsibility] (Athens: Euroekdotike, 1983). For ongoing efforts to provide the party with a distinct sense of identity that can make it a credible centre-right alternative to PASOK, see the special issue of *Epikentra* [Epicentres], a voice of the liberal wing of the party, which seems to have the support of the more enlightened and more modern sectors within the party: 'New Democracy at the Crossroads?', *Epikentra*, No. 34 (September-October 1983), pp. 21–69, as well as the editorial on pp. 2–3.

Continuity and Change in Portuguese Politics: Ten Years after the Revolution of 25 April 1974

Thomas C. Bruneau

The regime based upon the Constitution of April 1976 in Portugal continues to change although within the general parameters of a liberal democratic model, rather than outside it. There is little question at the present as to the continuity of this form of regime, but its precise nature and dynamic remain very much in question. The purpose of this short article is to characterise this regime, present its background and current dynamics, and highlight in particular the elements of continuity and change within this overall model.

PRE-1976 REGIMES

The present liberal democratic model of regime in Portugal stands in stark contrast to the governments which preceded it. We must touch upon these, however, so as to provide the material whereby the present regime can be understood, for the nature of the collapse of the earlier regimes has strongly conditioned it and its dynamics.[1]

The conservative-authoritarian regime founded in 1928 by Premier António de Oliveira Salazar grew out of the extremely unstable First Republic of 1910–26. In most respects the *Estado Novo* of Salazar was a direct contrast to the previous regime, and intentionally so. Many excellent books and articles have been published on the *Estado Novo*, and we need not dwell on it here but must indicate its bases: the system was explicitly anti-modern and anti-democratic; it sought to secure in Portugal an idealised vision of a simpler nineteenth-century society and political system without conflict and without threats; it relied on elements of Catholicism and nationalism for its legitimacy and negated the value of liberalism and ideologies arising from the Industrial and French Revolutions; the system did not allow the structured access to political power by the general population, either through the corporatist system or the parallel system of territorial representation; political decisions were made in the Council of Ministers, which was dominated by Salazar from the early 1930s until his incapacitation in 1968.[2] In sum, between 1930 and 1968 one political regime was in place, changed very little internally, involved a very small group of people which did not renew itself, and was the creation and project of one man – an austere, reclusive and strongly religious economist. When Marcello Caetano was appointed Prime Minister in 1968, there were promises and plans for a change within the system, for innovation and reform. However, Caetano never did master the system, considered himself its captive, and instituted no real reforms beyond the symbolic of changes in names and involving a handful of new politicians and bureaucrats, at least for a time.[3]

Most importantly, political inertia prevailed in this avowedly corporatist and non-democratic regime and innovation was not allowed, although the state did expand in size and responsibilty. It was particularly discouraged with regard to the most important policy, namely Portugal's commitment to retain an empire in Africa (twenty times the size of Portugal), despite the outbreak of guerrilla wars from 1961 which by 1970 led to the commitment of approximately one-half of the national budget for defence, a mass mobilisation of the population, emigration and continuing disruption of the economy. Change was clearly not possible within the political system, and it came from the only possible source which was the military, particularly the middle ranks of the officer corps, who knew the wars could not be won. The *Estado Novo,* then, was brought to an end on 25 April 1974 by means of a military coup, which immediately received the enthusiastic support of the vast majority of the population. As they had been denied a role in politics for the previous half a century, the Portuguese people greeted the complete overthrow of the regime with high expectations that Portugal would soon resemble other more modern countries.

The two years following the overthrow of the *Estado Novo* were characterised by a wide variety of models, strategies and tactics promoted by diverse social and political actors, all seeking to promote one or another political regime and socio-economic order. This period saw the emergence of fifty political parties, hundreds of pressure groups, and a score of factions within the armed forces. It was, in retrospect, a period of sorting through the possible systems which could be implemented in Portugal following the long period of the conservative-authoritarian regime and the resultant social and economic underdevelopment. There is no need to review all of the models which were bandied about in this period of effervescence and enthusiasm, but rather to indicate that most of them were completely unrealistic and were proposed only because there had been no previous opportunity for the people to participate in politics.[4]

The fact that a liberal democratic regime emerged is due to a combination of factors: the stalemate of other models; the impracticality of the vast majority of them; foreign involvement and support; and a commitment by a core group of Armed Forces Movement (MFA) officers and a small group of emerging politicians to this type of regime as they recognised its strengths in the light of weaknesses in the previous regime. It must be emphasised that the liberal democratic system emerged from a political, and at times military, process, and was not an outgrowth of the *Estado Novo* nor had it been previously worked out by those making the coup of 25 April. It was, in short, an improvised and tenuous process which carried tremendous implications for political participation in a society which had previously been denied almost all forms of participation.

THE CONSTITUTION OF APRIL 1976

Much of the enthusiasm, the structural changes brought about by revolutionary activity, long-range goals in the economy and society, as well as the liberal democratic regime, were formally enshrined in the Constitution of

April 1976. The constitution, with its 312 articles, was formulated by a Constituent Assembly which had been elected on 25 April 1975 – during the height of the radical transition and involvement. It was written by members of parties which had received the following votes in these elections: Socialist Party (PS) 38 per cent, Social Democratic Party (PPD and then PSD) 26 per cent, Communist Party (PCP) 12 per cent, and Social Democratic Centre (CDS) 8 per cent. In the 250-member Constituent Assembly, the PS had 116 members and the PCP 35 – a majority, although it must be noted that it was approved by all the parties in April 1976 except the CDS with 16 members, which had in fact participated in the elaboration of the document. The constitution enshrined the goals and gains from the coup of 25 April 1974 as well as the revolutionary processes which followed it.

According to one of the most respected constitutional experts, Dr Jorge Miranda, there are five main themes in the constitution: (1) National Independence which is dealt with in at least twelve articles defining the independence of Portugal in political, economic, social and cultural terms; (2) Fundamental Rights and Liberties which are treated in at least three articles, and in this form have no parallel in the constitutions of other countries, for they include an extensive series of guarantees, and indicate that all the rights must be interpreted in line with the Universal Declaration of Human Rights; (3) Political Democracy which is dealt with in at least twenty-three articles, specifying the liberal democratic system in terms of ideological and party pluralism. Guaranteed here are universal suffrage, the separation of powers, a central role for political parties, and a proportional representation electoral law. These guarantees apply not only to the national but also to the local level and to trade unions; (4) The State of Law is mentioned in at least five articles. They concern the protection of fundamental rights and limitations on government over the people; (5) The Transition to Socialism is dealt with in at least ten articles, which stipulate that Portugal is to move democratically toward a socialist economic system. This is not only an abstract statement, but includes specific and concrete items such as rights of workers, the role of workers' commissions, unions and the process of nationalisation. It must be emphasised that the movement toward socialism is viewed in the 1976 constitution as an integral part of the process of democratisation.[5] These 'transition' items loom large in the constitution and achieve prominence from the beginning with Item One on 'transformation into a society without classes', Item Two 'ensuring the transition to socialism', Item Nine on 'socialising the means of production', and Item Ten providing for the 'collective appropriation of the principal means of production'.

With the proclamation of this extremely detailed, programmatic and far-reaching constitution, Portugal in the spring and summer of 1976 also held elections for the Assembly of the Republic and the Presidency. In the Assembly elections on 25 April 1976, the PS with 35 per cent of the vote received 107 deputies and the PSD 73, the CDS 42, and the PCP 40. The PS of General Secretary Mario Soares decided to rule as a minority government rather than forming a coalition with the PCP to its left or the PSD or CDS to its right. Soares would not form a coalition with the PCP because the main claim of the PS was its opposition to the PCP during its struggle for hegemony during the height of radicalisation in 1975. Also, the foreign supporters of the PS, particularly in the Federal Republic of Germany, were adamantly against a coalition with the PCP. He did not form a coalition with the PSD, which was in fact encouraged by the Germans, because he, and several American embassy officials, thought that the PSD would lose its basis of support if not in the governing coalition. In addition, Mario Soares and the president of the PSD, Dr Sá Carneiro, were not on friendly terms. In the presidential elections General Ramalho Eanes, who had played a key role in putting down a left-wing military coup in late 1975 and had begun to professionalise the armed forces, became the candidate of the three main political parties, save the PCP which ran its own candidate. In these elections Eanes received nearly 62 per cent of the vote (against 16 per cent for Otelo Saraiva de Carvalho, his closest competitor who was a populistic military figure of the left, who had been central in the coup of 25 April 1974).[6]

GOVERNMENTS AFTER 1976

Between 25 April 1974 and the proclamation of the constitution two years later there were six provisional governments.The shifts from one provisional government to another, and particularly from the Second to Third, and Fifth to Sixth, represented shifts in potential regime types. From mid-1976 there have been nine constitutional governments which do not represent shifts from one type of regime to another, but rather reflect the balance of power among the political parties and different groups in the military. Thus, the theme of change was predominant between 1974 and 1976, and since then there has been substantial continuity within fairly broad limits.

The composition of the nine governments is indicative of these limits. The First Constitutional Government was a minority government of the PS which lasted from July 1976 until December 1977 when it fell on a vote of confidence (of 100 to 159). The Second, from January 1978 until July 1978 was an incohesive coalition of the PS and the CDS, which was presumably a party to the right and which had voted against the constitution. The next three governments were not based on party politics but were rather governments of 'presidential inspiration', which still had to have support in the Assembly if legislation were to be passed and, at least with the first two, stay in power. From the interim elections of December 1979 a coalition, the Democratic Alliance (AD) of the PSD and CDS, together with the very minor Popular Monarchists (PPM), ruled and this coalition was retained by the regular elections of October 1980. The AD continued, even after a shake-up in August 1981, until late 1982 when it collapsed internally. From the inability of the AD to regroup, elections were held on 25 April 1983 and the PS with 36 per cent of the votes and 101 deputies emerged as the largest party. (PSD 27 per cent and 75 deputies, PCP 18 per cent and 41 deputies and CDS 12 per cent and 30 deputies.) Following almost two months of negotiations and discussions,the Ninth Constitutional Government emerged as a coalition of the PS and PSD – or 'central block'.

This brief review highlights the 'flexibility' in the governments since 1976. Of the four main parties all but the PCP have been in power, and even the very minor PPM which had received only 0.52 per cent of the vote in 1976 has also been in government.The PS has entered into coalitions with both of the parties to its right, and these parties have been in coalition with each other as well. It is clear that, based upon a reading of the party platforms between 1976 and the present, the parties are very malleable in terms of goals and programmes. They can be in coalition with almost any other party, which in turn is also flexible. The exception, of course, is the PCP which was predominant for the part of the period of 1974–6, is consistent in its goals and platform, and is not a democratic party in any case. It exerts its influence through parallel organisations of workers in the urban and even rural areas. One outcome of the parties' flexibility in governing as well as their factions and instability is the opportunity for a wide variety of would-be politicians to participate. This observation is based not on statistics, but on the personal familiarity of many politicians, which suggests that the great majority of the intellectual elite (at least those with political aspirations) have now had the opportunity to take part in government. At a broad elite level, in any case, opportunities exist for political involvement in a manner undreamt of during the *Estado Novo*. This is not to imply that involvement leads to effective policy-making, but rather that the politicians at least can become identified with a system which they have been, are presently, or may be involved with again. It also suggests that there is still flexibility within the parties themselves. The PCP remains constant with the same general secretary and key elements of the secretariat; the PS, after extensive dissensions, has moved into line with Mario Soares; the PSD is currently in accord with Mota Pinto, vice- Prime Minister and Minister of Defence, but the party is severely split, wracked by crises and likely to evolve substantially in the near future; and the CDS is in fact without agreed-upon leadership. It should be noted that the president of the PSD, Sá Carneiro, and one of the two main leaders of the CDS, Amaro da Costa, were killed in an air crash in late 1980. If either had lived, there may have been more stability within the parties and in the relationships between them, but this is not certain either. In any case, two of the four parties are currently unstable, as is the party system itself generally speaking.

ELECTIONS AND PUBLIC OPINION

As the politicians have had substantial opportunities to participate in politics, so, too, has the general population been able to vote and become involved through parties and groups. This is in stark contrast to the *Estado Novo,* where the suffrage was severely restricted, in fact stagnant, and groups as well as parties were either outlawed or created and controlled from above. The country has thus experienced a major change in moving from the *Estado Novo* to the unstable period following it, and certainly continuing through the constitutional period. There have been presidential elections in 1976 and in 1980 in which Ramalho Eanes was elected and then re-elected. There have been elections for the Assembly of the Republic in 1976, 1979, 1980 and 1983. Local elections were held in 1976, 1979 and 1982. Without comparable surveys over time on voting intentions, it is difficult to say with certainty – but the regional breakdowns suggest – that there is great stability in voting. This seems obvious from the figures on the distribution of votes for the parties, and while there are shifts they are not in only one direction. We can note that between the national elections of 1976 and 1983 the percentages for the PS increased by 1 per cent, for the PSD by 3 per cent, for the PCP by 4 per cent, and decreased for the CDS by 4 per cent. Between the elections of 5 October 1980 and 25 April 1983 the results showed that the AD decreased by 7 per cent, the PS increased by 8 per cent, and the PCP increased by 1 per cent. There would seem to be no secular trend of change in anything but abstention rates, which have increased from 8 per cent of registered voters in 1975 to 16 per cent of registered voters in 1980 and 21 per cent in 1983. Continuity seems predominant, then, in the voter's participation, but there is a more important concern relating to continuity with the past.

What emerges most clearly from opinion poll after opinion poll is the distance between the general population and the structures of government. Thus, while a broad group of the elite has been deeply involved in politics since 1974 and the general population votes, may appear in demonstrations and freely discuss politics, in fact the latter is terribly ignorant of politics and has yet to identify with the liberal democratic regime. This is not to say that the people have identified with another possible model, except possibly the *Estado Novo,* but that they are reserved in their support for and identification with the present regime.

This ignorance and distance was obvious in our survey of early 1978, and has been found in virtually all surveys since then. Typical was a result of a survey conducted in late 1982. When asked about the most important or most positive action by a political figure in recent time, 58 per cent could not respond. After the constitutional revision, which was *the* stuff of politics in 1981 and much of 1982, 58 per cent of those interviewed did not know that it had been revised and 6 per cent indicated that it had not been. Only slightly more than one-third – 36 per cent –were aware of constitutional revision.[7] These kinds of results are commonplace in Portugal, and indicate an ignorance of key political actors and institutions as well as continuing lack of identification with the regime.

The combination of these two characteristics – governmental instability due to party fragmentation, and the political ignorance and reserve of the population – could be serious for the continuity of the democratic regime were it not for the President of the Republic. In elaborating the political system defined in the constitution of 1976, it was realised that the country had slight democratic traditions and faced severe socio-economic difficulties. The system, then, was formulated in a semi-presidential or bi-polar executive format.[8]

Item 193 states 'The Government is politically responsible to the President of the Republic and the Assembly of the Republic'. The President is popularly elected, and the Assembly presumably operates according to the will of the political parties (the existence of which is guaranteed in Item 47), which enjoy representation according to the results of the parliamentary elections. Authority is thus shared, and to the President's popular election were added his position as Commander-in-Chief of the Armed Forces and President of the Revolutionary Council. The President lacked executive powers except with regard to the armed forces. However, in conjunction with the Revolutionary Council with which he had to consult, his formal powers were extensive. They included the nomination of the Prime Minister after 'consulting with the Revolutionary Council and parties represented in the Assembly', 'and holding in mind the electoral results' (Item 190); dismissal of the Prime Minister; dissolution of the Assembly; (Item 136) an explicit veto which could be overridden by a majority or, in some cases, two-thirds; (Item 139) declaration of war, a state of seige or of emergency. In addition, due to the ambiguity of the text, the president also had a pocket veto and could dismiss the Prime Minister even though he might hold the confidence of the Assembly. The President presided at the Revolutionary Council which had exclusive jurisdiction regarding the armed forces, was the constitutional tribunal, and served as a council for the President. Thus, formally, particularly in recalling that the President presided at the Revolutionary Council, the political system was semi-presidential. However, as Duverger has shown, practice can vary greatly where formal powers are not utilised and where political parties can play supportive or opposition roles.[9]

In the five constitutional governments between July 1976 and January 1980, the President played an increasing role which served to draw power away from the Assembly as he sought to ensure some stability and effectiveness. However, he did not institutionalise this situation either through the formation of a presidential party or a revision of the constitution. That is, he employed the powers (broadly understood) of the constitution, but did not seek to identify them with himself or modify them for utilisation under different (non-minority government) situations.

The experience of the Second to the Fifth Constitutional Governments demonstrated that the powers of the President could be very great indeed. Not only did he dismiss Mario Soares (who lost his majority in the Assembly) in 1978, but he formed three governments on his own initiative with varying degrees of consultation with the political parties. He met extensively with ministers in the three governments of his initiation as well as the first two governments, utilised the pocket veto, and through public statements influenced policy as well. In foreign affairs he played important roles in defining Portugal's position on important issues. And, through visits within Portugal itself, he defined key issues of regional and even national policy. The Revolutionary Council did not veto any important legislation until May 1980, when it twice vetoed legislation on the delimitation of public and private sectors. However, even before this, the Revolutionary Council influenced policy as the assembly anticipated what it would veto, through statements by its members on legislation and through the President himself. The Council was particularly concerned with legislation regarding agricultural reform and nationalisations. It was, of course, predominant on legislation regarding the armed forces. It seems accurate to state that from 1976 to 1981 the Revolutionary Council acted as a balance or flywheel in providing a certain orientation to the unstable political system, and utilised a variety of means for doing so. These included its operations as an organisation as well as the involvement of its members in both the government and the armed forces.

The President, then, in the face of weak governments and unstable majorities in the Assembly became prominent at all levels of the governing process. However, it must be emphasised that he reacted strictly within the interpretation of the constitution and in line with the programmatic elements of this document. It could be argued otherwise, but my reading of the documents and my interviews indicate that the President would have been content to maintain a more limited role in governing – had there been a stable and effective government. There was not, and he thus assumed a much larger role. It must be emphasised that he did not form a presidential party which would have defined the political system along the lines of the French Fifth Republic. There were at least five proposals from a variety of politicians for such a solution which would have involved the formation of a party, revision of the constitution, and presidential support for certain candidates in the elections to the Assembly. He entertained the proposals, but remained aloof and did not offer support. His response was that he was the 'President of all the Portuguese' (and not only those of one party), and further that a political role would conflict with his position as Commander-in-Chief of the Armed Forces. Until 1980 the presidential orientation of the political system was not institutionalised, but was rather the result of a particular conjuncture arising from the elections of 25 April 1976. This conjuncture changed radically with the interim elections on 2 December 1979.

In preparation for these elections, the PSD and the CDS joined with the miniscule PPM to form the Aliança Democrática. They received 45 per cent of the votes (against 27 per cent for the PS, and 19 per cent for the PCP), and obtained 128 deputies in the 250-seat Assembly. In the agreement for the formation of the Aliança, the three parties envisioned a common proposal for revision of the constitution and a joint candidate for the Presidency who would not be the incumbent. From January 1980, when the Sixth Constitutional Government took office, the tensions were clear between the Aliança Democrática government on the one side and the President and Revolutionary Council on the other. The President travelled within Portugal and abroad, used the pocket veto, and the Revolutionary Council vetoed the key item in the AD programme on the delimitation of economic sectors. The orientations of the President and those of the government were clearly distinct and conflicting, and it is not difficult to provide evidence in this regard.[10] The resulting institutional arrangement was ambiguous: while the government, now based on a majority in the Assembly, tended to operate in a parliamentary fashion, the overall regime did not, as the President and the Revolutionary Council also enjoyed legitimacy and had broadly-defined roles in the system. What is more, their orientation was more in line with the legacy of 25 April, while the AD sought to change it. The AD increasingly presented itself in opposition to the system defined in the constitution, the Prime Minister – Sá Carneiro – proposed to revise the constitution, and the President and the Revolutionary Council continued to guarantee precisely this system.

It was hoped that the solution for the AD would be found in the elections to the Assembly in October and the Presidency in December 1980. The AD remained intact, while the PS continued to splinter, and received 47 per cent of the vote (against 28 per cent for the FRS (PS+), and 17 per cent for the APU (PCP+)) with 134 seats. The AD also backed a common candidate for

President – General Soares Carneiro. He promised if elected that the constitution might be revised by referendum if the Assembly could not provide the two-thirds vote required for revision (of more than a majority of deputies then serving). This candidate was clearly a creation of the AD and never generated popular support as a campaigner or spokesman for the right. Not only did President Eanes win easily with 56 per cent of the vote (against 40 per cent for Soares Carneiro) in the 7 December elections, but Sá Carneiro and the Minister of Defence from the CDS – Amaro da Costa – died in a plane crash just before the elections.

CONSTITUTIONAL REVISION

A constitutional referendum, on the initiative of the President was now out of the question, as Eanes had especially stressed his opposition to it during the campaign, and thus revision would have to be accomplished through the Assembly of the Republic. Revision required two-thirds of the Assembly, and there was no veto for the President or the Revolutionary Council. However, with its 134 deputies, the AD needed support from another party in order to achieve the 167 votes necessary for revision . The AD found this support from the PS which underwent an internal split as Mario Soares broke with President Eanes; Soares had promised President Eanes in the autumn of 1980 that the PS would not support a constitutional revision which diminished the powers of the presidency. During most of 1981 and the first half of 1982 constitutional revision, and the negotiations involved in achieving it, was *the* topic of politics in Portugal. Finally, revision was passed in the Assembly in August 1982 and promulgated by the president in late October. The main elements of this revision are as follows: the Revolutionary Council is eliminated and replaced by a Council of State which, given its composition, is likely to represent the party elites and the parliamentary majorities;[11] the President's power to dismiss the government is formally decreased to 'when necessary to assure the regular functioning of the democratic institutions, and consulting with the Council of State'; the pocket veto is abolished; it is forbidden to dissolve the Assembly six months after its election and in the last semester of the President; and the elimination of the political responsibility of the government before the President. According to a constitutional expert, who is also a politician, there were six items in the revision which strengthened the powers of the President and twenty-one which weakened it. It should be noted that the former are qualitatively as well as quantitatively less important.[12] Although the main public debate before the revision concerned the opposition of the AD to socio-economic items in the constitution, revision itself left these elements to ordinary law and focused mainly on changing the balance of powers between the presidency and the Assembly/government. From a semi-presidential or bi-polar system the system was turned much more clearly in the direction of a parliamentary system. It should be noted, however, that the President can still dissolve the Assembly almost at will.

    However, in light of the earlier observations on the fragility of the political parties and the distance from them of the population, the facts (again) have not followed the theory of the constitution (now revised). Shortly after the revision was promulgated, the AD government collapsed due to internal conflicts and personality clashes, and only with great difficulty was it able to propose another Prime Minister. The President, despite the fact that the AD still held a majority in the assembly, did not accept the AD's suggested candidate for Prime Minister, dissolved the Assembly and called elections. More recently, the President has tended to ignore elements of the revision concerning the appointment of the Chief of Staff of the Army. After several months of tension the President and Prime Minister came to an agreement whereby a Chief of Staff must enjoy the confidence of both the President and the Prime Minister. It is obvious that the revision of the constitution is not in line with the cultural and political factors which created and continue to allow for greater presidential powers, regardless of constitutional details. What has been obvious since 1976, even after revision, is the role of the President which increases or decreases depending on the stability of the party system and the presence or absence of a majority in the Assembly. At present there is indeed a majority in the Assembly, for the PS-PSD coalition, but the President still exercises his powers in a fairly broad mode. This may be due to the well-known fact that the Prime Minister, Mario Soares, is interested in becoming President in 1985, and would prefer not to occupy a position without power. Revision, in any case, with this different coalition in power has not had such serious consequences as many had anticipated.

The key political issue at present is whether the President will form a party on his own inspiration. Were he to do so, it would probably become the predominant party as the President's popularity, and his continued exposure, is unquestioned. The formation of such a party would substantially modify the current configuration of the party system, as it would necessarily draw support from at least the PS and PSD, and it would almost certainly benefit from the fluidity of the party system. There are proposals now, as there were in the past, for such a party, but so far there are no indications whether President Eanes will in fact act on this issue.

CONCLUSION

It should be emphasised that the context within which the political activities and strategies are played out is extremely confining in the sense of policy implications. Portugal is the most underdeveloped country of western Europe, has the lowest per capita income and her industries are not competitive. The country currently owes $13 billion, has an inflation rate of 25 per cent, and her trade balance in 1982 had a severe deficit of $3.2 billion or 14 per cent of GDP. Until now the previously-cited factors of political involvement and popular distance (or alienation) had much to do with this situation, and the policies of the nine governments in these regards have been either weak or inconsistent, or both. The EEC was previously viewed as some sort of panacea, but now serious reservations have arisen due to awareness within Portugal of the economic implications of opening the country fully to the outside and the problems involved in entry due to France's concern with Spain. The country is currently searching for some other solution, but is not likely to find one.

6

The acute awareness of constraint and these confining conditions are obvious from the very sombre and pessimistic party platforms for the 25 April 1983 elections. Little was promised but more austerity and difficult times ahead. The elections were followed by Mario Soares conducting an internal party referendum on the proposed coalition, requests for involvement by not only the PSD but also social forces such as unions and owners' groups in discussions, and an opinion by the Council of State. Through an extensive process of posturing, negotiating and consulting, Mario Soares sought to take over as head of government without oppositon except from the PCP and CDS, and with all other relevant political and social forces involved. He has, in short, sought to broaden the base of responsibility for what promises to be a difficult period in Portuguese history. The government has been formed, is governing, and times are indeed difficult. So far the government has not been effective and the future of the coalition of the PS and PSD remains in doubt. Within this context the themes of continuity in the liberal democratic regime remain, and there is no indication of a rupture in this model of regime.

This cautious optimism about the future of the new Portuguese democracy follows a decade of much uncertainty about the exact form it would eventually take, certainly more so than in the case of the other two southern European democracies under review; for, unlike in Spain and Greece, democracy was itself questioned. Portugal has only just, it seems, passed through a prolonged decision phase (if the constitutional revision represents a final stage in formulating the structure of her new political system which is an open question), and she has therefore hardly embarked on the habituation phase. In the formal sense, both the political elites and the general population have had ample opportunity to participate in the new system, but it cannot be said that Portugal has experienced the kind of 'remaking' of her political culture that would buttress the new democracy.The political system inaugurated after the 1974 revolution has continued to evidence serious elements of instability, notably those identified in the party system; but, nevertheless, it has shown as a whole a certain durability not least by surviving in unfavourable social and economic circumstances. So, while change was the predominant theme in the years immediately following the revolution, factors of continuity have gradually and sometimes hesitantly come to the fore-front of the new Portuguese polity.

NOTES

1. For an extensive treatment of the pre-1976 regimes and political processes during the constitutional governments I-VIII, see my *Politics and Nationhood: Post-Revolutionary Portugal,* (New York: Praeger Publishers, 1984).
2. The corporatist system and political dynamics of the old regime are analysed perceptively in the articles by Lucena, Schmitter and Wiarda in Lawrence S. Graham and Harry M. Makler (eds.) *Contemporary Portugal: The Revolution and Its Antecedents* (Austin: The University of Texas Press, 1979), and in Lawrence S. Graham, *Portugal: The Decline and Collapse of an Authoritarian Order* (Beverly Hills: Sage Publications, 1975).
3. For the Caetano period see Marcello Caetano, *Depoimento* (Rio de Janeiro: Distribuidora Record, n.d. but 1975) and José António Saraiva, *Do Estado Novo à Segunda República: Crónica Política de um Tempo Português* (Amadora: Livraria Bertrand, 1974).

4. For the various models see my 'The Left and the Emergence of Portuguese Liberal Democracy', in Bernard E. Brown (ed.) *Eurocommunism and Eurosocialism: The Left Confronts Modernity* (New York: Cyrco Press, 1979), and the mood is captured well in Phil Mailer, *Portugal: The Impossible Revolution?* (London: Solidarity, 1977).

5. Jorge Miranda, *Expresso* 1 April 1977. See also his *Constituicao e Democracia* (Lisbon: Livraria Petrony, 1976).

6. This period is dealt with reasonably well in Robert Harvey, *Portugal: Birth of a Democracy* (London: Macmillan, 1978).

7. The survey results on the recognition of political leaders may be found in *O Jornal* 11 February 1982, and for the revision of the constitution in *Expresso* of 19 February 1983. For a comprehensive discussion on the results of our 1978 survey, see Mario Bacalhau and Thomas Bruneau, *Os Portugueses e a Política Quatro Anos Depois do 25 de Abril* (Lisbon: Editorial Meseta, 1978). The data are summarised in my 1984 book.

8. On this type of system see Maurice Duverger, 'A New Political System Model: Semi-Presidential Government', *European Journal of Political Research* 8 (1980), pp. 165–87, and Werner Kaltefleiter, *Die Funktionen des Staatsoberhauptes in der parlamentarischen Demokratie* (Köln: Westdeutscher Verlag, 1970).

9. Duverger, passim. 1980.

10. For the details and a good discussion of the political structures see Pedro Santana Lopes and José Durão Barroso, *Sistema de Governo e Sistema Partidário* (Amadora: Livraria Bertrand, 1980). Another very useful political science-type book on Portugal is Emídio da Veiga Domingos, *Portugal Político: Análise das Instituições* (Lisbon: Edições Rolim, 1980).

11. For this argument see Joaquim Aguiar, *A Ilusao do Poder: Analise do Sistema Partidário Português 1976-1982* (Lisbon: Publicações dom Quixote, 1983), pp. 179-82.

12. Marcelo Rebelo de Sousa, *O Sistema do Governo Português Antes e Depois da Revisão Constitucional* (Lisbon: Cognito, 1983).

Spain: Parties and the Party System in the Transition

Mario Caciagli

The landslide victory of the PSOE during the election of 28 October 1982 and its entry into government with an absolute majority in the Cortes, permit us to consider the long transition period from authoritarianism to democracy in Spain as finally closed. Now it is possible to analyse the years from 1975 to 1982 as a single and complete cycle. The purpose of this analysis is to evaluate the role of the Spanish parties during this transition, their relations with both institutions and society and to define the configuration of the new party system.

It is necessary to say right away that one of the reasons for the long duration of the transition and the slow transformation of the Franco regime lies in the nature of the parties themselves, which have been insecure in their actions and weak in their structures. The fragility of the new democracy in Spain derived also from the insufficent penetration of the parties in society and the vagueness of their images. The rapid and profound changes in the choice of the Spanish voters, from one election to another until the cataclysm of 28 October 1982, confirmed the instability of the relationship between the parties and the electorate and do not yet allow us to single out a definite model for the party system. Table 1 describes the changes that occurred in the three general elections. Other popular votes (referenda, regional and municipal elections) and the attitudes of the public (registered in various ways) have sketched out a situation that is still difficult and changing. To offer a remedy or a chance of stability in this situation should be one of the hardest tasks awaiting an effective socialist government.

Among all the problems, the most outstanding one is the collapse of and the subsequent disappearance of the Unión de Centro Democrático (UCD), the party that held the government for five years and whose principal leaders had overseen a smooth end of the dictatorship. Other factors, however, relating to

TABLE 1

RESULTS OF THE CONGRESS ELECTIONS (PER CENT), SPAIN, 1977-82

	Years		
	1977	1979	1982
PSOE	29.3	30.5	48.4
UCD	34.6	35.0	6.8
AP	8.3	5.9	25.9
PCE	9.4	10.8	4.0
Others	18.4	17.8	15.0
	100.0	100.0	100.0

the events of that period, render a prediction of the future dynamic of the parties and their system difficult. These factors are: the crises of a historical party like the PCE, protagonist of the resistence against the Franco regime; the electoral increase and the new role of the Alianza Popular (AP), the conservative party that seemed destined to disappear after the elections of 1979; the changing fortunes of the many and between themselves differing nationalist regional parties; and also the exceptional success of the PSOE.

In comparative literature, many attempts to identify the factors that determine a party system can be found.[1] As in other cases, so also in post-Franco Spain, historical and social factors (most importantly nationalism) as well as institutional ones (most importantly the electoral system) have contributed to the formation of the party system. Above all, an important contributory factor, has been the modality of Spain's passage from authoritarianism to democracy, which occurred through the 'reforma pactada' or consensus-based reform of the old system, and not through a 'ruptura' or abrupt change. It was entirely managed from above. This modality has conditioned the parties' capacity for solid political and organisational development. The course of political life in the following years has not changed this initial situation, – in fact it has accentuated it.[2]

In each section of this article, I will show the effects of different factors: those which may be found in common with other party systems, and those which are peculiar to Spain. Perhaps inevitably, the first topic for consideration is the 'reforma' itself and the results of the first elections.

THE 'REFORMA' AND THE ELECTIONS OF 1977

Much rhetoric was used, in Spain and outside, to explain the 'Spanish Miracle' – this most unique event of the end of a dictatorship, without traumatic shocks and without the intervention of foreign agencies. Undoubtedly, the heirs of Francoism were very skilful in keeping the liquidation of the regime basically under their control, and in guiding the process of political change. The latter only really began to occur with the nomination of Adolfo Suárez as head of the government in July 1976, after the very critical and potentially polarising phase following Franco's death (November 1975), which was marked by the somewhat intransigent strategy of the government of Ariás Navarro on the one hand, and by the intense mobilisation at the popular level on the other.

The installation of Suárez as prime minister and those Francoist groups which supported him meant, however, the adoption of a strategy regulating any possible conflict through co-operation and compromise, in which the opposition was also involved and which continued to function during the following years as well.[3] This strategy has been judged the best in the circumstances because it brought a potentially uncontrollable situation under control and because it initiated, even though very slowly, Spain's transition towards democracy. This, of course, had its price. One of them was the limited interest of the various elites in taking part in the constitution of solid political parties, with vibrant roots in society. In 1976, organised parties in the real sense did not exist in the country, except for the communists. The anti-

Francoist opposition including the left showed itself at an early stage to be disposed towards collaboration among elites which the new leaders of the regime proposed. It therefore renounced the 'ruptura', that is, the option of an open and hard conflict which it claimed it could not support. It accepted this basis for agreement imposed by the government and negotiated, from a subordinate position, those conditions which it had considered as a necessary preliminary (amnesty, legalisation of parties and unions, etc.). In particular, the political left – the PCE, concerned about its legalisation and the many socialist parties, weak and competing with each other – did not want or could not achieve what they had continually promised: namely peaceful popular mobilisation.[4]

After the law of June 1976 finally legalised the political parties, they proceeded very slowly with their organisation. The very proliferation of the parties (more than two hundred were counted) in the months preceding the first free election should be considered as a very negative sign, namely of fragmentation. They were, of course, not real parties, but merely a 'sopa de letras' – a 'mixed soup of initials' – as they were immediately christened. Behind those initials stood few real personalities and few aspiring deputies ready to link their careers to the parties.

The inclination to found political parties normally manifests itself with great intensity after the fall of a repressive regime; but in Spain this phenomenon reached abnormal proportions. Many explanations have been offered: the division between the exiles and the 'insiders'; the international scenario (opposing blocks, the post-conciliar Church, the many socialist tendencies); the regionalist sentiments and parochialism which was so strong in Spain; the political culture of the Spanish (marked by a pronounced personalism and a lack of pragmatism).[5] One important factor cannot be neglected, however: there were no real party structures that would act as focal points with sufficient power and prestige to attract and organise activists and followers. One should not forget that the PSOE, destined to electoral triumph, had little more than 8,000 members in 1976, and its leaders were not in a position to project its future. The UCD, the party of the government, was constituted as a formal political party only in the autumn of 1977, after the electoral victory of the coalition of twelve small parties which were grouped around the leadership of Suárez. Moreover, during 1976, there emerged the most serious problem for the formation of a strong party system in Spain: the political weakness and organisational confusion of the centre-right and conservative front, which was found as much in the ranks of the democratic anti-Francoist bourgeoisie as with the heirs of the regime. The vicissitudes of the UCD, which seemed to be the ingenious invention of those years, eventually confirmed that genetic defect.

The elections of 15 June 1977 naturally had a great simplifying effect on this jungle of party lists. The system of parliamentary parties dominated the overall political situation and the attention of observers; the extra-parliamentary party system, however, continued underneath to maintain a certain vigour and remained capable of producing surprises. In this phase, the parties were mainly electoral entities, and were not functioning as structures within society. The selection among the lists presented was in any case ultimately determined by electoral competition and by the choices of the voters.It was narrowed down even more by the Spanish electoral system. The electoral system adopted in 1977, which then remained unchanged and was inserted in part into the text of the constitution,[6] is – as is known – a much modified proportional representation method that favours the major party lists and also the small constituencies in less populated and developed (and more conservative) provinces. It was tailor-made for promoting the success of the UCD. It certainly has, as was to be expected, influenced the configuration of the party system.

The election of 1977 rewarded two large formations, the moderate conservative and the moderate progressive, the first being represented by the UCD and the second by the PSOE. There also emerged two parties of medium size from the extremes of the political spectrum, the Alianza Popular on the right, and the PCE on the left. Apart from these four major party lists, there remained only the Basque nationalists (the moderate and Catholic PNV, but also Euzkadiko Eskerra) and the Catalan nationalists (the bourgeois list then called Pact Democrat de Catalunya, but also Esquerra Catalana). Ending up with no success were, other than the numerous lists on the extreme right and the extreme left, the Christian Democrats (which was the biggest surprise) and the other socialists (the PSOE *historico* and the regional socialist parties connected with the Partido Socialista Popular, which joined the PSOE the following year).

Much discussed at this time was the continuity or discontinuity of the new Spanish party system with regard to that in the past, particularly of the Second Republic of pre-Franco times. Major discontinuity[7] was evident in the disappearance of bourgeois republican parties of the centre-left, which had been dominant in the pre-Francoist Cortes; of a conservative-clerical party (the Confederación Española de Derecha Autónoma (CEDA)); of the movements of anarchist inspiration which were so important in the past; and in the appearance of a non-denominational conservative party: the UCD. At a regional level, the major sign of discontinuity had been the substitution of the Lliga Catalana by the Pact Democrat, which in turn became the Convergércia i Unió. In the Basque region, the party lists of the extreme left, decisively supported in the following elections and expressing the aspirations of the autonomist and independence movements, were a novelty. It was precisely in the Basque country that the most outstanding case of historical continuity, that of the PNV, the oldest Spanish party, occurred. Continuity is also true of the PSOE and the PCE, even though the elites of the former have been completely replaced and are hardly comparable to those of the past.

The existence of continuity is open to debate and strongly doubtful at a level of party organisation. However, it has been proven clearly in terms of areas of electoral strength. Tradition and 'historical memory' have weighed heavily in the geographical distribution of electoral support. In almost all areas in Spain, preferences in voting for the left or for the right have very faithfully reflected the preferences expressed during the Second Republic. Ecological correlations have indicated strong continuity between the vote for the CEDA during the thirties and that for the UCD, between the vote for the Popular Front and the PSOE and the PCE forty years later, between the vote for the PSOE of yesterday and the PSOE of today. The opinion polls have confirmed the inter-generational persistence of ideological sympathies.[8] It is because of this persistence of these cultural bases that the major parties had such a great opportunity to enlarge their presence in society. Furthermore, the elections performed a very important role in the legitimation of democracy, and in promoting 'party democracy' in particular.

As it happened, the parties became the main protagonists of democracy during the years of transition. They did not attempt, however, to establish contacts with those areas of the electorate that were inclined towards them and which were probably fruitful ground for mobilisation and recruitment. They ignored establishing any lasting ties, whether by using old or new forms of organisation and dialogue. The parties therefore lost the support of valuable resources that had become visible during the short but intense election campaign of 1977. The spring of 1977 was in fact a season of great enthusiasm. The masses, excluded from the decision-making processes, demonstrated profound confidence in the democratic mechanisms and in the actors that operated them. They showed through their participation a great wish to have a say in political matters. The very turnout at the voting booths, higher than even the most optimistic predictions, was a significant sign of these attitudes. The potential for mobilisation proved to be high: the elites could have utilised it by means of the instrument of the 'party', but this did not happen. There was therefore a large degree of disenchantment.

THE POLITICS OF THE 'CONSENSO' AND THE CRISIS OF THE PARTIES

The second phase of the transition (which is placed between the elections of 15 June 1977 and the attempted coup of 23 February 1981) lends itself to an interpretative schema based on three points: (a) the political compromise looked for at any cost by the major parties; (b) the few concrete results actually achieved; that is, the *contents* of this form of politics; and (c) the method of conducting politics; that is, the *style* of the political class. I will examine the essential features of these points.

The political system found its equilibrium and its shape in the network of agreements between the parties, practised with increasing openness and conviction by the participants. The strategy of the compromise was also named the 'consenso', with the justification that the seriousness of the country's problems favoured choosing the road of 'national unity'. The Pact of Moncloa (October 1977) involving agreed economic measures gave official sanction to this line; the draft of the text of the constitution (June 1978) was agreed upon by almost all parties, and was the most concrete, maybe also the best consequence of this approach. The parties of the left, particularly the PCE, did not however seek to activate political discussion among different social interests for the sake of speeding up the process of democratisation; instead, they looked tenaciously for contact and understanding with the UCD, and accepted the delaying tactics of the government. The two parties of the left (but also the AP of the right) gave the impression of wishing to participate in the daily management of the Francoist inheritance, if not to participate in the division of the spoils. Certainly, a model of a different society did not emerge from anywhere. The country was witness to a 'continuism' without any tangible results, and it abandoned its political points of reference.

What about the contents of the politics of 'consenso'? Many external aspects of the Franco regime were reformed, but nothing seemed to be radically new. The social policies projected by the Pact of Moncloa were not in fact achieved; instead, anti-inflationary measures were applied which favoured the so-called 'national economy', but hurt the living standards of large sectors of society. No changes of the social order were carried out (even the fiscal reform of the minister Fernández Ordóñez was blocked!). In the state ordinance, everything remained as before; no intervention against the corruption of the public administration; Francoist personnel were maintained at the head of the military, the police and the courts; and the local elections were continuously postponed, seriously damaging local political and democratic life. Graver than anything else were the delays and ambiguities in the running of local administrations, a crucial matter affecting the entire Spanish system: it was in the face of resistance from centralism that the parties committed their worst mistakes, either out of misunderstanding or because of loyalty to their statist ideologies. Judgement on the contents of the politics of 'consenso' may still be a controversial subject; and it could be true that energetic measures would have presented risks in the face of possible blackmail from reactionary forces (primarily the military with its coup-inclined groups).

Within the framework of the compromise, the essential differences between the parties faded until they almost completely vanished. The energies of political elites were consumed in trying to converge. The major responsibility of the Spanish parties *vis-à-vis* society during this period was to regulate the mode of behaviour of their elites, which I would term the *style* of the political class. Hardly had it been reawakened, when political life was reduced to contracts and dialogues between 'professionals'. The Pact of Moncloa also facilitated secret relations between the party leaderships and between them and the government. The constituent process itself was conducted inside the committees of the Cortes, but the decisive phase was carried through in secret meetings held in private places. The attention of the elites seemed encapsulated within the institutions, and the leaders of the parties were effectively cut off from political communication with the wider electorate. The grey, daily routine of politics could not but follow the extraordinary events of before. But this chosen strategy had a direct influence on the style of the politicians: politics became merely games of manoeuvres in the corridors of power, because the energy for courageous choices and the will to devise a general political purpose was lacking. The original expectation and hope had for its answer the 'normalisation' of political affairs.

The parties thus neglected their other, more important function: to be the clasp between society and the state. In order to agree among themselves, they not only reduced the differences between their programmes, but also those of image. It was then that talk of the 'crisis of the parties' began.[9] The first and major effect of this crisis was the appearance of 'desencanto' (disenchantment). No other word was used so often in Spain between 1978 and 1980. It expresses, above all, the wave of rejection of the party system. This rejection of politics and of the parties which were held responsible did not only come from the young (the 'pasotas' or 'apathetic ones'), the ecologists and the outsiders; it also came from more politicised groups from the working class, intellectuals and members of the parties themselves. Surveys made during those years[10] revealed a disillusionment and bitterness that seemed to bring back in renewed form the 'political cynicism' already nourished by Francoism. These surveys also showed that the Spanish possessed little identification with parties, that they judged parties very negatively, and that these were all viewed as similar and only interested in power.

The results of the elections of 1 March 1979, even though they essentially repeated the party strengths of those in 1977, showed clearly signs of apathy on the one hand and protest on the other. The growth of electoral abstention was correctly considered a clear signal of apathy and protest as well. Table 2 shows the figures of this phenomenon during the span of a few years. A further sign of protest was the vote for the nationalist parties, especially for those which succeeded in winning seats for the first time (in Andalusia, the Canary Islands and the Basque country). This reflected voters' particular concern with their own regions at the same time as being a condemnation of the 'statist' parties; it all coalesced into a general detestation of central government.

TABLE 2
SPAIN: VOTING TURNOUT FROM 1976 to 1979 (PER CENT)

Referendum 1976	General Elections 1977	Referendum 1978	General Elections 1979
77.7	79.1	67.1	68.3

The crisis of the parties involved not only their relations with society, but also their state of internal relations. The parties were not in a condition to work out well-defined programmes and to present clear ideological guidelines. Immobile and elitist, they soon manifested little internal cohesion and tended to be obstructive of democratic participation.[11] These elements of extreme weakness and internal confusion of the parties had catastrophic effects. Where they still persist today, they present a danger for the democratic evolution of the country. Its lack of internal cohesion and the elitist character have destroyed the UCD and nearly also the PCE. Only the PSOE, which demonstrated in a similar fashion confused internal conflict in 1979, succeeded in finding unity under the near-charismatic leadership of Felipe González.

The crisis of the parties can also be measured according to their low capacity for recruitment. During the years of 'desencanto', a crisis of activism emerged which was interpreted as a failure of integration by the parties within sections of the electorate and a failure to satisfy demands for participation. Contrary to what happened in other systems after the collapse of dictatorship, a sudden and considerable increase of party-membership did not occur. The explanations are all valid: mistrust for political parties instilled by Francoist propaganda and the memories of the Civil War; an individualistic culture with little inclination for associationalism; and a previous lack of party-political activism during the Second Republic.

The figures furnished by the parties are few and hardly reliable. In every case, they are so low as not to raise the membership ratio (ratio between registered party members and voters) of the Spanish party system even to 1 per cent. Only in some months of 1978 did the total of registered party members approach almost half a million. We know that the UCD reached in 1980 a maximum of 130,000 registered members, that the PSOE recorded around 100,000 (which increased after its election success of October 1982); that the PCE fell rapidly from 200,000 registered members in the first years of the transition to some tens of thousands during the last years; and that the AP showed numbers oscillating between 50,000 and 100,000.

In the best study on the subject,[12] José Ramon Montero has sought the reasons for the crisis of activism among the decisions of the parties. If the parties were the only channels for participation, then they were also the upholders of those practices that had defined the limits of political space (such as the 'reforma pactada', the 'normalisation' and parliamentarisation of political life and the strategy of the 'consenso'). The parties have been widely perceived as the principal creators of the syndrome called 'desencanto'.

However, to explain the crisis of activism by 'desencanto' alone is too much of a simplification. Montero writes that with all the good reasons for the disillusionment and the decrease of involvement, one has to add another: 'the structural negligence with which the parties have treated their own members and any politics of recruitment . . . when the falling political temperature required an effort by the parties to organise, solidify and enlarge the range of party enrolment.' This means that the political elites had intentionally renounced their 'resources of enrolment because of the costs that could arise for them during this brief period and supposedly superior benefits which were implicit in their leading roles and their high visibility during the years of the transition'.[13]

It is possible that the membership party may be a phenomenon destined to disappear from the European scene, and that the Spanish have already shot ahead toward this 'modern' state of affairs. Well-organised and well-rooted parties, however, are still a useful instrument in society in keeping contemporary democracies functioning and are, in fact, necessary for their reconstruction after the experience of an authoritarian regime.

The crises of the UCD and the PCE could obviously have had different outcomes with parties of different dimensions and characteristics. As for the PSOE, its leaders and sociologists have always maintained the importance of creating a real membership party, but until now they have not been able to do so. Precisely because of its position in the government, the PSOE needs well-defined structures and a numerous membership in order to be more receptive to the moods and demands of society. Opinion polls which are still favourable after some months of government and the undiminished great popularity of the prime minister cannot be sufficient in the long run. Paradoxically, it is precisely because of its present position of power that the PSOE should think of strengthening itself as a party and of also encouraging other political forces to do the same, thus promoting a smoother balance to democratic politics.

PARTIES AND CLEAVAGES

Along with the increase in abstention, the most important feature of the election of 1979 was the success of the nationalist and regionalist parties. The matter of nationality, apparently of little relevance just after the first elections, became a crucial point of reference during the draft of the constitution, and as a consequence of the ambiguity of motives shown by the state-supporting parties in the process of elaborating and carrying into effect regional autonomy. In 1979, the numerous regionalist and nationalist parties won almost one and a half million votes, equal to 8.6 per cent and 29 seats in the Congress.

The question of nationality has provoked the most serious cleavage in present-day Spain, and it is only natural that this is reflected in the configuration of the party system. Some parties that were successful in 1979 seemed to be marginal and transient phenomena, linked to the protest against the delay in granting regional autonomy – which was seen as a remedy for economically and socially depressed conditions. Once regional autonomy was granted, the Partido Socialista de Andalucia and other parties of the extreme left of Galicia and the Canary Islands practically disappeared in the 1982 election. This does not mean that the nationalist issue will not resurface in the above regions and others as well during further election campaigns in the event of future tensions.

The nationalist strongholds remain in the Basque region and in Catalonia. That their strength will last was demonstrated by their rise there in electoral support in the election of 28 October 1982. Next to the larger parties, both in the centre, the Basque PNV and the Convergencia i Unió, there are moderate leftist parties such as the Esquerra Republicana in Catalonia and extreme leftist ones such as Euzkadiko Eskerra and Herri Batasuna in the Basque region. Since the socialists themselves have their autonomous branches in the two autonomous regions, and in view of the fact that separate communist parties exist at least in Catalonia, one can justly speak of two party subsystems or of a fragmented party system.[14] The presence of these parties makes the structure of the Spanish party system more complex. The long history of cultural and linguistic diversity which Francoism sought to suppress was bound to lead to this situation. But the positive aspect to the existence of these parties is that they might be useful in absorbing centrifugal forces and preserving a balance that the 'nationality' cleavage could severely compromise.

In the past, class identification has played an important political role in Spain. The class conflict was a determining factor in the Second Republic, and contributed considerably to the Civil War. The cleavage 'social class' still matters in present-day Spain, but it has assumed features similar to those of other modern societies. Moreover, in Spain the class structure has undergone a remarkable transformation during the past few decades. The agricultural sector has been much reduced and the agrarian question, battlefield of the harshest clashes between the classes, belongs to the past. The tertiary sector has grown, and with it the middle classes. Moreover, the diffusion of more homogeneous life styles in large sections of society has contributed to the fading of the traditional divisions of classes.

The parties took note of these changed circumstances, and adopted suitable electoral strategies as well as less strongly antagonistic ideologies. The conservative parties declared themselves to be interclass, and turned even towards a working-class electorate. The PSOE and the PCE openly looked for the support of the middle classes, and enlarged their concept of the working class to the point of including medium-sized and small entrepreneurs. Ideological differences were toned down considerably, and electoral promises tended to sound very similar as they were addressed to a general audience.[15] In spite of this strategy of the elites and changed social conditions, large sectors of Spanish society have still retained outlooks and orientations which are based on class background. This is true of the structure of cognitive values of voters and party members, and it also affects the image of the parties.

The Spanish electorate continues to place itself on the continuum of right to left, as linked to class interests. The parties of the centre and of the right are considered as the defenders of the interests of the higher classes. Those of the left are seen by their voters (and even more so, by their members) as representatives of the working classes. The same voters of the left, whatever their status may be, tend to place themselves among the working classes.[16] If one section of the workers had earlier voted for the UCD, it is easy to imagine that in 1982 the overwhelming majority chose the PSOE with the strong movement then in electoral preference. The PSOE has continued to increase its support among the middle classes, certainly among the urbanised and modern ones, while the traditional classes (small agrarian proprietors, medium-large entrepreneurs, businessmen) went in 1982 to the AP. The economically priviledged classes therefore identified themselves decidedly with the centre and the right.

The great economic and social changes of recent years have thus not yet produced uniformity in the political behaviour of the Spanish. Apart from class identification, there are secondary cleavages that could explain some continuities in political attitudes. Unfortunately, these aspects have been little studied. It would be useful, however, to understand how the structure of peasant property and traditions of clientelism foster individualism and particularism as political motivations in Galicia or in Castile-Leon; or how behind the PSOE in Andalusia there are found motivations rooted in the outlook of collective interests.

A primary cleavage in the political battle in Spain was religion until the murderous outcome of the Civil War. In the new democratic system religion seems to be destined to play an important role, but not a dramatic one. The break-up of areas of large landed property has removed the role of a great socio-political actor from the Spanish Catholic Church; and the Second Vatican Council has pushed it into a severe identity crisis in the subsequent drive for renewal. The rapid process of secularisation of society has deprived religion of much of its influence; practising Catholics are now more independent in their political preferences. Finally, relations between Church and state have also changed with the advent of the new party system. First, a denominational party was not founded. The failure of the plan for a Christian Democratic force seems to be definite, in spite of some recent, vain ambitions on the part of the Partido Demócrata Popular. Second, the parties of the left have almost completely abandoned anti-clericalism; believers are found among left voters, and even also among the leaders of the PSOE.[17]

In spite of this, religion has still retained some importance as a variable. Religious practice is most directly correlated with a vote for the centre or the right, and sentiments toward the Church as an institution are different according to sympathies for the parties. Moreover, problems such as abortion, divorce and above all private schools and religious education have reawakened the involvement of the Church hierarchy, and are creating a series of conflicts with the socialist government. However, solutions by compromise are likely to gain the upper hand, and no radical conflict is envisaged.

WHICH TYPE OF PARTY SYSTEM?

Almost all scholars who have concerned themselves with the definition and classification of the Spanish party system have explicitly referred to the typology of Giovanni Sartori, especially since his work has become the dominant analytical approach among Spanish political scientists.[18] I, too, will refer to the typology presented by Sartori. None of the types can however be assumed for certain, which confirms Sartori's thesis that a long time has to elapse before a system becomes classifiable.

The *two-party system* has been advocated with much conviction by Miguel Martinez Cuadrado.[19] This author does not consider one of Sartori's criteria, namely the *format* ('whenever the existence of third parties does not prevent the two parties from governing alone'), and assesses rather another, the *'mechanics'* ('alternation in power') taking an historical perspective. He recalls the experience of the Restoration period after 1875, when the conservative and liberals agreed on prearranged alternation (*turno pacifico*), excluding those parties that were against the system. The conditions of today and the present scenario are very different, and the PSOE has switched roles into government against the UCD, while the format of the system has changed anew.

The concept of *polarised pluralism* has received greater approval among scholars. This schema seemed the most explanatory to José María Maravall for the system arising from the elections of 1977 and 1979: a system with many parties, with bilateral oppositions for the major parties, with a party in a central position (the UCD), with the presence of anti-system parties, and with the risk of a polarisation of the political game toward the further extremes of the political spectrum.[20]

The concept of polarisation is of course the most debated one in Sartori's theory. Also, in the Spanish case it is debatable at which point of the scale of the anti- and pro-system parties the AP and PCE would be placed. One can observe, however, that the true anti-system parties are irrelevant, and have neither coalition use nor the power of intimidation (in looking at Fuerza Nueva on the extreme right and the Basques at the extreme left) and that, above all, the events of the transition have revealed the existence of centripetal and not centrifugal movements among the parties that matter.

Juan José Linz has been prudent in attributing in his various contributions on this subject[21] the qualification *polarised* instead of *moderate* to the multi-party system. Linz has no doubts that the 'borderline' indicated by Sartori for speaking of *extreme multi-partyism* has been fully passed in Spain. This author evaluates, with great care, the nationalist parties: he defines their system as *segmented pluralism*,[22] and here he finds confirmation of the centrifugal-polarisation thesis. Linz, too, is inclined to cast the AP and the PCE in the roles of bilateral opponents, but acknowledges objective centripetal tendencies in the attitudes of their elites during the politics of the 'consenso'.

It was the end of the politics of the 'consenso' itself that set in motion the full mechanism of the party system again, however, towards completely unexpected and traumatic outcomes. The subsequent excess of dynamism has almost entirely distorted the scenario, changed the weight of the actors and the quality of relations between them. Thus, Jordi Capo is right when he suggests a new term for the Spanish type – that of a *fluctuating system*.[23]

It is not possible to reconstruct here in detail how the results of 28 October 1982 came about. I just want to recall the crucial stages: the motion of the socialist censure of May 1980 which started the PSOE on the road to alternation (with some 'stops' during the period of 'arrangement' with the government of Calvo Sotelo); the deep crisis of the UCD, along with the exasperations of its internal battles and the fall of Suárez; the coup attempt of 23 February 1981, and the renewal of popular mobilisation which favoured the PSOE; the elections in Galicia and Andalusia which prepared the ground for the general election. In 1982, the PSOE managed to aggregate the votes on the left of the political spectrum (extra-parliamentary elements, autonomists, communists, moderates of the centre-left) and to triumph with 48.4 per cent of the vote winning a majority of the seats in Congress (202 out of 350) and the Senate (134 out of 208). The AP emerged, based on the ashes of the UCD, as the main opposition to the PSOE.

Let us now look at the new situation from three angles: the relations of the parliamentary forces, the opposition's role in society and, finally, the party system as a whole. The results produced a further concentration of the parliamentary vote: in 1977 UCD and PSOE obtained together 63.8 per cent, in 1979 65.5 per cent, while in 1982 PSOE and AP obtained 74.3 per cent. Between the two major forces polarisation, understood as ideological distance, has increased. The PSOE is still more moderate and its centripetal path has continued, but its new partner in dialogue (the AP) is further away than the UCD. This polarisation could correspond to a radicalisation among the public. The electorate of the AP, certainly anti-socialist is entirely conservative, that is, it is available as a loyal opposition and faithful to the democratic institutions, but does it nevertheless feel nostalgia for the authoritarian regime? It is legitimate to retain doubts concerning the democratic commitment of the right-wing electorate. At best one might consider it a heterogeneous and contradictory pole, more sensitive to authoritarian calls than the previous centrist pole of the UCD. In Spanish society, as before in history, the most dramatic problem is the formation of a social and electoral block that is conservative and democratic at the same time. Once more, it is a matter of the political organisation of the bourgeoisie.

At the level of the party system, the AP demonstrates the same ambiguity and arouses the same suspicions: it is still a party in a phase of *semi-acceptance* of the system, as Sartori would say. Its ally, the Partido Democráta Popular,

FIGURE 1

SPAIN: DRAMATIC CHANGES IN PARTY SUPPORT 1982

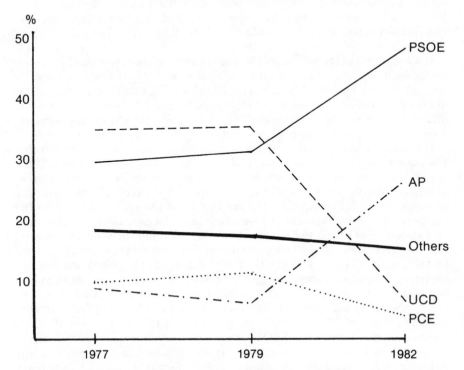

might have a moderating influence on the AP. However, it is this very existence of the PDP that makes the right-wing weaker and confirms that the present AP cannot offer a credible and cohesive alternative to the PSOE. Only the transformation into a moderate and democratic party of the centre-right can legitimate the AP as an alternative to the moderate party of the centre left, now in power.

The problem of the future dynamic of the Spanish party system lies in this conundrum. One can speak of a strong bipolarism in Spanish society, where a biparty-ism in a sense does not obtain.[24] For the latter, there are not even the required electoral figures: 25.9 per cent for AP is too far away from the 48.4 per cent the PSOE.

If one wants to name a type, one could define the Spanish system at present as a 'predominant-party system', as some have already proposed. It is possible that the PSOE will succeed in maintaining its predominance, at least as long as the expectation of an alteration is not yet feasible. This means that the party system is not yet structured in a stable and lasting manner, but remains open to the appearance of new actors on the scene.

After the end of the transition, a new phase of refounding of the party system began. In this new phase a very important task, maybe even of historical importance, awaits the PSOE. This party has to concern itself with the preservation of the hegemony of the left in order to avoid the risk of fragmentation on the left of the spectrum, and has also to perform the decisive role of a mediator between the institutions and society. To do so, it has to conduct itself effectively in government, but also to establish itself as a genuinely organised party that penetrates and manages to guide society. However, in its strong position in government, the PSOE could also have an effect on the other side of the spectrum. Thus, it should act upon the right, in order that it clearly becomes a valid interlocutor which thoroughly accepts the rules of the game and provides an opposition fully embedded in the system. With the resources at its disposal – power, consent, but also tradition – the PSOE could find the means and ways to assume this pedagocical function.

In conclusion, therefore, the new Spanish party system has during its founding period of 1975–82 demonstrated a capacity for adaptation and change and is, particularly in the way in which the party system determined the course of the fledgling Spanish democracy, in line with the central role played by parties in other West European democracies. Certainly, system-supportiveness has been widespread among the Spanish party elites. This commitment to democracy is one important reason why Spain's party system may indeed be seen as a *new* rather than a refounded party system, which is not surprising in view of the longevity of the Franco regime. Nevertheless, party development in Spain has been top-heavy, for the individual parties have evolved more as institutional than as socio-political forces. Their resulting potential for instability is the principal reason why this new Spanish party system is really unclassifiable.

NOTES

1. Among the most recent suggestions, see Gordon Smith, *Politics in Western Europe* (London: Heinemann Educational Books, 1980), Chapters 2 and 4.
2. In the important contribution of Antonio Bar, 'El sistema de partidos en España: ensayo de caraterización' *Sistema,* 43 (March 1982), pp.3–46, these characteristics are thoroughly analysed (youth, the weakness and lack of consolidation, the presence of other social and political powers, the sub-system of regional parties), but the conditions and causes of these characteristics of the party system are not explicitly examined.
3. An accurate analysis of this strategy and the use of the interpretative schema of consociative politics is found in Carlos Huneeus, 'La transición a la democracia en España. Dimensiones de una política consociacional', in Julián Santamaría (ed.), *Transición a la democracia en el Sur de Europa y America Latina* (Madrid: Centro de Investigaciones Sociologicas, 1982), pp.243–86.
4. A very severe critique can be found in Julio R. Aramberri, 'Origen y evolución del sistema de partidos en la España democratica: Un ensayo de interpretación', in Fernando Claudín (ed.), *Crisis de los partidos políticos?* (Madrid: Dédalo, 1980), pp.65–152.
5. Jorge de Esteban and Luis López Guerra, *Los partidos políticos en la España actual* (Barcelona: Planeta, 1982), pp.45–6.
6. See my article, 'El sistema electoral de las Cortes según los articulos 68 y 69', in Alberto Predieri and Eduardo Garcia de Enterria (eds.), *La Constitución española de 1978* (Madrid: Editorial Civitas, 1980), pp. 505–51.
7. Juan J. Linz, 'The New Spanish Party System', in Richard Rose (ed.), *Electoral Participation. A Comparative Analysis* (Beverly Hills and London: Sage Publications, 1980), pp.102–10. A perspective that takes into account tradition is found in Manuel

Ramírez, 'Aproximación al sistema de partidos en España (1931–1981)' in *Estudios sobre historia de España,* Vol.2 (Madrid: Universidad Internacional Menendez Pelayo, 1981), pp. 211–25.

8. Cf., among others, José María Maravall, *La política de la transición* (Madrid: Taurus, 1981), pp. 39–44.
9. Among all, see Fernando Claudín (ed.), *Crisis de los partidos políticos,* op. cit.
10. It is sufficient to look at the data of the polls on which *Informe sociológico sobre el cambio político en España, 1975–1981* (Madrid: Euramerica, 1981), edited by Fundación Foessa, is based.
11. A study that thoroughly reconstructs those bleak and difficult years of the relations between parties and society is missing. The climate that dominated can be estimated from the press of that time, from polls, from acknowledgements even by the politicians and from many written accounts.
12. José Ramon Montero, 'Partidos y participación política; algunas notas sobre la afiliación política en la etapa inicial de la transición española', *Revista de Estudios Políticos,* 23 (September-October 1981), pp. 33–72.
13. Ibid., pp. 64–5.
14. For this argument, see Isidre Molas, 'Los partidos de ambito no estatal y los sistemas de partido', in Predo de Vega (ed.), *Teoria y práctica de los partidos políticos* (Madrid: Edicusa, 1978), pp. 192–3. On the Basque subsystem, see Alberto Pérez Calvo, *Los partidos políticos en el País Vasco* (Madrid: Tuscar, 1977) and on the Catalan one see Joan Botella, Jordi Capo and Joan Marcet, 'Aproximación a la sociologia de los partidos políticos catalanes', *Revista de Estudios Políticos,* 10 (July-August 1979), pp. 143–206.
15. I refer to the convincing analysis included in Giacomo Sani, Richard Gunther and Goldie Shabad, 'Estrategia de los partidos y escisiones de masas en las elecciones parlamentarias españolas de 1979', *Revista de Derecho Político,*11 (Autumn 1981), pp. 141–86. The original essay was published in *World Affairs,* 143/2 (Autumn 1980).
16. This is based on the numerous polls conducted in those years, mainly by DATA and the Centro de Investigaciones Sociológicas, the results of which were used in many of the texts so far quoted.
17. An exhaustive description can be found in Eusebio Mujal-León, 'The Left and the Catholic Question in Spain', *West European Politics,*Vol. 5, No. 2 (April 1982), pp. 32–54.
18. Giovanni Sartori, *Parties and Party Systems. A framework for analysis* (Cambridge: Cambridge University Press, 1978), Chapters 5 and 6; Spanish translation, *Partidos y systemas de partidos* (Madrid: Alianza, 1980). See also the essays in Italian collected in *Teoria dei partiti e caso italiano* (Milano: Sugar-Co, 1982).
19. See in particular Miguel Martinez Cuadrado, *El sistema político español y el comportamiento electoral regional en el Sur de Europa* (Madrid: Instituto de Cooperación Internacional, 1980), pp. 77–83.
20. Maravall, p. 38.
21. Linz, pp. 110–35.
22. Juan J. Linz, 'Il sistema partitico spagnolo', *Rivista italiana di scienza politica,* Volume VIII, No. 3 (December 1978), p. 374.
23. Jordi Capo, 'Estrategias para un sistema de partidos', *Revista de Estudios Políticos,* 23 (September-October 1981), p. 166.
24. See Manuel Ramírez, 'El sistema de partidos en España tras las elecciones de 1982', *Revista de Estudios Políticos,* 30 (November-December 1982), p.15.

Political Parties in Post-Junta Greece: A Case of 'Bureaucratic Clientelism'?

Christos Lyrintzis

INTRODUCTION

The fall of the military regime in July 1974 was immediately followed by a reappearance of political forces, for they had to regroup hastily in order to participate in the national election of the following November. This set in motion a restructuring of the Greek party system resulting in the three-party alignment of today. Even though the dictatorship which preceded had – unlike the long-lasting Iberian dictatorships of Franco and Salazar – been in power for only seven years, its interruption of party-political development nevertheless allowed for a new departure here with the resumption of democracy in 1974.

The study of Greek political parties has remained a remarkably neglected area of research, and this is especially true of the most recent period since 1974. The reason has been partly the lack of sufficient and relevant empirical and especially survey data coupled with the overall absence of adequate research resources. In particular, the individual political parties have been reluctant to open themselves to scrutiny or even to publish significant material on their activities, social base and functioning which reflects on their internal problems and unity. Furthermore, work on the modern Greek parties has been strongly inhibited by a number of strongly-held myths, such as that they are simply 'personal parties' or alternatively that they are exclusively clientelistic. In view of such one-dimensional interpretations, any new research on this subject is bound to be revisionist.[1]

This chapter therefore seeks to provide some new direction in assessing the nature of the Greek party system that has developed since the fall of the junta government in 1974. It will focus on three major questions. First, to what extent are the post-1974 political parties different from the primarily clientelistic parties that dominated postwar Greek politics up to 1967? Second, what form have new elements in the party system over the past decade taken; for example, how far have they adopted new patterns of mobilisation and of representing the various social interests? Third, to what extent is it possible to argue that the year 1974, apart from the transition to parliamentary politics, also signalled a transition from clientelistic/particularistic party politics to mass politics?

PATTERNS IN THE PRE-1967 GREEK PARTY SYSTEM

It is useful to begin with a short description of the forces which formed the postwar party system and of their major characteristics, in order to trace the background of the political parties of today and to determine the continuities and discontinuities between the pre-junta party system and that which succeeded the junta. The complex of political parties that emerged after the occupation of Greece by the Axis forces (1941–4) and the subsequent civil war (1946–9) consisted of three major groups which may be conventionally identified as the right, the centre and the left.

The ancestry of the modern Greek right goes back to the interwar People's Party (Laiko Komma) which was at the forefront of the monarchist movement. Its policies and ideology were mainly defined in opposition to those of its main rival, the Liberal Party (Komma Fileleftheron), founded in 1910 by Greece's most prominent statesman, Eleftherios Venizelos. The Liberal Party's conflict with the People's Party over the issue of the monarchy strongly marked interwar Greek politics, and created what became known as the 'National Schism' which was the cleavage between republicans and monarchists (Venizelists and anti-Venizelists).[2] After its poor showing in the 1950 and 1951 elections the People's Party was gradually absorbed by the 'Greek Rally' (Hellinikos Synagermos), founded in 1951 by Field-Marshal Alexander Papagos, the victor of the civil war. The Rally's landslide victory in the 1952 parliamentary elections was to establish a long period of uninterrupted right-wing rule (1952–63). After Papagos' death in 1955, his successor, Constantine Karamanlis dissolved the Greek Rally and founded his own party, the 'National Radical Union' (Ethniki Rizopastiki Enossis-ERE). ERE was, however, not a new party but merely the old Greek Rally under a new name and with a few changes in its leading political personnel. Under Karamanlis's leadership ERE remained in power until 1963 and continued to play a central role in Greek politics until the 1967 military coup.

During the same period, the centre did not manage to remain united or to provide a credible alternative to the right. The fragmentation of the Liberal Party and other centre forces only ended in 1961, when the Centre Union (Enossis Kendrou) was formed. This brought together the various centre groups under the leadership of George Papandreou. The Centre Union won the 1963 and 1964 elections but remained in power only until 1965 when, after the King's intervention in party politics, the party split and its right-wing defected to form a new government with the parliamentary support of ERE. This so-called 'apostates' government marked the beginning of a period of governmental instability, and at the same time sparked off a process of political radicalisation which found a symbol and a leader in Andreas, son of George Papandreou, who had entered Greek politics in 1964.[3] The elections scheduled for May 1967 were expected to result in a comfortable majority for the Centre Union dominated by its centre-left faction led by Andreas Papandreou. The military coup of April 1967 pre-empted such an outcome and temporarily destroyed any hope of political change.

The Greek left has traditionally been identified with the Communist Party of Greece (Kommounistiko Komma Hellados, hereafter KKE). Unlike most of its European counterparts, the KKE did not emerge out of a split within the socialist movement. Instead, in 1920, the second congress of the Socialist and Labour Party of Greece (SEKE) – founded in 1918 – decided that the party should join the Third International, and changed the party's name to KKE, without causing any major crisis within the young and fragile Greek socialist movement. Following this decision, the party's ideology, organisation and policies developed along the lines prescribed by the international communist movement. This gave the KKE a well-organised mass base and a highly centralised structure, while at the same time increasing the party's dependence on the 'foreign centre', which in 1931 intervened to nominate a whole new leadership of the party. The KKE, however, remained a marginal political force throughout the interwar period, and it was only during the Axis occupation that the KKE managed to revive its clandestine organisations, which then became the driving force of the resistance movement; and it developed as the major component in the 'National Liberation Front'(EAM), the most effective of the resistance organisations, which by the end of the war was in control of the major part of Greek territory. However, for a variety of reasons – among which British interests and generally foreign interference played a crucial role – EAM and the KKE eventually became involved in an armed confrontation with the forces of the right.[4] The civil war (1946–9) resulted in the total defeat (military and political) of the left, and created a new schism between the victorious 'nationally minded' (Ethnikofrones) Greeks on the one hand and the communists and their sympathisers on the other. The KKE was proscribed and the left-wing sympathisers were systematically suppressed and harassed by the right-wing governments and their specially designed 'extra-legal' and 'para-state' mechanisms. The left then found a new source of political expression in the 'United Democratic Left'(EDA), founded in 1951 with the help of the clandestine communist organisations. This party attracted not only communists, but also the majority of left-wing, socialist-orientated groups. The electoral appeal of EDA remained limited, however, with the notable exception of the 1958 elections, when the party received 25 per cent of the vote. It could be said, therefore, that to the extent that the EDA was a front for the KKE, the latter dominated and monopolised the Greek left during this period.[5] Occasional attempts, mainly on the part of a few intellectuals, to create a viable and independent socialist party proved stillborn.

In summary, it could be argued that a three-block party system emerged in postwar Greece. However, it was a system in which one of the participants (the left) as a result of the dominant anti-communist ideology, the authoritarianism of right-wing governments and the repressive mechanisms at the disposal of the state had no real chance of winning power. The army, being the guardian of the existing political order, was always ready to intervene in order to avert any real or imaginary threat from below. The main features of the other postwar political parties were their organisational weakness and clientelistic nature. Both the Centre Union and ERE were parties built structurally around a network of local notables; while their unity and electoral appeal depended on the personalities of their national leaders and on the effectiveness of their clientelistic relationships. In terms of policies, the differences between the non-communist Greek parties were ones of degree rather than substance. Thus, clientelism at the organisational level and anti-communism at the ideological level distinguished the nature and performance of the postwar political parties. By arguing that clientelism was the major characteristic of Greek political parties, we do not imply that clientelism is the main or only explanatory variable of political behaviour in Greece as some analysts have asserted.[6] Undoubtedly class cleavages, historical background and foreign dependence have also played a central role in shaping Greek politics. By emphasising the clientelistic nature of the Greek political parties, however, we intend to stress that at the organisational level it was clientelistic relations through which the non-communist parties mobilized mass support and through which they communicated with the electorate.

Thus, in order to understand how and why these features came to characterise Greek party politics, one has to take into account a number of factors, which from the creation of the independent Greek state strongly influenced if not determined Greek politics. First, the Greek political system had to operate under the shadow of foreign interference. The resulting dependence here which was both economic and political became a structural feature of Greek politics, whose effects were evident in every phase of modern Greek history.[7] Second, the state emerged as a powerful and omnipresent entity whose mechanisms were extensively employed by the parties in power – that is, mainly right-wing parties – to consolidate their power and expand their clientelistic networks. Owing to the country's belated and limited in scope industrial development, the state played a dominant role not only in the economy but also in every aspect of social and political life.[8] The ever-increasing involvement of the state in socio-economic and political development became even more apparent during the postwar years. By allocating huge economic resources received in foreign aid, and by playing a central role in the rapid economic development of the 1950s and 1960s, state-controlled agencies acquired a significant role in the Greek political system. The state and the parties thus became closely related and often interdependent forces, the former defining the scope of the parties' activity and the latter depending on and at the same time influencing the former by using its mechanisms to consolidate their power and attract mass support. Thus, at the risk of over-generalisation, it could be argued that Greek politics were marked by the combined effects of this dependence and the state's key role in socio-economic and political developments.

These factors are directly related to the weakness of the political institutions, the fragility and clientelistic nature of the political parties and the oscillation between authoritarian and democratic regimes. Unable therefore to become autonomous and well-organised forces, the Greek political parties tried unsuccessfully to copy foreign models and remained attached to the state mechanisims in order to maintain their electoral bases and secure their survival. These features of Greek party politics are particularly helpful in understanding the close identification of the political right with the state and the lack of identity and organisational independence that characterised almost all non-communist Greek political parties. Another aspect of this situation was the limited appeal of the communist left during the interwar years – although the KKE had attracted a large percentage of the small working class – and its difficulty in elaborating a strategy and articulating a consistent appeal during the postwar years which could rally the dissatisfied under the banner of a left-wing party. The combination of clientelism, anti-communism and the all-pervasive state resulted in the effective blurring of class cleavages mainly through the development of vertical clientelistic networks. The middle class that regrouped in the postwar years, as a result of both the state's role as the major employer in the economy and of the country's rapid economic development and the related rural exodus, was easily drawn into the clientelistic networks of the right. Together with the farmers, the middle class provided the electoral backing that secured the parliamentary dominance of the right-wing parties during this period. In conclusion, serious antagonisms between political leaders, the clientelistic nature of the Greek political parties, the failure to integrate all social and political forces into the political system by excluding the communist and left-wing forces from every access to power and by isolating them both politically and ideologically and, last but not least, the attempts to control from above every social and political development that could lead to social and political change were the key aspects of what has been described as a system of 'guided democracy' or 'restrictive parliamentarism'.[9]

It was only in the 1960s that a process of social and political mobilisation got under way. It was motivated by the inequalities that resulted from the Greek model of economic development and the rapid and abrupt economic changes that accompanied it. For this reason, the middle and lower classes became ready to shift their allegiance towards parties that advocated policies which seemed beneficial to their interests. Since the communist left had no real chance of gaining power, the Centre Union and particularly its centre-left faction led by Andreas Papandreou became in the middle sixties the representative of these newly mobilised and radicalised forces. The centre-left emerged as the only force whose message – consistent and quite radical for the standards of that period – rallied support for 'democracy' and social and political reforms. The prospect of an electoral victory for the Centre Union and this centre-left provoked the overthrow of the parliamentary system. The 1946–67 system had failed to pass the crucial test of any democracy: it could not survive changes of power.

Within this context, several qualifications to the clientelistic nature of the Greek political parties should be made. The system of power developed by both right-wing and centre parties had not been one based simply on the influence of local notables – as was the case in nineteenth- and early twentieth-century Greece – but one very similar to what has been described as 'party-directed patronage', in which the central party leadership and particularly the leader himself played a central role at the expense of the influence of local factions.[10] The increasing importance of the party leadership in allocating favours and spoils, in combination with the central role played by the state apparatus in the functioning of the clientelistic system allow one to speak of 'bureaucratic clientelism' rather than merely 'party-directed patronage'.[11]

Bureaucratic clientelism is a distinct form of clientelism and consists of systematic infiltration of the state machine by party devotees and the allocation of favours through it. It is characterised by an organised expansion of existing posts and departments in the public sector and the addition of new ones in an attempt to secure power and maintain a party's electoral base. When the state has always played a central role in both economic and political development, it is very likely that the parties in government turn to the state as the only means for consolidating their power, and this further weakens their organisation and ideology. Such a political party becomes a collective patron, with the clientelistic networks based on and directed through an intricate combination of party mechanisms and the state apparatus. In a system such as this the public bureaucracy is orientated less towards the effective performance of public service than towards the provision of parasitic jobs for the political clientele of the ruling sectors, in exchange for their political support.

Postwar Greek politics exhibited many characteristics of a system of bureaucratic clientelism; however, the fragile organisational structure of the ruling postwar political parties and the presence of well-known politicians heading strong local or regional factions among their ranks do not allow us to speak of a genuine system of bureaucratic clientelism. The latter requires a sufficiently well-organised political formation whose party machine organises and directs the allocation of favours through the state machine. It was after the fall of the junta when new parties emerged which, ostensibly, were better organised and less susceptible to the power of their leading members that one can identify a real trend towards bureaucratic clientelism.

THE EMERGENCE OF A NEW PARTY SYSTEM

Before looking individually at the three main political forces which have come to dominate post-junta Greek politics, it is necessary to establish the general context of the party-political scene – one which was characterised by a certain ideological fluidity and organisational fragmentation. This is best done by describing briefly the electoral fortunes of the various parties during the 1974–81 period.

Parliamentary elections were held in November 1974 with the participation of four major political parties. The right was represented by the 'New Democracy' (Nea Democratia – hereafter ND) founded by Karamanlis, and the political centre by a revival of the old Centre Union under a new label 'Centre Union-New Forces' (Enossis Kendrou-Nees Dynamis, EK-ND). The traditional left took the form of an alliance of the two communist parties, which included the remnants of the old EDA. Under the label 'United Left' (Enomeni Aristera) the communist left concealed the deep divisions within its constituent parts. The fourth party that contested the 1974 elections was an entirely new one created by Andreas Papandreou. The 'Panhellenic Socialist Movement' (Panhellinion Socialistiko Kinima – PASOK) presented itself as a socialist party advocating radical change in Greek society. The 1974 parliamentary elections gave an easy victory to Karamanlis' ND, which received 54.3 per cent of the vote and an overwhelming majority of the seats in parliament; the centre was confined to 20.5 per cent of the vote and the communist left to 9.4 per cent; while PASOK received 13.6 per cent of the vote and 12 seats in parliament, far fewer than the party's leadership had anticipated.[12]

In November 1977, after three years in office, the New Democracy party called for elections, a year earlier than scheduled, on the grounds that the country's domestic and international problems (Greece's entry into the EEC and the renegotiation of its relations with NATO were the two main issues) demanded a government with a fresh mandate. The elections of 20 November 1977 redressed the balance of power between the major parties. ND retained its parliamentary majority, but its share of the vote decreased by 13 per cent and its number of seats in parliament declined from 220 to 171. The main victory of the election was won by PASOK, which doubled its vote and became the second largest party in parliament. The centre represented by the

TABLE 1

ELECTIONS TO THE GREEK PARLIAMENT, 1974, 1977 AND 1981

	1974 %	1977 %	1981 seats	1981 %	European Parliament 1981 %
National Democratic Union (EDE)	1.0				
National Front[1]		6.8			
Progressive Party			–	1.7	1.9
New Democracy (ND)	54.3	42.8[2]	115	35.8	31.5
Centre Union-New Forces (EK-ND)	20.5				
Union of Democratic Centre (EDIK)		11.9	–	0.4	1.4
Democratic Socialist Party (KODISO)			–	0.7	4.1
Panhellenic Socialist Movement (PASOK)	13.6	25.3	172	48.0	40.2
United Left	9.4				
Alliance of Progressive and Left-Wing Forces[3]		2.7			
Communist Party of Greece (Interior)[4]			–	1.3	5.1
Communist Party of Greece (KKE)		9.3	13	10.9	12.6
Others (extreme Left/independents)	1.2	1.1	–	0.9	3.9

Notes

1. The National Front was the successor of the National Democratic Union; in 1981 the National Front was absorbed by New Democracy.
2. The 1977 vote for New Democracy includes that for the New Liberals (1.0 per cent) who merged with New Democracy immediately after the 1977 election.
3. In 1977 the Communist Party of the Interior and four other parties formed a common 'Alliance', similar to the United Left of 1974, but without the KKE.
4. Communist Party (Interior) is the Eurocommunist party; the 1981 election was the first it fought independently.

Source: C. Lyrintzis, '*The Rise of PASOK: The Greek Election of 1981', West European Politics,* Vol.5, No.3 (July 1982).

'Enossis Demokratikou Kendrou' (Union of Democratic Centre – EDIK) – which was the new name of the 'Enossis Kendrou-Nees Dynamis' – saw its share of the vote shrink to 12 per cent, while the traditional left slightly increased its strength. PASOK's electoral gains meant an increase in its parliamentary seats from 13 to 93. This enabled the party to present itself as a serious contender for power and as the only alternative to the ND.

Between 1977 and 1981 the centre disintegrated into several small groups. Decimated by defections, EDIK was finally left with two MPs, and with a negligible organisational infrastructure. A small number of its MPs joined ND in 1977, while in 1979 four EDIK MPs formed the 'Party of Democratic Socialism' (Komma Democratikou Socialismou – KODISO), which was a serious attempt to salvage the centre from oblivion by creating a new party that saw itself as the representative of social democracy in Greece. At the same time, Mavros, the leader of EDIK between 1974 and 1977, created his own group which also aspired to represent the Greek centre. This situation was exploited by PASOK and ND, who both tried to attract the centre voters. Eventually it was PASOK which managed to attract the larger part of the floating centre electorate. By 1981, PASOK had established an image of itself as a party ready to win power, and was expected to emerge as the strongest party in parliament. However, the extent of its victory in October 1981 was hardly to be expected. No other parties apart from PASOK, ND and the KKE managed to win parliamentary representation, and thus the new parliament was marked by a tripartite structure. Since it was the performance of these three parties that shaped the post-junta Greek party system, the discussion will now look at their organisation, ideology and leadership in an attempt to understand their role as social and political forces.

NEW DEMOCRACY: A NEW INTEGRATIVE FORCE OF THE RIGHT?

The creation of New Democracy by Constantine Karamanlis in September 1974 represented a significant attempt to regroup and modernise the traditional right. He presented New Democracy as a new centre-right party which had nothing in common with its predecessor (ERE), for it abandoned the ERE's passionate and all-embracing anti-communism and adopted more progressive socio-economic policies. However, although the party did introduce new personnel into Greek politics (127 out of its 220 MPs ran for office for the first time in 1974), its leadership consisted exclusively of ex-ERE members.[13] New Democracy failed essentially to project a convincing image of a modern, centre-right party, and this was directly related to its inability to formulate and articulate a coherent ideology and to create a well-structured mass organisation.

Although several attempts to develop a well-organised mass party were made, culminating in the April 1977 'pre-congress' and the 1979 congress, when a new organisational plan was accepted and a new 'administrative committee' was elected, New Democracy remained basically a party of notables which relied on MPs and their clientelistic networks for com-municating with the electorate and rallying mass support. The efforts of a small progressive and centre-orientated group to reorganise the party and to establish a mass membership were frustrated by the entrenched power of well-known personalities and most of the party's MPs, whose vested interests would have been endangered by the development of a more structured organisation. As a political analyst close to the party has himself acknowledged, 'the party was far less significant as a mass organisation than as a group of leaders and professional politicians'.[14]

Although the party's basic ideological principles were described by Karamanlis at the 1979 congress as 'radical liberalism', also making clear that it did not represent social democracy, New Democracy never elaborated on these ideas nor did it define exactly what was meant by 'radical liberalism'. New Democracy failed to put forward a clear 'neo-liberal' ideology of the kind for instance adopted by the British Conservative party under Thatcher; similarly, it hesitated to adopt whole-heartedly a moderate, centre-orientated and catch-all strategy as the Christian Democrats had done in Italy. Hence, the party oscillated between policies which aimed at the modernisation of the social and economic system (e.g. reforms in the field of education, the extension of state control over the whole of the Greek banking system) and a set of conservative policies reminiscent of the ERE period and its related anti-communist mentality (e.g. the trades unions and anti-terrorist legislation). New Democracy, therefore, came to suffer from a confusing and contradictory image, the implications of which became evident during its electoral campaigns from 1977 and eventually contributed to the party's defeat in 1981.

New Democracy capitalised and depended heavily from the beginning on its founder's charisma and immense prestige as the leader who had restored democracy to Greece. This was clearly illustrated during the 1974 electoral campaign, when the slogan 'Karamanlis or the tanks' showed how the party's leader was projected as the sole guarantor of the preservation of Greece's newly-won democratic freedom, and this accounted most of all for the party's outstanding performance in the elections of that year.[15] At the same time, the party's neutrality during the December 1974 referendum on the monarchy marked the end of the close identification of the Greek right with the Crown, for the 69.2 per cent of votes registered for a republic was decisive in settling the historical question of the monarchy in Greece. For the time being, it seemed that New Democracy's political future was secured as a force integrating the right, especially as the extreme right proved to be weak (the National Democratic Union (EDE) gained only 1 per cent in 1974). This tended to suggest that traditional anti-communist hysteria had indeed declined if not disappeared, although in 1977 the National Front which replaced the EDE won nearly 7 per cent of the vote. This party attracted arch-conservatives and pro-junta supporters who viewed ND as a centre-right party which had betrayed the basic principles of the traditional right. The relative success of the extreme right account for ND's loss of 10 per cent over its 1974 showing, although it must be pointed out that a significant percentage of ND voters defected to the left and supported PASOK, which in 1977 managed to double its share of the vote and to become the official opposition in parliament.

During the period 1977–81, ND in office had to deal with a number of basic and challenging problems, and did so with only limited success. Economic recession and rising inflation (running at over 20 per cent in 1980) were problems for which the party failed to provide satisfactory solutions. The government's ad hoc interventions in the economy caused the hostility of private capital, and this together with the world energy crisis probably accounted for the poor state of the Greek economy between 1978 and 1981. In the field of foreign affairs, where the government's policy was determined by the dictum of Karamanlis that 'Greece belongs to the West', Greece's entry into the EEC was presented as the party's major achievement, but this was bitterly contested by the opposition parties, PASOK and KKE. More controversial even was the issue of Greece's relationship with NATO and the 'Rogers agreement' providing for Greece's reintegration into the Atlantic Alliance, again sharply opposed by both PASOK and the communist left.[16]

The election of Karamanlis as President of the Republic in May 1980 deprived the party of its undisputed and highly popular leader, and of the only person who could guarantee the party's electoral prospects. Karamanlis' successor to the party leadership, George Rallis, elected by a narrow majority over his main rival Evangelos Averoff, lacked charisma and failed to impose his authority on the party. His election not only did little to solve the basic leadership question, it also brought to the surface significant differences of opinion within ND and illustrated the ideological confusion of the party. Rallis, representing the party's moderate centre-orientated wing was continuously challenged by his right-wing rival Averoff, who never accepted his defeat at the leadership contest as definite. Under pressure from the party's right-wing, Rallis was gradually forced to abandon appeals to the political centre, initiated by his predecessor, and to adopt an increasingly right-wing strategy. Afraid of the possible loss of votes to the extreme right, ND tried to win over the most prominent figures of the National Front into the party's ranks, and was eventually successful, but this destroyed the party's credibility as a centre-right formation, appealing to a large part of the political spectrum. Thus, it was a divided party which fought the 1981 election and one which had a markedly right-wing image. Within this context, the lack of a consistent ideology became more damaging, and it failed to present a dynamic set of policies for the future that could deflect the growing challenge from PASOK. At the same time, its organisational weaknesses now became more pernicious, since the party conspicuously failed to mobilise its supporters and to project its ideas in a manner comparable to that achieved by PASOK or the KKE.

In conclusion, it can be argued that ND had two alternative model courses to follow: either to become a modern mass party and independent of clientelistic networks, with a well-structured organisation serving as the channel for elaborating a convincing ideology and programme; or to rely on the personal influence and clientelistic networks of its leading members and to adopt policy positions in a more ad hoc fashion. The available evidence suggests that Karamanlis opted for the first alternative, but failed to implement it successfully. The fact that the party was in power from its creation, together with the vested interests of its leading personnel, impelled the ND to follow the second model, even though some efforts were made to develop a mass organisation. Thus, ND as all previous conservative parties relied heavily on the resources of the state machine and used these for party purposes. Although the party played a crucial and important role in launching and consolidating parliamentary democracy in Greece from 1974, it failed to function as an effective and well-institutionalised political and social force. Its weaknesses in this latter respect might have been contained, but ND's eventual lack of substantial policy success in office especially over the country's mounting economic and social problems, together with the retirement from the leadership of its charismatic figure Karamanlis (on whom the ND had depended so much for its public appeal), meant that its intrinsic defects as a political party undermined its impact. Thus, ND can hardly be viewed as a new integrative force of the right, despite the considerable efforts made by its founder and a small group within the party towards that direction. The election of Averoff to the party's leadership did little to restore the internal unity of the party and the recurrent discussions about a new leadership and the need to renew the party's ideology and policies showed a deep division between a conservative and a progressive, centre-orientated wing within ND. It seems that the party is going to need considerable time in order to bridge the differences between its constituent parts to become a coherent and homogeneous political formation succesfully integrating all those forces opposed to the left. Whether New Democracy in opposition will remain a united political force, even possibly reforming itself, or will split into a right-wing party or a centre-orientated one is a question with important consequences for the future of the new Greek party system.

THE RISE OF PASOK

As noted earlier, a short period before the 1967 coup, the Centre Union's centre-left faction led by Andreas Papandreou emerged as a radical force representing newly mobilised classes. The dictatorship did not destroy the centre-left as a political force, for most of its leading members, together with new political activists, joined the 'Panhellenic Liberation Movement'(PAK), one of the major resistance organisations, created by Papandreou in May 1968. During his absence abroad for the period of the dictatorship, Papandreou dissociated himself and PAK from the Centre Union and chose not to take the leadership of that party after the death of his father in 1968. He concentrated his efforts instead on making PAK an effective political force with a radical programme for change, and which could become the basis for a new political party.

On his return to democratic Greece in August 1974, Papandreou refused to join a refounded Centre Union. Instead, he founded PASOK as a new political party which distinguished itself from both the old centre and the traditional communist left. Thus, the opportunity provided by the interruption of the military regime was taken to establish a viable and independent socialist party in Greece.

The new party drew together the PAK group, members of other resistance organisations and cadres that had emerged during the struggle against the military regime, as well as assorted independent figures from both the traditional left and the old centre and centre-left. It was the PAK group, however, that played the dominant role in creating PASOK in September

1974. Ex-PAK members occupied many of the key positions in PASOK's
executive organs – numerically the PAK group was the largest in the central
committee during 1974-5. Also, PAK's ideas and policies characterised the so-
called 'Third of September Declaration', which became the basic ideological
and political text of PASOK.[17]

It is clear that PASOK's historic roots relate to the Centre Union and
particularly the 'centre-left' but this does not mean, however, that there is a
simple continuity between the Centre Union and PASOK. PASOK itself has
claimed that it has integrated three different currents in Greek politics: the
first current goes back to the war-time resistance EAM movement and those
organisations associated with it; the second current refers to the Centre Union
and its centre-left faction; and the third one includes the forces that emerged
during the resistance against the junta. The analysis of the background of
PASOK's leading political personnel, however, suggests that this claim is only
partly true. For example, the party's central committee and parliamentary
personnel include only a small number of members who had participated in
the EAM.[18] The overwhelming majority of PASOK's leading members
emerged from the centre-left and the resistance organisations during the
dictatorship, while a considerable number of other such members were new
figures in Greek politics. Although PASOK's links with the EAM movement
are really very weak, it would be misleading on the other hand to view PASOK
simply as the continuation of the Centre Union. It seems more arguable to
treat the party as essentially a new force in Greek politics, which both achieved
an extensive renewal of political personnel and brought new ideas and
practices to the Greek party-political arena.

There is ample evidence to show that the party introduced a large number of
new personnel into Greek politics. It is significant that out of 170 MPs elected
in 1981, only 14 had been elected before 1967 on Centre Union lists and 6 had
been elected in 1974 on the EK-ND list. The remaining 150 MPs were all
elected for the first time on PASOK's lists. Among these 150 new MPs only 12
had been parliamentary candidates for parties other than PASOK; the
remaining 138 entered Greek parliamentary politics for the first time through
PASOK. In contrast, New Democracy's parliamentary group in 1977
included 68 MPs who had previously run as ERE or 'Greek Rally' candidates
in the postwar period, and 10 who had run for the Centre Union. Almost all
members of PASOK's 1977 central committee had not held any significant
position in any of the pre-junta political parties, and in this sense they were
newcomers in Greek party politics. It could be said, therefore, that to the
extent that PASOK relied strongly on new leadership personnel it can be
viewed as a new force in Greek politics.

PASOK also introduced several novel ideas and policies. The party's
ideology was based on the concepts of national independence, popular
sovereignty and social liberation. With these as its main objectives, PASOK
advocated Greece's withdrawal from NATO and the EEC, the removal of the
US military bases in Greece, the socialisation of the means of production (to
be distinguishd from nationalisation), self-management and decentralisation.
These basic policies were complemented by a set of social and institutional
changes aiming at the establishment of a welfare state and the democratisation

of the state machine. Altogether, PASOK presented itself as a radical socialist party advocating a road to socialism different from both the communist and social democratic model. PASOK emphasised its Third World orientation and its nature as a 'liberation movement'. This in combination with the ill-defined manner in which the party presented its policies led many observers to argue that, in fact, PASOK was a populist party and so different from the mainstream western European socialist parties.[19] PASOK's 'green socialism' (green was the official colour of the party in contrast to the red of the communist left and the blue of ND) by stressing the idea of national independence appealed to all social strata concerned about the problems and implications of foreign interference. By advocating a 'Greek road to socialism' and identifying the enemy as the 'foreign factor' (imperialism and multinational capital) and those few 'privileged' associated with it, PASOK was able to mobilise large sections of the population. It was an achievement that the communist left had failed to realise in the postwar years, mainly because of the impact of the civil war, but also because of its orientation towards foreign models and the recurrent crises within its ranks over strategy and tactics. In a society in which it was anathema to be a communist, and where anti-communism had for decades dominated the ideological sphere, PASOK by presenting itself as an independent socialist party created a force that was progressive and belonged to the left without bearing the stigma of communism.

Against this background, it was not surprising that PASOK did not commit itself to seeking the support of a specific social class. Instead, the party claimed to represent in general 'under-privileged' Greeks, the latter being defined as a broad social bloc encompassing 'farmers, workers, employees, craftsmen and artisans, the youth and all the people who are subject to odious exploitation by modern monopoly capital, local as well as foreign'.[20] Thus, PASOK aimed to appeal to its followers not as a class but as the people or 'the nation'. By appealing to the 'under-privileged' in this all-embracing way, PASOK adopted a 'catch-all' strategy and so strengthened its position for uniting under its banner all those who for one reason or another opposed New Democracy.

PASOK's most important innovation, however, was its establishment of a well-structured mass organisation. In a relatively short time PASOK managed to build a mass organisation, so that by 1977 the party could claim a membership of 27,000 members, while by 1980 the total membership exceeded 60,000. This membership was organised in local and departmental units which were supposed to function in a manner very similar to that of PASOK's western European counterparts. According to the party's statutes, the national congress is the most powerful party organ, with the central committee acting as the leading unit of the party between congresses. The president and the executive bureau occupy a special position within the party hierarchy, with responsibility for formulating the party's programme, implementing party policies and supervising and co-ordinating organisational matters.

Despite its impressive development in this respect, PASOK did not function internally as envisaged in the party's statutes. The party failed to implement democratic procedures within its ranks, and the personality and charisma of Papandreou influenced powerfully its development and nature. A special bond developed between the president and the party structures: Papandreou's charismatic authority and appeal to the masses maintained the party during its initial period of internal crises, and later it was his influence that brought about the reconstruction of the party organisation and the subsequent steady growth of the party. It was he who articulated and presented the party's ideology and served as its dominant spokesman. As a result of this situation, the mass membership was never involved in the decision-making process because the president and the eight-member executive bureau controlled party activity. The primacy of Papandeou's role has been officially acknowledged by PASOK's leading members who have described his presence within the party as 'a crucial parameter of the existence and operation of PASOK, determining it as a unified, organised movement and as a unitary political entity'.[21] However, although the party has lacked institutionalised democratic processes – and, notably, a national congress has not yet been held – its organisation cannot be dismissed as merely playing a passive role, as shown by its central importance in PASOK's election campaigns.

Despite its shortcomings, PASOK's organisation was nevertheless a major novelty for a non-communist Greek political party. From its foundation, PASOK appeared determined not to rely on clientelism as a means for communicating with the electorate and rallying mass support. The available evidence suggests that its leading personnel, and particularly its parliamentary group, did not adopt or develop clientelistic practices. Their rise was, with few exceptions, due to the general advance and appeal of the party and to their role in the party organisation. This phenomenon, it must be emphasised, constituted a considerable departure from previous practice in Greek party politics, and in the contemporary context sharply contrasted with the political practices of New Democracy.

It could be said, therefore, that in combining a radical ideology with charismatic leadership and organisational activism, PASOK appeared not only as a novel force in Greek politics, but also as a hybrid type of political party, articulating populist elements (of the kind familiar to students of Latin American populist parties) and mass-organisational socialist elements (of the kind exhibited by west European socialist parties). The presence of a dominant and charismatic leadership together with its relatively vague Third World orientated ideology have reinforced this populist image of PASOK. However, as the 1981 elections approached with the prospects of victory increasing, PASOK began to abandon much of its Third World-style ideas in an attempt to present a moderate image and to strengthen its appeal to voters of the centre. For instance, although its 1981 electoral manifesto reiterated PASOK's commitment to withdraw Greece from NATO and remove the US military bases, it was recognised that a transitional period was necessary, that 'PASOK would never allow the capability of the armed forces to be undermined' and that withdrawal from NATO was part of PASOK's long-term objective towards the abolition of the two military blocks. As far as Greece's position in the EEC was concerned, PASOK repeated its pledge to seek a referendum on the issue, but it also made clear that in the meanwhile it would participate in the Community's structures in order to mitigate the negative effects of Greece's participation in the EEC. Similarly, references to socialisation and self-management were minimized throughout the 1981 campaign, and the manifesto made no reference to a 'socialist constitution' as had the 1977 one. The word 'socialism' was rarely used by Papandreou in his public speeches; instead, the slogan 'Allaghi' (Change) came to dominate PASOK's message.

PASOK did indeed succeed in attracting moderate centre voters in 1981, thus confirming its gradual displacement of the old centre as the main alternative to the right; and it also challenged successfully the communist KKE's previous monopoly over the Greek left. In a period marked by ideological fluidity, PASOK had emerged as a convincing and appealing force, but it would be a stark and misleading oversimplification to say that the party was elected with a mandate to bring about a socialist transformation of Greek society. This was the vision of a relatively small group of party militants, but for the majority of the party's voters in 1981 PASOK's pledge to establish a welfare system, reform the civil and penal law, democratise and modernise the state machinery and to reorganise and rationalise the economy was enough to convine undecided voters to support the party. The slogan 'Change' captured the imagination of the electorate and gave PASOK a remarkable electoral victory.

Nevertheless, beneath PASOK's broad appeal lay a potential instability within its electorate, for it is difficult to say that the party has – at least yet – established itself as a socially integrative force despite its widespread organisational presence. Although it is very difficult to draw any major conclusions about PASOK's social base, the 1981 electoral results suggest that the party's catch-all tactics paid off in terms of electoral gains and that it attracted voters from different socio-economic backgrounds. PASOK's remarkably broad appeal to all sections of the electorate is illustrated by the distribution of its vote in urban and rural areas. The difference between the degree of its support in urban and rural areas was smaller in PASOK's case than in that of any other party in Greece. This was already evident in 1977, but in 1981 there was virtually no difference between PASOK's percentage of the vote in urban and rural areas. It sould be pointed out, in contrast, that ND was more successful in rural than in urban areas, thus following the pattern of electoral performance set by all postwar right-wing parties in Greece. New Democracy, however, attracted a larger percentage of the women's and older people's vote. Specifically, ND received 36 per cent of the women's vote and 33 per cent of the men's vote, while PASOK received 48.8 per cent of the men's vote but 47 per cent of the women's.[22] The available information suggests that PASOK's programme of change did not appeal to any one specific class or group within a class. It appears that PASOK had succeeded in persuading the electorate that it was a party for all 'the people' and it was elected as such by all sections of the population. In this sense it can be argued that PASOK's electorate was a mirror image of Greek society: the relatively moderate image projected by PASOK between 1980 and 1981 certainly contributed to this achievement.

It must not be forgotten, however, that PASOK'S victory in 1981 owed

much to the personality of Papandreou, who dominated its campaign and
monopolised all its public rallies and demonstrations; and that, accordingly,
his eventual disappearance from political life must be a major factor of
uncertainty in PASOK's future. In this particular sense, PASOK invited
comparison with the traditionally personalistic nature of Greek parties.
Furthermore, as the party in power, PASOK or at least groups in it may seek
to consolidate their positions by developing new clientelistic practices. As the
party organisation may possibly prove ineffective in maintaining mass
support, and in addition as PASOK may see good reasons in wanting to purge
the state machine of its numerically dominant right-wing cadres as a necessary
precondition for implementing its policies, a process of clientelisation by the
political left cannot be discounted. Moreover, a failure to fulfil the policy
expectations aroused in the 1981 campaign would be likely to strengthen this
temptation. Whether PASOK follows a clentelisation process (of which there
are already some signs) similar to that previously adopted by the political right
in power, or whether alternatively it will attempt to institutionalise and
expand its own organisational roots as a party, or even combine both methods
for the sake of maintaining its newly acquired power position is a fundamental
question, the answer to which must be crucial in determining how far the
Greek party system since 1974 has permanently taken a new departure.

THE COMMUNIST LEFT: A PRISONER OF ITS IDEOLOGICAL GHETTO

The dictatorship brought to the surface the problems of internal division that
has characterised the communist left throughout the postwar years. The then
EDA's strategy and policies had already been a cause of disagreement between
the section of the leadership of the KKE which remained outside Greece in
eastern Europe and the leading party members – both communists and non-
communists – who had stayed inside Greece. The 'pure and hard' line adopted
by the communist leadership abroad and the concomitant disagreements and
divisions were among the factors which accounted for the generally limited
appeal of the EDA. The differences over serious political issues re-emerged in
a more acute form during the military dictatorship, when the whole leadership
of the communist left found itself abroad, and this led to a definite split in
1968. The dissident members formed an interior bureau of the KKE which,
after the fall of the junta, became the KKE Interior party and held its first
congress in 1975. Attitudes towards the Soviet model of socialism, the
question of loyalty to and dependence on Moscow and the opening to
Eurocommunist ideas were the main lines of difference between the two
branches of the Greek communist left.[23]

Despite the differences, however, the KKE and the KKE Interior joined
forces for the elections in 1974 and formed the United Left (EA). The United
Left was a precarious alliance formed purely for the election. After its poor
showing in the 1974 elections (9.4 per cent of the vote), the alliance split into its
constituent parts and relations between the two KKEs were characterised by
vitriolic attacks and mutual hatred. The KKE opposed the New Democracy
government on fundamentalist grounds, regarding it as an instrument of
western imperialism. In contrast, the KKE Interior had adopted a strategy of

unity of action of all democratic forces, from the communist left to the democratic right, aiming at consolidating democracy in Greece and thus in its view facilitating the road to socialism. At the same time, the KKE, apart from predictably denouncing the KKE Interior as revisionist and opportunistic, was also in conflict and competition with PASOK.

This antagonism between the three parties that claimed to represent the Greek left sprang out of their desire for hegemony over the left. The 1977 elections proved determinant in that while the KKE won 9.3 per cent of the vote the rival KKE Interior received only 2.7 per cent so consolidating the dominance of the KKE over the communist left. This dominance, however, was only a qualified success in view of the rise of PASOK in 1977. As already shown, the 1981 election corroborated what was already known in 1977, namely PASOK's ability to offer a radical message while frequently out-flanking the KKE by accusing it of aligning itself with Soviet positions. Even so, the KKE still won 10.9 per cent of the vote against the odds. Although the party still attracts a large section of the working-class vote (the KKE's electoral strongholds are the predominantly industrial areas in Athens, Pireaus, Salonica, Larissa and Volos), it failed to achieve any significant advances among the rural and middle-class strata. Thus, the limited mass of communist voters remained loyal to the KKE, but for reasons of internal division and adherence to traditional and 'foreign' ideas the communist left had failed to break out of its ideological ghetto.

THE GREEK PARTY SYSTEM AFTER 1974: NEW ELEMENTS AND OLD PRACTICES

In the period after 1974 the Greek party system operated under various different conditions compared with the party system prior to the period of the military junta. First, anti-communism ceased to be such a dominant feature of Greek political life, and the communist parties were free to compete as legalised forces. Second, the historically divisive question of the monarchy was swiftly taken off the agenda of Greek politics by the referendum late in 1974, related as this was to the King's controversial behaviour shortly before and during the military dictatorship. Third, PASOK's rise in popular support and eventually to power demonstrated the impact of a new type of political force.

In spite of these important differences, one can also identify limitations to change and even several similarities and thus continuity between the pre 1967 and post 1974 party systems. First, the political right as represented by New Democracy failed essentially to become a modern mass party similar to most of its western European counterparts. In particular, it relied heavily on traditional practices of 'bureaucratic clientelism', and it became plagued by strong internal division over its very identity. Second, PASOK notwith-standing its establishment of a mass organisation and enunciation of a radical programme has failed to institutionalise itself as a political party in the full sense, and thus there still exists considerable ambiguity and confusion over the party's nature and future. PASOK projected itself as a force for social and economic change and capitalised on the failures and weaknesses of New Democracy very effectively, but it has all the same evidenced a certain ideological inconsistency. In other words, PASOK has been both an expression as well as a beneficiary of the ideological fluidity which has characterised the Greek party system in this period. Furthermore, the strongly personalistic nature of its public appeal through the figure of Papandreou and the possibility that it might itself adopt clientelistic practices in power additionally suggest the picture of a party still in search of its political identity. Certainly, PASOK cannot continue forever to use the strategy which enabled it to emerge as the champion of all those sections of the electorate that were dissatisfied with the policies of ND. Thus, systematic efforts may be made to institutionalise charisma and to reinforce the role of the mass organisation and/or to embark on a process that may eventually lead to some form of 'bureaucratic clientelism'. The first alternative, however, may offer a greater chance to PASOK to develop as a stable and effective force, successfully integrating the social and political forces of the Greek left.

For these various reasons, it could be argued that the major non-communist Greek parties have failed to institutionalise those mechanisms and procedures that would link them to their electorates, elaborate and articulate their programmes and hence guarantee their effectiveness and longevity as social and political forces. Party politics since the fall of the military junta has continued to be very dependent on the personalities and policies of party leaders; and, moreover, the familiar interplay between the state machine and party figures in the form of clientelism has not ceased to exist. These different aspects therefore favour the view that the extent and nature of the new elements introduced in the post 1974 party system in Greece have not constituted a profound change.

In summary, it can be argued that the post-1974 Greek party system is characterised by a combination of new elements and old practices. With the exception of the extreme right, the post 1974 political parties played a positive role in securing the smooth transition to parliamentary democracy and in creating a relatively stable party system. The creation and development of PASOK, its organisation and ideology and its eventual rise to power provided the major novelty, but this was due first and foremost to a process characterised by charismatic leadership, populist ideology and tactics and organisational activism. A process such as this could not effectively integrate the masses into party politics, and it could not ultimately develop the means to cope successfully with clientelism and with the problems related to the role and nature of the Greek state machine. On the other hand, the fact that the political right has failed to renew itself and thus grow out of the old clientelistic practices reinforces the image of a party system struggling between renewal and traditional practices. Finally, the communist left, although the only political force with a well-established and institutionalised mass membership, did not manage to integrate new elements. Given this context, the electoral victory of PASOK in 1981 and its performance while in office can be viewed as a possible historical turning-point in Greek party politics. The persistence of the personalistic and clientelistic elements depend to a considerable extent on the policies and practices of this party in power.

NOTES

1. See G. Mavrogordatos and E. Nicolacopoulos, 'Report on Greece', presented to symposium of the ECPR standing group on Southern European Politics, on Parties and Party Systems in Southern European Countries, Barcelona, November 1982.
2. The most thorough and in depth analysis of interwar politics and society in Greece is G. Mavrogordatos, *Stillborn Republic,* University of California Press, 1983. For an historical account of the social and political developments in Greece since the formation of the Greek state (in English) see J. Campbell and P. Sherrard, *Modern Greece* (London, 1969); also R. Clogg, *A Short History of Modern Greece* (London, 1980).
3. Andreas Papandreou had been a professor of economics in the United States. He returned to Greece in 1963 and joined the Centre Union; in 1964 he was elected MP in the department of Achaia and became minister in his father's government. With a group of personal friends and party militants he organised the centre-left (Kendroaristera), and became the leader and representative of the party's left-wing.
4. The literature on the resistance and the civil war in Greece is marked by conflicting interpretations. The most recent work on this subject (in English) is a collective volume edited by J. Iatrides, entitled *Greece in the 1940s: A Nation in Crisis,* (University Press of New England, 1981).
5. On the relationship between KKE and EDA and on the various debates and arguments within the KKE during the 1960s see V. Kapetanyiannis, 'The Making of Greek Eurocommunism', in *Political Quarterly,* Vol. 50, No. 4 (Oct.–Dec. 1979). Also, M. Papayiannakis, 'The Crisis in the Greek Left', in H. Penniman (ed.), *Greece at the Polls. The National Elections of 1974 and 1977,* pp.130–59.
6. See K. Legg, *Politics in Modern Greece* (Stanford: Stanford University Press, 1969).
7. On the role of foreign influence in Greek politics see, N. Mouzelis, *Modern Greece: Facets of Underdevelopment* (London, 1978). Also, T. Couloumbis, J. Petropoulos and H. Psomiades, *Foreign Interference in Greek Politics* (New York, 1976).
8. On the role of the state in Greek society see N. Mouzelis, 'Capitalism and the Development of the Greek State', in R. Scase (ed.), *The State in Western Europe,* (London, 1981). It must be pointed out that the special role and nature of the Greek state is not a postwar phenomenon, but one that has characterised Greek politics since the creation of an independent Greek state.
9. See G. Katephores, *He Nomothesia Varvaron* [The Barbarians' Legislation] (Athens, 1975). Also, N. Mouzelis, *Modern Greece,* op. cit., pp.115–33. On the repressive nature of the postwar Greek state, see N. Alivizatos, 'The Emergency Regime and Civil Liberties', in J. Iatrides (ed.), *Greece in the 1940s,* op. cit., pp.220–8.
10. The term 'party-directed patronage' is used here in the sense developed by A. Weingrod; see A. Weingrod, 'Patrons, Patronage and Political Parties', in *Comparative Studies in Society and History,* Vol.X (July 1968), pp.376–400. On the nature and role of clientelism in Greece, see N. Mouzelis, 'Class and Clientelistic Politics: the Case of Greece', in *Sociological Review,* (August 1978).
11. The term 'bureaucratic clientelism' has often been employed by both oligarchic and populist regimes in Latin America; see A.E. Van Niekerk, *Populism and Political Development in Latin America,* Rotterdam: Rotterdam University Press, 1974). Also H. Jaguaribe, *Political Development* (London, 1973), pp.475–80.
12. On the post-junta political parties and elections, see H. Penniman (ed.), *Greece at the Polls,* op. cit. This work covers the parties' role and performance between 1974 and 1977.
13. J. Loulis, 'New Democracy: The New Face of Conservatism', in H. Penniman (ed.), *Greece at the Polls,* op. cit., pp.49–83. See also, *Nea Democratia: Ideologikes Arches ke Katastakiko* [New Democracy: Ideological Principles and Statutes], a publication of the New Democracy Party, Athens, 1979.
14. Loulis, op. cit., p.72.
15. On the 1974 elections and Karamanlis' performance during the period 1974–5, see R. Clogg, 'Karamanlis, Cautious Success', in *Government and Opposition* (Summer 1975).
16. The Rogers agreement was negotiated by the Rallis government in 1981; PASOK committed itself to a new vote in the next parliament in order to achieve its annulment.

17. The 'Third of September Declaration' includes the basic ideological principles of PASOK, its major political objectives and the main policies in order to achieve these objectives; it is significant that this text cannot be changed even by a party congress.
18. Most of the information about PASOK presented in this article is based on research conducted in Greece between 1980 and 1981 for the preparation of the author's Ph.D. thesis.
19. On the debate over the socialist or populist nature of PASOK, see N. Mouzelis, 'The Greek Elections of 1977', in *New Left Review,* No. 109, pp.59–74.
20. A. Papandreou, article for *Athinaiki,* Athens daily newspaper, 29 October 1975.
21. Report of the executive secretariat to the First Panhellenic Conference, published in *Exormisi,* PASOK's official weekly newspaper, 15 September 1977.
22. See *Epikendra,* a political periodical published by the Research Centre of New Democracy, Athens (Sept.–Oct. 1981).
23. See Papayiannakis, 'The Crisis in the Greek Left', op. cit., pp.149–59.

Social Cleavages and Electoral Performance: The Social Basis of Portuguese Political Parties, 1976–83

J.R. Lewis and A.M. Williams*

INTRODUCTION

Since the military coup of 25 April 1974 ended the 48-year old dictatorial regime in Portugal, there have been four elections for the National Assembly and ten constitutional governments (in addition to the six provisional governments of 1974-6). At the same time, two presidential elections have led to the election and subsequent re-election of one individual to the post of President of the Republic. To date there have been few systematic studies, published in English, of the changing patterns of party allegiance displayed in these elections.[1] There are a number of ways in which the social bases of party support can be investigated, one of which is through electoral geography. This paper seeks to provide such an analysis, focusing on the spatial distributions of the electoral results in the belief that these reflect many of the socio-economic structures which condition political relationships in Portugal. This seems particularly apposite in the Portuguese case, because the processes of uneven regional development within the country have produced a distinctive territorial organisation of social classes. Political relationships have also been shaped by the absence of a democratic tradition, especially during the years of the Salazar-Caetano dictatorship.[2] New political parties have had to be created after (or just before) 1974 and these stand in varying relationships with the power groups of the previous regime.

The dictatorial regime personalised and essentially shaped by Salazar was not monolithic in character, for it experienced two major and linked changes in the course of its development. The first was in the late 1950s and early 1960s when there was a shift in economic policies from autarky to international-isation, facilitating rapid industrial growth. This led to the expansion of both the urban industrial proletariat and the bourgeoisie.[3] The political development of both these groups contributed to demands for reform of the political system. After Salazar, incapacitated by illness, had been replaced as prime minister by Caetano, it seemed as though the regime might be capable of reform from the inside. A number of 'liberals' were brought into both the party and government apparatus, while a number of opposition deputies and deputies from the liberal wing of the União Nacional (UN) were elected to the Assembly in 1969. Although Caetano later retracted some of the liberalisation moves in face of right-wing reaction, this was an important phase in the sense that it encouraged opponents of the regime to aspire to further reforms, while

*The authors wish to acknowledge the assistance of the Nuffield Foundation and of the University of Exeter in financing part of the fieldwork on which this paper is based.

the opposition and liberal UN deputies were to form the nuclei of some political parties after 1974.

The failure of the regime to carry through its own liberalisation policies and, more fundamentally, to end the prolonged colonial wars led eventually to the military coup of 25 April 1974. The events which followed – such as the succession of six provisional governments between 1974 and 1976, the supposed attempted coups in 1975 and rapid decolonisation – are described in detail elsewhere.[4] Here, it is sufficient to identify two elements which contributed to political change after April 1976, the date of the first constitutional elections. The first was the attempt by the *Partido Comunista Português* (PCP) to capture power in 1975 and, belatedly, its support for programmes of nationalisation and collectivisation. This contributed in no small part to the alienation of some social groups from the PCP, benefiting the *Partido Socialista* (PS) which actively opposed the aspirations of the PCP, and Ramalho Eanes who played a significant military role in blocking an attempted far left coup in November 1975.[5]

The other important development in this period was the formulation by the constitutional assembly of a new constitution. In addition to guaranteeing basic democratic freedoms, this distributed power between the president, the assembly and the *Conselho da Revolução* (council of the Revolution). The latter was a constitutional committee, dominated by the military which had veto powers over legislation passed by the assembly. The role granted to it was probably a condition whereby the MFA, the *Movimento das Forças Armadas* (Armed Forces Movement), which had organised the coup, agreed to hand over power to the civilians. The office of president also carried extensive powers which, at least until 1982, included the right to appoint and dismiss prime ministers. Otherwise, the tenor of the constitution reflected the post-revolutionary atmosphere of 1975, for it emphasised the 'transition to socialism' in Portugal whilst enshrining both the 'collectivisation' of land in the Alentejo and the nationalisation of key manufacturing industries and the banks.

The Constitution was ratified in February 1976, paving the way for elections to the assembly in April and for the presidency in June. Subsequently, the new political parties have sought to establish and consolidate the social bases of their support, while constantly reassessing their relationships with each other. An examination of the electoral geography of the period 1976–83 provides the most relevant and practicable means of studying these developments, because Portugal's basis of social organisation is territorial and there is a lack of individual data on this subject.

ELECTIONS FOR THE ASSEMBLY AND PRESIDENCY

The new constitution provided for 24 multi-member electoral districts as the spatial framework of elections: 18 of these corresponded to the *distritos* of the mainlands (which resemble British counties in area),while the other districts were for the emigrants, the islands of Madeira and the Azores and the colony of Maçau. Only the 18 mainland *distritos* will be considered here, given the peculiar features of the other electoral districts, but these do account for 251 of

TABLE 1

ELECTIONS FOR THE ASSEMBLY (PORTUGAL) IN 1976, 1979, 1980 AND 1983[1]

	Percentage of vote (number of deputies)			
	1976	1979	1980	1983
% of votes cast	85.6	87.2	83.9	78.6
{Socialist Party (PS)	35.0 (107)	27.3 (74)	1.1 (3)	36.3 (101)
{Republican and Socialist Front (FRS)			26.7 (71)	
{Communist Party (PCP)	14.6 (40)			
{United People's Alliance (APU)		18.8 (47)	16.8 (41)	18.2 (44)
Social Democratic Party (PSD)	24.4 (73)	2.4 (7)	2.5 (8)	27.0 (76)
Social Democratic Centre Party (CDS)	16.0 (42)	0.4 (0)	0.2 (0)	12.4 (29)
Democratic Alliance (AD)		42.5 (121)	44.9 (126)	
(AD + PSD + CDS)[2]	40.9 (115)	45.3 (128)	46.7 (134)	39.9 (105)
Total[3]	100.0 263	100.0 250	100.0 250	100.0 250

Notes:

1. Includes the non-continental electoral districts.

2. Totals include the Monarchist Party (PPM) in all elections; figures for the 1976 and 1983 elections represent the totals for the parties of the AD (which did not then exist); the separate figures for the PSD and CDS in the 1979 and 1980 elections are for the islands where they campaigned separately.

3. Totals include other small parties.

the total of 263 (a number later revised to 250) deputies in the Assembly.[6] Those over the age of 18 are entitled to vote, and the votes are distributed amongst candidates by the *d'Hondt* rule, a system which tends to exaggerate the strength of larger parties and coalitions. Somewhat in contrast, the presidential elections require an absolute majority, and if necessary two ballots may be held.

There have been four elections for the Assembly, the results of which are summarised in Table 1. There was an exceptionally high turnout in the first election and, although this later declined, there was still a high turnout in the 1983 election by northern European standards. No single party obtained an absolute majority of either the votes or the deputies in 1976. The PS obtained the largest share of the vote and about two-fifths of the deputies, followed by the *Partido Popular Democratica* (later renamed the *Partido Social Democratica,* the PSD) with 73 deputies, while the *Centro Democratico Social* (CDS) and the PCP each had about 40 deputies. The socialists decided to govern alone, forming a minority government which lasted until late 1977. They then formed an alliance with the most right-wing party, the CDS, for a short-lived government which lasted until the summer of 1978. At this point, the president used his constitutional powers to appoint two successive presidential governments: the first failed to secure the initial support of the assembly, and the latter also failed to win a vote of confidence after only a few months in office. In the summer of 1979, thwarted in his attempts to appoint a viable government, President Eanes called fresh elections, a year ahead of schedule (under the 1976 constitution these must be held every four years).

In the 1979 election two of the major parties, the CDS and the PSD, formed an electoral coalition, the *Aliança Democratica*[7] (AD). The share of the vote obtained by the Alliance in 1979 was only 4.4 per cent higher than that obtained by its component parties in 1976. However, their number of seats increased from 115 to 128, while the representation of the socialists fell to 74 seats. As the total number of deputies was smaller at the latter date, the proportion of seats obtained by the AD increased from 43.7 to 51.2 per cent, while that of the PS fell from 40.7 to 29.6 per cent. In part the decline of the socialists was also due to the gains of the PCP, which increased both its share of the vote and its number of seats (to 47). A polarisation of Portuguese politics was occurring with, it seemed, the centre-left (the PS) being squeezed. Some commentators likened this to an 'Italianisation' of national politics – the establishment of a centre-right ruling coalition, with the Communist Party becoming the major opposition as the PS declined.[8]

These expectations were partly borne out by the 1980 elections, for the AD further increased its number of deputies to 134 (53.6 per cent of the total). However, the PS which contested the election in a coalition with minor parties maintained its position, and it was the communists who slipped, losing two percentage points in their share of the vote and six deputies. Both the 1979 and 1980 elections are significant in that they were the only two of the four post 1974 elections which directly produced working majorities for the newly elected governments. These elections, in a sense, were the peak of the AD's achievements rather than the start of four years of stable government. The prime minister and leader of the alliance, Sá Carneiro, died in an air crash on 4 December, only days before the presidential elections and his successor, Balsemão, found increasing difficulties in maintaining the unity of both the coalition as well as his own party.[9] By 1983, the alliance had fragmented and new elections were called; these were contested separately by the major parties. The share of the vote obtained by the ex-alliance partners fell by more than six percentage points, while their deputies were reduced in number by 29. Overall, in comparison with the 1976 election, the PSD emerged far stronger than the CDS from the alliance. However, it was the PCP and especially the PS which made the major gains in this election. The latter obtained its highest ever proportion of votes, and emerged as the largest single party in the assembly. After lengthy discussions, it formed a coalition government, the *bloco central,* with the PSD. Arguably, this was the only remaining feasible coalition which had not hitherto been attempted.

While the assembly elections produced a varying sequence of governments, the presidential elections resulted in seeming stability and continuity (see Table 2). Ramalho Eanes obtained an absolute majority on the first ballot in both the 1976 and 1980 polls. However, the opposition to and support for his candidature changed considerably between these two dates. In 1976 Eanes was largely unknown, his reputation being based on his role in opposing the

TABLE 2

ELECTIONS FOR THE PRESIDENT OF THE PORTUGUESE REPUBLIC, 1976 AND 1980

	1976*	1980
Percentage of votes cast	75.5	84.2
Ramalho Eanes	61.5	56.5
Otelo Saraiva de Carvalho	16.5	1.5
Pinheiro de Azevedo	14.4	
Octávio Pato	7.6	
Soares Carneiro		40.2
Galvão de Melo		0.8
Pires Veloso		0.8
Aires Rodrigues		0.2

*All the candidates in 1976 were military officers.

attempted left-wing coup in November 1975. Supported by all parties to the right of the PCP, he secured 61.5 per cent of the vote, defeating amongst others, Otelo, a charismatic and key figure in the MFA, and Octavio Pato of the Communist Party. Many were apprehensive about Eanes' own inclinations, but he was also seen as a bulwark against anti-democratic movements; in the event, his political views proved to be slighty left of centre.

By the time of the 1980 election, Sá Carneiro was already established in his second government. The AD viewed Eanes as being too closely associated with the PS,[10] and as being an opponent of their attempts to reform the constitution. They therefore put forward their own candidate in the election, the uninspiring Soares Carneiro, who was given strong personal backing by Sá Carneiro.[11] Indeed, he died while flying to the the north of the country to support Soares Carneiro's campaign. Therefore,the main support for Eanes this time came from parties to the left of the AD, initially from the PS (though not from their leader Mario Soares) and eventually from the PCP, whose own candidate, Carlos Brito, stood down at the last moment. The election result saw a decline in the share of the vote obtained by Eanes, but he was still able to secure victory on the first ballot. The differences between the two elections are significant; whereas in 1976 Eanes was elected largely as an all-party (bar PCP) non-partisan candidate, by 1980 he was elected with the support of the centre-left against centre-right opposition. Moreover, Eanes performed far better than might be expected from the current electoral strength of the parties supporting him – even gaining the largest share of the vote in many northern districts. In this specific case, this seems to demonstrate the importance of personality over party[12] but, in more general terms, it also shows the capacity of the system to produce a president and government which are politically opposed.

This brief review of the elections has highlighted a number of important issues, including the seeming 'inevitability' of coalitions, the changing relationships between parties and between these and the president, and significant shifts in electoral support. These are best investigated through a consideration of the social bases of the parties.

POLITICAL PARTIES AND THEIR SOCIAL BASES

In the post-1974 period, four major political parties have established themselves in the assembly: the PCP, PS, PSD and CDS. The parties have different lineages, and it is important to note how they have developed.[13]

The Communist Party has the longest roots of all the major parties, having been founded in 1921. It was banned during the long years of the Salazar-Caetano regime, but it established a strong clandestine organisation, especially amongst the rural and the urban proletariat. After the coup in 1974, its leaders were welcomed back from exile, and they were invited to participate in government – perhaps in order to keep the labour force in check. The party was careful to avoid conflict with the MFA, and it gradually strengthened its hold on successive provisional governments. The greatest threat to its power seemed to come from the working class itself, for there were a number of largely spontaneous protest movements in urban neighbourhoods, the *latifundio* areas and the larger factories during 1975. One of the major aims of the party, therefore, was to 'capture' such movements and bring them under central control. This it successfully achieved, managing to consolidate its strength both in the trade unions,[14] through the inter-union association *Intersindical,* and the collective farms in the Alentejo.

In many ways, it can be argued that the party has been conservative in outlook since 1974, and that it has consolidated rather than extended a social basis which already existed before the coup. In a different form, its conservatism is reflected in its pro-Moscow line in international affairs, a position which has been criticised by the more Eurocommunist parties of Spain and Italy.[15] It is this political stance, combined with suspicions regarding the PCP's involvement in the attempted coup of 1975, which help make the political gap between the PCP and the PS far larger than that between the PS and the parties of the right.[16]

In comparison, the Socialist Party is a much newer organisation. It was actually only formed in West Germany in 1973, drawing together elements from diverse socialist groups, mainly united by their common opposition to the regime. Stock and Rother write that 'without doubt such antecedents considerably enriched the PS, giving it an open and pluralistic structure and image but, inevitably, in this also lies the cause of many of its internal cleavages and lack of ideological clarity'.[17] The same authors identify six distinctive tendencies within the PS, and consider that only in the 1980s did Soares become leader of a majority tendency within the party; this partly explains the intensity of factional conflict within the first two socialist governments, a feature which greatly undermined their effectiveness.[18] The social base of the party's support and the origins of its militants have not been clearly established. However, its leaders tend to be drawn from the urban middle classes, while fragmentary evidence suggests its electoral base is much more broadly-based than most other parties, although the skilled working class and the non-agricultural self-employed seem to be particularly important.[19]

The PSD has something of an 'instantaneous' nature, having been established in May 1974 in the wake of the coup. Its leaders – Sá Carneiro, Magalhães Mota and Pinto Balsemão – brought together members of the liberal wing of the old UN and also some of its opponents within the 1969 parliament. The party's initial image was as a non-Marxist centre-left group, which was social democratic, pro-capitalist and pro-Europe. In reality, it has turned out to contain important right and left-wing factions. After 1976, the charismatic Sá Carneiro moved it decisively to the right (causing the resignation of many of its deputies), but since his death tensions between the factions have re-emerged while, overall, the party under Balsemão shifted back towards the centre. The electoral basis of the party's support is again largely unknown, but it is considered to be most strongly based amongst the urban and rural bourgeoisie; this is partly confirmed by data on its membership, indicating that about 85 per cent are drawn from the upper and lower middle class.[20] Overall, it somewhat resembles the PS in the diversity of views it encompasses and, to a lesser extent, in being a nationally-based party.

The Social Democratic Centre Party is the youngest and, in terms of support, the smallest of the major parties. It was formed in July 1974 by Freitas do Amaral and many of its leaders had strong links with the UN, the party of the regime, being associated in particular with the reformist ideals of the Caetano government.[21] In fact, many CDS deputies had only been prevented from holding high office in the regime because of their relative youth.[22] However, it would be wrong to see it as a neo-fascist party or as a Christian Democratic party on Italian lines. Instead, it is essentially a conservative party akin to the British one, formed to represent moderate liberals and right-wingers who had been alienated by the excesses of 'revolutionary politics' in 1974–5, and its major 'ideology' is strengthening private enterprise. Again, hard data on its electoral support are absent, but its party membership, in comparison with the PSD, tends to be older and to be drawn more from the upper and upper-middle classes. It has also significantly less representatives of the skilled working class, but greater representation amongst the commercial bourgeoisie.[23]

It is clear that the poles of the political spectrum in Portugal are far more clearly defined than the middle ground. On the left, the PCP has adopted a strong pro-Moscow line while, on the right, the conservative CDS has some roots amongst the reformist elements of the Caetano regime. In contrast, the middle ground of politics, where the two largest parties – the PS and the PSD – are located, seems rather cluttered. Both parties started to the left of centre, and it is clear that they have overlapping areas of ideology as well as of membership. Their initial ideological postures differed – if only in terms of acceptance or not of Marxist vocabulary – but today they both seem to be largely pro-capitalist, pro-NATO and pro-EEC in orientation. The PS under Soares has moved rightwards, while the PSD under Balsemão has moved leftwards. By the time they 'met' to form the *bloco central* government in 1983, their differences on policy isssues were relatively minor.[24]

SPATIAL PATTERNS OF ELECTORAL RESULTS

In the absence of data at the individual level on the social bases of party support, it is useful to consider the spatial patterns of electoral results. As was noted in the introduction,this is particularly useful in Portugal because the process of uneven regional development has produced a distinctive territorial organisation of social classes.[25] Agriculture has a dualistic pattern with *latifundios* or large landed estates dominant in the south (the Alentejo) and *minifundios* or small 'peasant' farms in the north. Industrial development is largely concentrated in the littoral, but whereas large-scale and more capital-intensive units are dominant in the south (in the Lisbon metropolitan area), the centre and north are characterised by diffuse industrialisation – small and medium-scale enterprises, often labour-intensive, dispersed throughout the small towns and villages of the regions. However, it is the tertiary sector which is most localised, and the centralisation of the state as well as the availability of communications has led to a massive concentration of service employment in Lisbon and, to a lesser extent, Oporto. These economic conditions have produced a remarkably distinctive spatial distribution of social classes: the Alentejo is characterised by a rural proletariat; the Lisbon metropolitan region by an industrial proletariat; the north-west littoral by an industrial and a semi-industrial proletariat; much of the 'rural' north by peasant agriculture; and Lisbon, Oporto and the other cities by the new petite bourgeoisie, including important segments of office workers.[26]

This thumbnail sketch of the spatial organisation of socio-economic structure provides a basis for interpreting the geography of electoral behaviour. Figures 1–3 represent the distribution of support for the four major parties in the elections of 1976, 1980 and 1983.[27] It is simplest to consider each party in turn, beginning with the PCP. In all three elections support for this party was highly localised, being concentrated in the Alentejo (notably the *distritos* of Setúbal, Evora and Beja). Elsewhere its electoral base is weak, for it has rarely obtained more than 10 per cent of the vote in any *distrito* in the centre or the north. Over time, the party has strengthend its position in almost all areas, but the relative gains have been greatest in the north; for example, its share of the vote in Viseu and Braga has doubled. In contrast, support for the PS is far more evenly distributed and, in 1976 for example, ranged between 22.6 per cent in Bragança and 44.7 per cent in Faro. In this election its support was greatest in Faro, Lisbon, Oporto and the centre-south zone, while its support was least in the northern interior. By 1980 the party's support had slipped in all *distritos,* but especially the south and Lisbon. When the party recovered its position nationally in 1983, it was notable that while in the north and centre it secured a level of support greater than that of 1976, in the south it still lagged behind those levels by up to six percentage points.

The regional patterns of support for the PSD and CDS are largely the inverse of those of the communists – that is, their main strength in all three elections was in the north and centre. There are differences in their precise patterns of support (which are exaggerated considerably at finer spatial scales), but more important for our present purposes are the shifts over time.

FIGURE 1

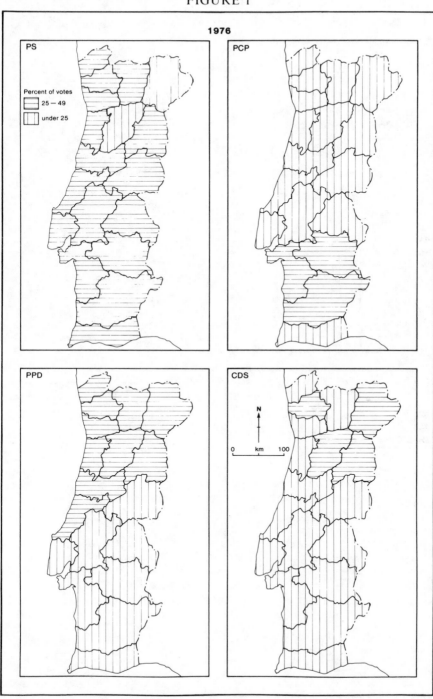

FIGURE 2

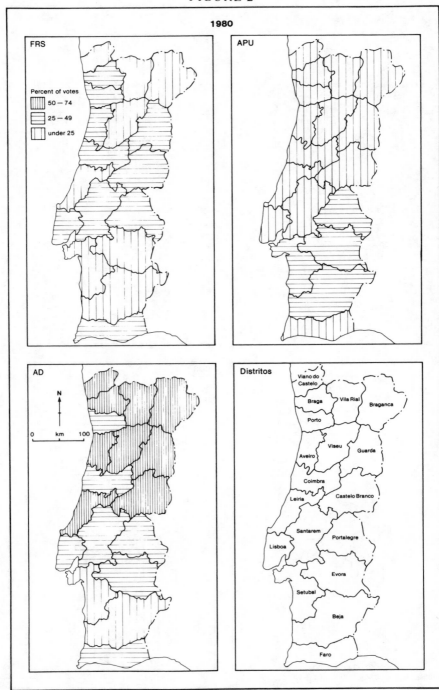

FIGURE 3

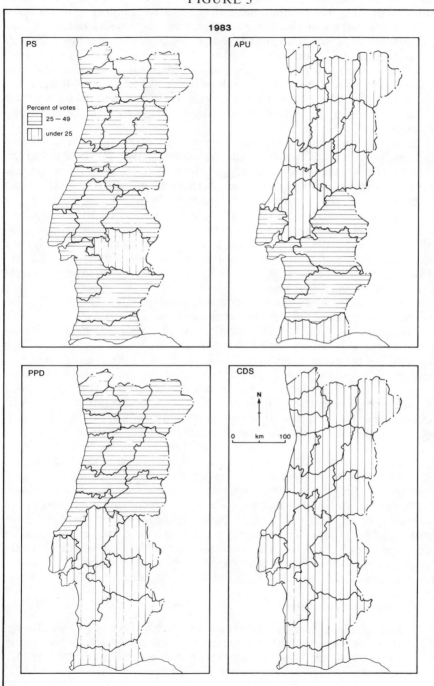

Comparing the results for 1976 and 1980, it is evident that the AD made gains throughout the country (compared with aggregated support for the PSD and CDS). However, the most substantial gains were in the centre and south, with support in some *distritos* in the latter being almost doubled. Further comparison of the results of the 1976 and 1983 elections shows that the PSD and to a lesser extent the CDS, despite their national reverses, were able to sustain their votes in the south at levels well above those of 1976. It was in the north that they suffered the sharpest electoral reversals, and the CDS's share of the vote was up to a third below that it had obtained in 1976 in many *distritos*.

These distributions do emphasise very clearly the spatial associations amongst the levels of support for the individual parties. The PCP's electoral base is obviously the Alentejo, where it obtains up to ten times the percentage of vote it acquires in the north. In less extreme forms, both the PSD and the CDS have their strongest electoral bases in the north and centre of the country. In contrast, the PS is the only party which has a 'national' electoral base, having obtained more than 20 per cent of the vote in all *distritos* in 1980. Between 1976 and 1983, however, its electoral base has shifted relatively from the south to the north, so that its support is now more similar to that of the PSD and to a lesser extent the CDS. In many ways the Alentejo represents the key to interpreting the electoral shifts, for this is where the greatest polarisation in voting behaviour occurred, with the PCP and the PSD/CDS increasing their shares of the vote at the expense of the PS.[28]

Examination of the spatial distribution of voting in the presidential elections can also illuminate the relationships between the parties, as well as highlighting the remarkable shift which occurred in the support for Eanes between 1976 and 1983 (see Figure 4). In the first election, supported by all the parties to the right of the PCP, Eanes secured the highest levels of support in the north and centre. In fact, he polled better in right-wing *distritos* than in PS areas for, in the latter, both Pinheiro de Azevedo and Otelo performed quite well. However, Eanes was also able to secure the largest share of the vote even in the Alentejo *distritos* of Beja and Evora. This was due to the left vote being split between the PCP candidate, Octavio Pato, and the populist left candidate, Otelo. It is perhaps indicative of the PCP's temporary loss of control in the region that their candidate received less votes than Otelo. By 1980, the overall patterns had been almost completely inverted, and Eanes, with the support of the PS and PCP, now secured his highest share of the vote in the south. In Beja, for example, the proportion of the vote he obtained increased from 34 to 73 per cent between 1976 and 1980. Elsewhere, he topped the poll in all *distritos* except Bragança, Guarda, Vila Real and Viseu, that is, the north-eastern region. His support and the swings were not just based on party allegiances.

Pimlott has written that

> In 1976, Eanes had depended on his party backers and his vote, though large, represented only 80 per cent of the total cast for the parties supporting him. Now, on a much higher turnout the president did nearly as well as four years earlier despite the opposition of the PSD and CDS

FIGURE 4

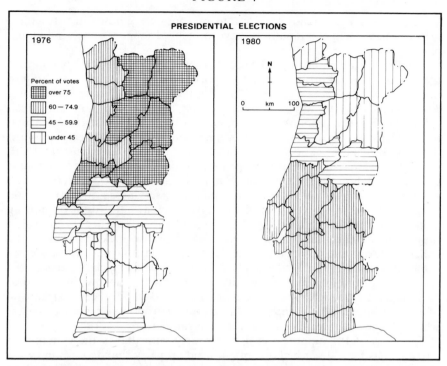

PRESIDENTIAL ELECTIONS

1976

Percent of votes
over 75
60 — 74.9
45 — 59.9
under 45

1980

N

0   km   100

which together had taken more than half the popular vote two months before. Indeed, Eanes succeeded in doing better than the two parties backing him, the PS and PCP, in every single electoral district.[29]

Clearly, Eanes had a personal following which exceeded that of his party backers. Whether this stems from his key role in the events of 1975, or from the stability he seems to represent amongst the turmoil of party politics is not clear. But it does underline one of the fears of the PS, and of Soares in particular that, given the ineffectiveness of the PS in government and opposition, Eanes may have become the 'natural' leader of the left.[30] The successful re-election of Eanes also highlights a potentially discordant feature of the electoral system. This allows a party or coalition to have a majority in the assembly with less than 50 per cent of the vote, yet this will not be sufficient to secure the presidency for their candidate. This condition is exaggerated because, since the 1982 constitutional reform, presidential and assembly elections need no longer be held even in the same year.

While there is little dispute about the spatial distribution of party support, it is less easy to determine those structural features of society which determine this. Amongst the many features which could be highlighted, clientelism, emigration, religion, industrial and rural proletarianisation, the system of values of the peasantry and the growth of a new urban middle-class seem particularly relevant.[31]

SOCIAL BASES OF PARTY SUPPORT

We will end our discussion of elections by considering how these structural features, in varying combinations, have influenced support for the individual parties.

The PCP's electoral base in the south is rooted in its organisation amongst the urban and rural proletariat. Its support amongst the former is greatest in those industrial branches where the PCP-dominated group of unions, *Intersindical*, is strongest. Typically, these include the iron and steel, shipbuilding, metal manufacturing, paper and chemical industries which tend to be located in and around the Lisbon metropolitan area. Its base amongst the rural proletariat is in the Alentejo. During the Salazar regime the PCP, through its active support of rural protests, established a firm hold amongst the landless labourers in the region. For a brief period in 1975 it seemed that, having been drawn into the state apparatus (serving in the provisional governments), the party would be outflanked by far left groups organising land seizures in the region. The PCP eventually re-established its control in the region by encouraging these seizures, while also seeking to bring the collective farms and co-operatives under centralised control.[32] Subsequently it has established itself as the main defender of working-class gains in the region and, through control of local government, has dominated local patronage. Its two major social bases are in fact linked, for there is a tradition of emigration from the Alentejo to the Lisbon metropolitan region, a process which provided for a radicalisation of the southern proletariat.

The basis of PS support contrasts strongly with that of the Communist party. It has been described as both 'a residual party'[33] and as a 'somewhat nebulous following drawn from all classes'.[34] It is certainly true that it tends to draw support from a broad range of social classes and from most regions. In turn, this reflects its ability to draw support from different social groups in different regions: from the lower-order professional and white-collar workers in Lisbon, Oporto and other towns, from the industrial proletariat and semi-proletariat in the north, and from the small and medium-size rural proprietors in the Alentejo.[35] What is clear is that it lacks a solid base amongst the rural and urban proletariat. Initially, it only had a weak hold in the trade unions – in some of the smaller white-collar branches – and this has only partly been remedied by the establishment in 1978 of the socialist UGT confederation of unions as a rival to *Intersindical*.[36] It also has a relatively weak base in the Alentejo, for the PS's role in redistributing land from the collective farms has alienated it from the rural proletariat; at the same time, the more aggressive anti-collective policies of the AD government secured support for it amongst the family- and medium-sized farms in the region.[37] The PS, therefore, seemed largely irrelevant in the real conflicts which occurred over agrarian issues, and it has found its base in the region substantially weakened.

In a sense then, the PS can indeed be viewed as a residual party, securing electoral support where the other parties are not dominant. It can be argued that, in 1976, given the newness of the parties and the ambiguous ideological stance of the PS, the room for a residual party was considerable; consequently, it secured a role far in excess of what could be expected given its social base. The PS's relatively poor economic performance while in government and the rise of a viable alternative – the AD – led to its electoral support being squeezed in 1979 and 1980. However, by 1983 the demise of the AD had, once again, created more space for the residual party of the centre.

It has been argued that for many it was a matter of whim whether they joined the PS or the PSD in 1974–6.[38] However, their electoral support does seem to vary in social and spatial terms for, compared to the PS, the PSD has a much stronger base amongst rural proprietors and industrialists, as well as the peasantry, although like the PS it also draws significantly on the lower-echelon bureaucrats and white collar workers.[39] This is also reflected in the party membership, amongst which the professions and farmers are well represented while the rural and industrial proletariat are under-represented.[40] It has been argued that, under Sá Carneiro, the party established a firm base in the rural areas and smaller towns of the north and centre. However, its appeal has been broadened under Balsemão, and comparison of its vote in 1976 and 1983 reveals a tendency for this to become more evenly distributed. The comment that the PSD operates in 'a fluctuating electoral space' seems particularly apposite,[41] and it is probably the PS which is its main partner in these fluctuations.

Fluctuations in the PSD vote are not entirely accounted for by its relationship with the PS, for changes in the level of support for the CDS are also important. At the level of the *distrito* the areas of support for the PSD and CDS are broadly similar, but there are considerable variations at the level of the 274 *concelhos* (municipalities). Clientelism may explain the continuation of such differences, but it does not explain their existence. Cabral has suggested that the less market-orientated peasantry tend to vote for the more catholic and conservative CDS, while those more involved in the market may have preferred the less traditional and more aggressively pro-capitalist PSD.[42] It is certainly true that support for the CDS has always been greatest in the poorest areas, in the north east, which also has the least penetration of capitalism in agriculture. The CDS is also relatively strong in Braga, the *distrito* where church strength is greatest, although the church's stand has mainly been anti-communist rather than pro-CDS.[43] Finally, it can be noted that both the PSD and the CDS are likely to benefit from the votes of returned emigrants, whether from Europe or the '*retornados*' from the ex-colonies.[44]

CONCLUSIONS

The study of electoral geography provides a valuable insight into socio-spatial structure and so highlights the distinctive social bases of party support, suggesting reasons for fluctuations in these. Both the PCP and, to a lesser extent, the CDS have strong regional electoral bases while the PS, and increasingly so the PSD, have broader regional and social appeal. Since 1976, and especially since 1980, the two major parties have become more alike in terms of ideology and specific policies; this, in itself, combined with the 'overcrowded' nature of the centre of Portuguese politics, has contributed to important fluctuations in 'electoral space'. In addition, the failure of either party to dominate the all-important centre ground of politics, and therefore to capture an absolute majority, helps to explain the series of failed governments and coalitions since 1976. Rother has argued that, given the apparent solidity of the PCP vote since 1979, the PS increasingly has to look to the right and to the urban middle-classes in order to increase its vote.[45] Fluctuations in the centre ground of electoral politics are therefore likely to increase.

Coalitions would appear to be the most obvious strategy whereby absolute majorities could be secured in the Assembly. These have proved difficult in practice, because the diversity of views within both the PS and the PSD makes it difficult for both to form coalitions with either the left or the right, without risking fragmentation of their own parties. The PS is in a particularly difficult position because the PCP is not an ideologically acceptable partner while, during the life of Sá Carneiro, his right-wing populism and personality clash with Soares made an alliance with the PSD unlikely. The AD coalition appears to have been held together mainly by the strength of Sá Carneiro's leadership, for after his death the alliance quickly fragmented as a result of within-party tensions. The present coalition, between the PS and the PSD, is the final combination to be attempted and, in many ways, the most logical. There is much speculation as to its future: would its success lead to the creation of a single centre party, or would its collapse lead to total ungovernability?

One point is clear, however; for a 'new' democracy, the patterns of party politics, party competition and party support have very quickly achieved a consistency. Both the CDS and the PCP, for example, are restricted electorally by their narrow social bases, as is clearly shown in the distribution of their vote. However, the structural conditions which determine the relative weight of social groups within Portuguese society are not themselves fixed. Further changes in agriculture (perhaps, the decline of the rural proletariat and of the non-market orientated peasantry) or in industry (perhaps, further growth of a semi-proletariat in the zones of diffuse industrialisation) may fundamentally alter the electoral bases of the major parties before the end of this century.

In general, it may be said on the positive side both that the main party-political actors have been clearly identified – Portugal's has evolved into a four-party system during the first decade since the 1974 revolution – and that the nature of their electoral support has shown a certain continuity. Furthermore, the electorate taken as a whole has indicated a marked preference for political forces placed around the centre, so that altogether the Portuguese party system shows a potential for future stability, bearing in mind too that three of the four parties are system-supportive (doubts about the PCP on these grounds remain). However, for a party system which is essentially new, it is perhaps no surprise that it has continued to reveal unsettled characteristics. These have been most evident in a certain ideological fluidity especially around the centre of the spectrum, the scope for individuals as distinct from party structures to mobilise opinion (noticeably in the appeal of the president) and above all the fact that underlying the continuity of electoral patterns likely changes in social structure hold out the possibility of significant future shifts in the bases of party support.

NOTES

1. A number of studies of the elections have been published in Portuguese – for example, see J. Gaspar and N. Vitorino, *As Eleições do 25 de Abril: Geografia e Imagem dos Partidos* (Lisbon: Livros Horizonte, 1976). Studies of the elections, rather than of the parties *per se*, are relatively few in the English language. Notable exceptions are J. L. Hammond, 'Electoral Behaviour and Political Militancy', in L. S. Graham and H. M. Makler (eds.) *Contemporary Portugal: the Revolution and its Antecedents* (Austin: University of Texas Press, 1979), and D. B. Goldey, 'Elections and the Consolidation of Portuguese Democracy: 1974–1983', *Electoral Studies*, Vol. 2 (1983), pp. 229–40.
2. Elections were frequently organised by the Salazar regime, but these had no democratic legitimacy.
3. For a discussion of changes in the relative sizes of social classes, 1950–70, see A. Marques and M. Bairrada, 'As Classes Sociais na População Activa Portuguesa: 1950–70', *Análise Social*, Nos. 72–73–74 (1982), pp. 1279–98.
4. Useful summaries are T. Gallagher, *Portugal: a Twentieth Century Interpretation* (Manchester: Manchester University Press, 1983); R. A. H. Robinson, *Contemporary Portugal: A History* (London: George Allen and Unwin, 1979), and M. C. L. Porto, 'Portugal', in A. M. Williams (ed.), *Southern Europe Transformed* (London: Harper and Row, 1984).
5. The precise involvement of political groups, especially the PCP, in the attempted coup in November 1975 is still unclear.
6. As the number of deputies reflects the population, their distribution between *distritos* varies enormously: the Azores have a single deputy, Portalegre has 4 and Lisbon has 56.
7. Note that, in Madeira and the Azores, the component parties of the AD campaigned separately in the elections.
8. This is discussed in T. Gallagher, *Portugal: a Twentieth Century Interpretation* (Manchester: Manchester University Press, 1983).
9. Balsemão had to resign as party leader and reorganise his government in September 1981 in an attempt to hold together the fragile coalition; he still failed in his objective. For a discussion of conflicts within the AD see E. Rosa, *O Fracasso dos Governos de Direita em Portugal* (Lisbon: Edições Um de Outubro, 1982).
10. The leader of the PS, Mario Soares, still smarting at his 'dismissal' in 1978, opposed the re-election of Eanes, perhaps also seeing him as a serious opponent for the leadership of the centre-left.
11. There are reputed to have been serious personality clashes between Eanes and Sá Carneiro; and the latter openly declared that he would refuse to continue as PM if Eanes was re-elected. Note that Sá Carneiro and Soares Carneiro were not related.
12. Goldey also emphasises the ability of the presidential candidate to cut across party lines; see D. B. Goldey op. cit.
13. Portugal has little history of a western European style of parliamentary democracy, bar the republic 1910–26; see B. Kohler, *Political Forces in Spain, Greece and Portugal* (London: Butterworth, 1982).
14. The evolution of *Intersindical* is discussed in U. Optenhögel, 'A Evolução das Centrais Sindicais Concorrentes (CGIP-IN/UGT) Após O 25 de Abril – Consequências par a Defesa dos Interesses dos Trabalhadores', unpublished paper presented at the Colóquio sobre Formação e Modos de Acção de Grupos Sociais em Portugal Depois de 1950, Bad Homburg, December 1983.
15. The evolution of the Communist Party since 1974 is discussed in T. Gallagher, 'The Portuguese Communist Party and Eurocommunism', *Political Quarterly*, Vol. 50 (1979), pp. 205–18.
16. This is certainly the view of the public, as indicated in a questionnaire survey reported in J. M. D. Barroso, *Le Systeme Politique Portugais Face A L'Intégration Européenne* (Lisbon: April 1983).
17. This is discussed in detail in M. J. Stock and B. Rother, 'PS: a Trajectória de um Partido', *O Expresso*, 14 May 1983, pp. 37–44.
18. Discussed in T. Gallagher, 'Portugal's Bid for Democracy: the Role of the Socialist Party', *West European Politics*, Vol. 2 (1979), pp. 198–217.

19. The evidence available on the social base of electoral support for the PS is reviewed in B. Rother, 'A Representação de Interesses Sociais no PS', unpublished paper presented at the Colóquio sobre Formação e Modos de Acção de Grupos Sociais em Portugal Depois de 1950, Bad Homburg, December 1983.
20. There is an excellent discussion of the social base of support for the PSD and the CDS in M. J. Stock, 'A Base Social de Apoio e o Recrutamento dos Líderes de PSD e do CDS', unpublished paper presented at the Colóquio sobre Formação e Modos de Acção de Grupos Sociais em Portugal Depois de 1950, Bad Homburg, December 1983.
21. Xavier Pintado is a notable example of a young technocratic minister in the Caetano government who later joined the PSD.
22. This is the view expressed in N. Portas and S. Gago, 'Some Preliminary Notes on the State in Contemporary Portugal', in R. Scase (ed.), *The State in Western Europe* (London: Croom Helm, 1980).
23. See M. J. Stock, op. cit.
24. The major issues in the discussions leading to formation of the coalition appear to have been denationalisation of the banks, Soares' eventual candidacy for the presidency, and the inclusion of Mota Pinto (of the PSD) in the cabinet.
25. Reviewed in J. R. Lewis and A. M. Williams, 'Regional Uneven Development on the European Periphery: the Case of Portugal', *Tijdschrift voor Economische en Sociale Geografie*, Vol. 72 (1980), pp. 81–98.
26. There is an excellent analysis of the territorial organisation of social classes in J. Ferrão, *Classes Sociais e Indústria em Portugal* (Lisbon: Universidade de Lisboa, Centro de Estudos Geográficos, 1982).
27. The results of the 1979 election will not be considered here for reasons of brevity, but these are broadly similar to the 1980 election results. Analysis is confined to the *distrito* level, the meaningful level for electoral results, but it is possible to disaggregate these to the smaller levels of *concelhos* (municipalities) and even *freguesias* (parishes).
28. The association between the distribution of votes for the parties can be indicated by a coefficient of location: for any two parties, this measures the percentage of their vote which has to be reapportioned to give them identical relative spatial distributions. In 1976 the index values were as follows: PS-PCP 33.5; PS-PSD/CDS 21.0; and PSD/CDS-PCP 51.0.
29. B. Pimlott, 'Portugal – Two Battles in the War of the Constitution', in *West European Politics* (October 1981), pp. 294–6.
30. T. Gallagher, 'Portugal's Bid', op. cit., stresses this view in light of the experience of the PS in government 1976–9. It is a view which may require modification since the PS victory in the 1983 assembly election.
31. The importance of these structural influences on electoral behaviour has been indicated in a number of statistical analyses using aggregate data. See J. Gaspar and N. Vitorino, op. cit.; J. L. Hammond, op. cit.; and J. Gaspar *L'Abstention Electorale au Portugal 1975–1980* (Lisbon: Universidade de Lisboa, Centro de Estudos Geográficos 1982).Examples of correlations obtained at the *distrito* level for 1976 are as follows:

	PSD/CDS	PS	PCP
% wage labourers in agricultural labour force	−0.84	0.35	0.85
% of population resident in urban areas	−0.50	0.16	0.38

32. On agricultural movements, see M. V. Cabral, 'Agrarian Structures and Recent Rural Movements in Portugal', *Journal of Peasant Studies*, Vol. 5 (1978), pp. 411–45; and S. McAdam Clark and B. J. O'Neill, 'Agrarian Reform in Southern Portugal', *Critique of Anthropology*, No. 15 (1980), pp. 47–74. For a discussion of the relationship between the PCP and urban social movements, see J. Gaspar, 'Urbanization: Growth, Problems and Policies', in A. M. Williams (ed.), *Southern Europe Transformed* (London: Harper and Row, 1984).
33. J. L. Hammond, op. cit., p. 260.
34. N. Portas and S. Gago, op. cit., p. 235.
35. J. L. Hammond, op. cit., and M. V. Cabral, op. cit.
36. However, Rother, op. cit., considers that only marginally more of the industrial proletariat vote for the PCP than for the PS, although of course there are regional variations.

37. See E. Rosa, op. cit.
38. This argument is advanced in J. Aguiar, *A Ilusão do Poder: Análise do Sistema Partidário Português 1976–1982* (Lisbon: Publicações Dom Quixote, 1983).
39. This is asserted in K. Maxwell, 'The Emergence of Portuguese Democracy', in J. H. Herz (ed.), *From Dictatorship to Democracy: Coping with the Legacies of Authoritarianism and Totalitarianism* (Westport, CT: Greenwood Press, 1982).
40. See W. C. Opello, 'Actividades, Papéis e Orientações Ideológicas de Sociais Democratas Portugueses: Estudo de uma Amostra', *Análise Social*, Nos. 72–73–74 (1982), pp. 947–58.
41. J. Aguiar, op. cit.
42. M. V. Cabral, op. cit.
43. W. Opello, op. cit., p. 949, found that only 40 per cent of PSD party members in his study area were practising Catholics. Comparable data is not yet available for the CDS.
44. No precise data is available on the electoral behaviour of returned migrants. *Retornados* are usually considered to have right wing – perhaps, even neo-fascist – inclinations, but there is no firm evidence to support this. Emigrants, while abroad, certainly tend to be more right-wing than the electorate at home: those living in western Europe tend to support the PSD, whilst those living outside western Europe give overwhelming support to the CDS. However, their voting behaviour after their return is not known. C. Brettell, in her article 'Emigration and its Implications for the Revolution in Northern Portugal', in L. S. Graham and H.M.Makler (eds.), *Contemporary Portugal: the Revolution and its Antecedents* (Austin: University of Texas Press, 1979), considers that emigration tends to alienate the children of the emigrants from local society, making them disinterested in Portuguese politics. Furthermore, it can be argued that the self-denial involved in emigration, in order to improve consumption standards, is likely to encourage right-wing political affiliation.
45. B. Rother, op. cit.

Southern European Socialism in Transition

Salvador Giner

INTRODUCTION

More than any other political animals, socialists live by hope; hope, however, mixed with a great deal of apprehension when socialist governments took office in southern Europe not so long after the fall of dictatorships in Greece, Portugal and Spain. Electoral outcomes later in France and Italy meant that, by 1983, the entire European Mediterranean region had come under either socialist-majority rule or under coalition governments headed by a socialist premier.

Through many successive failures and setbacks – ever since the great debacle of the First World War and the rise of Stalinism – socialists everywhere have grown wise to the complexities of history. As a result, especially in western Europe, many have accepted the slow reformism of social democracy as the viable way of proceeding. Yet, for many radical, albeit essentially 'liberal' socialists, the social democratic path does not necessarily have to be the only possible alternative to the totalitarian brand of socialism advocated by the Marxists-Leninists. They have accordingly been in permanent search for a principled and democratic solution which should avoid, on the one hand, the barbarism of the police state and, on the other, the social democratic management of the capitalist order. It is for this reason that, within the sphere of democratic and pluralist socialism, two largely differing conceptions can be found, one cautiously meliorist and another far more radical, with revolutionary or quasi-revolutionary implications. For a long time, only the first current has had any chance to gain lasting access to power, while the second has either remained the preserve of left-wing minorities within parties and movements or has been confined to parties permanently in opposition. This has led some observers to distinguish between 'government' socialism and 'opposition' socialism. They equate the former with slow reformism and the latter with radicalism. The implication in this distinction is that, given the current constraints of the western political and economic order, radicalism must be permanently condemned to play a merely oppositional role.[1] Mediterranean radical socialist parties, often banned in the past, and hardly ever in power, have thus been seen as endemically of the oppositional sort. Hence, their peaceful and 'normal' advent to power was greeted by many principled socialists everywhere with a mixture of hope and apprehension.

Reasons for scepticism at the hour of triumph were abundant: the entire Mediterranean region has a recent dictatorial past, often militaristic; all the countries concerned had suffered fascist or *fascistisant* regimes at one time or another; all of them possess powerful conservative social classes or groups apparently capable of stiff and efficient resistance to the implementation of structural changes; there is now an awareness among many of the possible close relationship between any form of institutionalised power (including socialist power) and conservatism; there are direct international pressures against radical 'experiments' that may smack of 'communism', and last, but not least in that part of Europe, the example of the failure of democratic, socialist radicalism (such as the overthrow of Salvador Allende's government in Chile in 1973) constitutes an important warning against extremism for socialist militants and voters.

In contrast with all this, the region has not been tainted with what are seen as the equivocations of the more northern kind of socialism. The semi-peripheral position of southern Europe in the context of European economic development, the sharpness of its class cleavages, and its long tradition of radicalism have seemed to give it a number of advantages and opportunities towards the end of the twentieth century which had been missed by socialists elsewhere. Likewise, the much more fundamentalist electoral programmes of the southern European socialists[2] showed that they were fully aware of the scope of their historical chances. Moreover, although international hostility to radicalism by the major western powers had not vanished, at least it seemed to have diminished partly by virtue of changes in the conditions of the Cold War. The abandonment by several communist parties of a wholly subservient line to the Soviet Union (the rise of Eurocommunism) finally created a new climate, more propitious for a peaceful and entirely democratic change towards socialism. Moreover, the new electoral successes of the socialists were greeted with less alarm by the 'bourgeois' forces: the more adventurous among the conservatives in some quarters even spoke of giving the socialists a chance. And, in the eyes of many liberals in southern Europe, the socialists' access to power was not seen as a cataclysm: a change in attitude with hardly any precedents in the history of the region. These conditions, together with the inherited radicalism of the socialist movements of the area, seemed to promise the establishment of an interesting alternative to the north-western European pattern of socialist development.

This essay explores some aspects of the predicament and prospects of socialism in southern Europe, beginning with a brief consideration of the historical background of socialism in Mediterannean Europe and its vicissitudes and limitations within the political framework of their respective countries. It then examines the position and strategy of the socialist parties (and movements) across the several countries in the 1970s and 1980s in order to look at the likely direction of their future conduct and to assess the chances of socialism in the region. In doing this the author assumes that, despite substantial differences between them, significant comparisons are possible between the countries in question and that so are certain cautious generalisations about several societies in Mediterranean Europe.[3]

ORIGINS AND TRADITIONS: THE SOCIALISM OF A BACKWARD EUROPE

From its very inception, the history of socialism in southern Europe was dominated by a lack of congruence between the structural backwardness of the societies concerned and the advanced tenets of socialist ideology, benefiting as this did from easy communication and proximity with the advanced European centres of the age. Thus, Italian and Spanish socialists participated in the work of the First International and formed their respective 'regional sections'. In Portugal and Greece, however, they remained more marginal: it was a group of Spanish exiles, themselves part of a socialist backwater, who brought with them socialism to Lisbon in 1871. Meanwhile, until the formation of distinct 'socialist' parties, the anarchist, Bakuninist forces of the International were extremely influential in the ranks of the nascent movement; and they were to remain powerful for a long time to come, especially in Spain. Southern European socialists, therefore, faced from the start the immensely difficult odds created by this incongruence. Theirs was a doctrine (and a strategy) best suited for industrial and urban environments of which there were few and far between in their societies. Their own national bourgeoisies, who could have provided intellectual and political leaders amongst their disaffected members or, alternatively, might have accepted the socialists as a legally recognised oppositional force, were weak and relatively small. The exclusion of mass political participation was maintained for a much longer time in the Mediterranean countries than elsewhere in Europe. Such exclusion, in fact, extended to other groups and as a consequence, for a long time, socialists did not have a monopoly on radicalism. Other alternatives, such as anarchism, but also liberal anti-clerical and 'free-thinking' liberalism were as powerful in their opposition to the established order, and often more so than socialism itself.

All this was complicated further by the low organisation density, politically speaking, of those countries. Their civil societies were weak, and thus unable to counterbalance the resources and ambitions of army, church and state bureaucracy. This, together with a 'non-zero sum' conception of power made peaceful negotiations for the solution of national problems very hazardous indeed. Largely for this reason, trade unions and radical political parties and movements were far more mistrusted by the establishment forces in the south than anywhere else in the continent, save in Europe's other periphery, the east. In terms of official recognition and legalisation, parties and unions lagged behind all other similar groups elsewhere in Europe. Repression of radicals and socialists became the normal stuff of politics. Revolt and a loss of faith in constitutionalism were the inevitable reactions from the excluded. However, efforts on the part of established political forces to break this mould of oppression and violence were made at a relatively early date. Thus, an explicit programme of legalisation for socialists was significantly but unsuccessfully put forward by liberals in Spain as early as 1871, despite bitter opposition from the very militants in the International whom they were trying to help. These saw such legalisation as a bourgeois plot, and some predicted that its ultimate price would be domestication. Deradicalisation by incorporation was Giovanni Giolitti's explicit aim in his policies towards the Italian socialists. It was with a sense of achievement after a long and strenuous struggle that he announced to the Italian Parliament in 1911 that socialists had finally become acceptably moderate and that their mentor, Karl Marx, had finally been 'relegated to the attic'.[4]

Today, a century after these issues became clear, any general discussion about the realisation of socialism still has to grapple with its oldest and most fundamental practical dilemma: whether to accept a measure of rejection from the legitimate political realm and therefore confront it as a revolutionary force, or to enter the sphere of legality and therefore also that of political integration and social reform. Given the particular circumstances of the Mediterranean countries the dilemma has remained intensely alive in them, especially in the three countries whose periods of dictatorship and repression have lasted longest. But even in Italy, historians of socialism are quick to underline the similarities which exist between today's arguments and debates and those which took place at the onset of the socialist movement, practically a century earlier.[5] This, no doubt, reflects the permanence of old political problems and social conditions in the midst of change, but it must also be attributed to the confrontational nature of the inherited ideologies, for they have their built-in momentum. The political culture of the south still continues to make maximalism and radicalism a plausible proposition for many. Socialist parties, accordingly, are particularly busy in southern Europe trying to explain to their constituencies how they are, at heart, as radical as anyone. Theirs is not only a struggle for an ideological space no longer securely occupied by the communists, for these have in most parts lost their radicalism as well. It is, also, a new version of the old aim of all true radicals: *pas d'ennemis à gauche.*

Historically, in Great Britain, Scandinavia and the United States revolution was not so much defeated as ruled out. In southern Europe it was either defeated through civil war, or smothered violently by dictatorship, or both. Paradoxically, if radicalism in that region still has deep roots, it is because it was suppressed time and again rather than being made unnecessary by a more tolerant polity. The history of that suppression does not need to be retold here. Suffice it to say that what could be termed the 'Giolittian' solution to the incorporation of the left into the legitimate political arena was tried in every country concerned but, in the long run, it met with ultimate defeat. In Portugal, the liberals and republicans themselves who spearheaded political change and on whose ultimate success the small socialist component depended for survival were routed definitely in 1926; democracy then vanished from the country until 1974. In Greece, the vicissitudes of the similarly small socialist or left-wing camp were far more tortuous, and the relationship with the liberals more complex: it was the republican and hypothetically progressive element of the Greek bourgeoisie under Venizelos who carried out the task of political exclusion against them. Thus, the 'special law' (*idionym*) of 1929 made attempts to 'undermine the existing social order' illegal, i.e. it banned socialism, communism and free trade unionism from the realms of legitimate politics. The original Greek development of a 'parallel' constitution or set of general laws set alongside the more democratic constitution, and in direct contradiction with it, permitted conservative politicians to obtain results that, in other countries, required a fully-fledged dictatorship. Yet, even this was not enough, and as in Spain, a large-scale civil war (1946–9) was necessary to suppress the enemies of 'the social order'. The difference of course, is that in Spain (1936–9) the conflict had been led by fascists and reactionaries against a democratic republic, based on an uneasy coalition of socialist, republican and anarchist forces (and to a much lesser extent of communists and other groups). In both cases, however, warfare was the ultimate solution found against socialism. In Italy, a full civil war was not necessary, since the victory of fascism, largely organised as a weapon against the threat of left-wing revolution, made that impossible. But it is difficult not to treat the fascist terror that, for instance, reigned through vast parts of the countryside in the early twenties or the fascist elimination of socialist and communist activity in the urban and industrial areas as a case of warfare. The chief difference between Italy and the other Mediterranean countries is that, through fascist defeat in the Second World War and Allied intervention, the Italian socialists and communists found accommodation and later integration into liberal democracy at a much earlier date.

A shared past of repression, persecution and the corresponding maximalism that must be their consequence is not the only common element in the historical experience of southern European socialists. More fundamentally, perhaps, is the fact that precisely through such processes the socialist camp everywhere split into a democratic socialist and a Marxist-Leninist, communist sector. The relative strength of each varied not only from country to country, but also through time in each country. In all of them communism at one time or another was successful, with its uncompromising attitude towards a 'bourgeois' order that had proven its incapacity to cope with fascism and dictatorship and had afforded no protection to socialists and radicals when the crunch had come. Socialist parties were reduced to significant minorities within the left (Italy) or to insignificant ones (Greece, Spain). In some countries (Portugal, Greece), socialists only re-grouped and actually founded their parties on the very eve of democratic change and in the most inauspicious circumstances. In Spain, the old and once powerful Socialist Workers' Party in exile never dissolved, but there were very long periods under the Franco dictatorship when it was non-existent for all practical purposes: it had become as weak and evanescent as that once vast organisation of the working classes, the anarcho-syndicalist movement. Communists either drove out socialists from the ranks of the left, or confined them to small enclaves. The reasons for their success included unity of purpose, discipline and ideological commitment as well as effective support from the Soviet Union at crucial moments. Important among them was the earlier 'failure' of the democratic socialists to stem the fascist tide. A result of the communists' rise and near identification with the left was that for a long period they appeared to have taken over the revolutionary tradition of the south and presented themselves as the carriers of the political counterculture. Though communists had never monopolised the resistance and revolt against fascism, foreign occupation and repression (not even in Greece during the civil war),they reaped the fruits of their combat at the forefront of those movements and exercised hegemony over the entire left. They thrived above all because they were or had been best suited for the struggle against the sordid world of reactionary dictatorship.

THE SOCIALISTS IN THE TRANSITION TO DEMOCRACY

Fascism, dictatorship and war did not bring about a real solution of continuity in the evolution of the socialists' attitude to parliamentary democracy. At the level of principle, their will to participate in and accept the rules of the government-opposition system was not supposed to drive out the essential radicalism of socialism. But, precisely for that reason, some important practical problems became immediately apparent. Thus, when early participation of communists in certain postwar governments ceased, the socialists in the only Mediterranean countries enjoying a fully constitutional government, France and Italy, were left to maintain their revolutionary aims *and* to uphold pluralism. Once again, the radicalism of the south made a successful strategy very difficult. While, for instance, the German socialists – out of power for the first two decades following the war – steadily veered toward the explicit rejection of radicalism and Marxism, which finally took place at the Bad Godesberg conference of 1959, the southern European parties could not easily risk such official transformation. When a sector of the Italian party attempted it, that party simply split it into two smaller ones: Saragat's moderate social democrats and Nenni's socialists, who refused to isolate the communists and therefore isolated themselves. The French, for their part, engaged in a curious and ultimately suicidal exercise in political schizophrenia: while their party, the SFIO, regularly participated in government until the Fourth Republic's demise in 1958, they steadfastly stuck to their quasi-marxist ideology and phraseology. Whether in government or out of it – as in Italy, where the Christian Democrats were to rule unmolested and indefinitely – the question of radicalism and the support of pluralism was for socialists not wholly resolved under liberal democracy, for neither the political culture nor the class structures of the region permitted substantial advances in ideological deradicalisation. Socialists were forced on the 'principled' path from both their flanks; on the one hand, the communists imposed a 'lefter than thou' attitude on any other left-wing groups and, on the other, old fashioned reactionary forces were still strong enough to kindle, as ever, the fires of traditional radicalism.

In the decades after the war, the situation under the dictatorships of Spain and Portugal or under the 'guided democracy' (alternating with dictatorship) of Greece was quite different from that of Italy. In those countries, the destruction of socialism had been an essential part of the several regimes' repression of democracy in general and of the left in particular. Their assimilation of socialism to communism was often very successful both in creating confusion and in making many believe that any opposition to tyranny must be communist-inspired. Meanwhile, the understandable hopes harboured by socialists that an Allied victory against fascism would also bring with it the restoration of democracy in their countries never materialised. Even worse, with the onset of the Cold War, they had to witness how western democracies and especially the United States provided economic, military, political and moral support to the dictatorial governments that persecuted them. Bitterness towards the 'West', and towards the systematic inclusion of their countries into the so-called 'free world' by western ideologists, generated a serious disappointment with liberal democracy. It played at the time a decisive role in the political migration of socialists and potential socialists towards communism.

It is all the more surprising therefore, that, from the late 1960s onwards, democratic socialists in all those countries were able to recover from the effects of this extremely unfavourable and adverse situation, and began to gather strength again. So much so that, in the following decade, they were able to become a substantial component in their respective country's passage to democracy. This, in turn, opened the way for their full passage to participation in government. Besides, socialist parties in Greece, Spain and Portugal were to play a strikingly similar role in the consolidation of democracy after dictatorship as well as in the necessary tasks of political modernisation. Yet, the political vicissitudes differed significantly in each case. Let us look briefly at the socialist's role during each national transition.

Greece

The communists had already begun to lose much of their charisma before the collapse of the military dictatorship in 1974, so that serious opposition to this regime could no longer be wholly identified with them. In particular, their split into two separate parties after the Soviet invasion of Czechoslovakia in 1968 and the imperviousness of the larger one, the pro-Moscow KKE, to criticisms of Soviet imperialism and of Stalinism helped to undermine their appeal. The newly-founded PASOK was able to take advantage of this situation and soon was able to present itself as the principal left-wing alternative to the conservative party, New Democracy, under Karamanlis. This they did despite the legalisation of the communists. Their intransigence and purism as leftists – opposition to NATO and the EEC, their view of Greece as a Third World country – was possible in the aftermath of the junta's downfall largely because PASOK, as such, had not played a role in the restoration of democracy. Founded shortly after the event, PASOK remained 'outside' the restoring groups though it was firmly 'inside' the new sphere of legitimacy. In so far as it encompassed a number of groups – chiefly the Panhellenic Liberation Movement (PAK), formed by Andreas Papandreou in 1968 – which had suffered persecution and had most vigorously opposed tyranny, PASOK amalgamated the most serious grudges against the fallen regime as well as against its friends abroad. Hence its simultaneous espousal of socialism and traditional xenophobic feelings, centring this time upon the CIA, Dr Kissinger, Turkey and other apparent sources of Greece's ills. PASOK's new role then quickly became that of protagonist of the opposition in the newly established 'government-opposition' dichotomy which is essential to the western form of democracy. It itself endorsed that liberal system despite the presence in its ranks of a number of then still-unpurged 'non-pluralist' dissenters. The reappearance in this new guise of the old ambivalence between socialist fundamentalism and pluralism forced PASOK to limit its initial demands to the abolition of the monarchy and the punishment of the leaders of the dictatorship, including the trial of their collaborators and torturers. In this sense the party, despite its extremism, played a key role in the earliest stage of democratic consolidation. Its extremism appeared to threaten stability, but the non-communist, democratic credentials of its members and the keenness of its followers in strengthening the liberal democratic process became a guarantee as to its ultimate political intentions.

Portugal

Just over one year after the Portuguese Socialist Party's foundation in exile, its General Secretary, Mário Soares, joined the first provisional government; while the Portuguese Constitution of 1976 itself was largely shaped by the socialists, and so was its revision later.[6] Its influence upon the immediate events in the aftermath of the military coup in Portugal was much greater, therefore, than that of PASOK in Greece. Yet, in both countries, the formation of the party coincided with the final crisis of dictatorship, and in both countries small beginnings were followed by spectacular expansion and access to power, though in Portugal this occurred at the earliest possible stage in the process of transition to democracy. Radicalism, likewise, was the hallmark and common denominator of both socialist parties.

Of all the transitions to democracy in southern Europe, the Portuguese one was the most turbulent. Given the reaction against Salazarism, the legitimation of the new political order was bound to be on a left-wing basis; but once the communists were defeated in their attempt to create a state along Marxist-Leninist lines, the attainment of socialism (enthroned in the Constitution) was postulated through pluralism. Why did events take that turn? Why was the originally very small and organisationally unprepared Socialist Party thrust into a position of power? Very schematically put, it would appear that Portugal's dependent position *within* the economic and political order of the West precluded state socialism. Clear statements to that effect were made by leaders of NATO countries at crucial points in the 'revolutionary' process. Internally, even the restricted, though significant, measures of revolutionary change implemented by organisations or by spontaneous movements began to encounter a very stiff resistance – especially during the so-called 'hot summer' of 1975 – in several parts of the country. Localised violence and widespread hostility was not only directed against the PCP, but extended also to the Armed Forces Movement (MFA). This warned the government that, should drastic reforms be pressed any further, civil strife could easily degenerate into a much graver form of conflict. Soon the brakes were applied upon the revolutionary process with the *de facto* victory of the moderate branch of the Armed Forces Movement (their plans had already been put forward in the midst of the critical summer of 1975, in the Document of the Nine). The way was thus opened for the democratic socialist control of the government. The Document of the Nine advocated a form of pluralist socialism. (The fact the pluralist socialism may, in turn, be open to the penetration of other, non-socialist forces was, then, another matter, but one of a crucial importance at a later stage.) Once the MFA moderates had won the day and the PCP lost its chance, power could only revert to a party possessing both the aims that were congruent with those of the constitution (socialism) and a genuine affinity with pluralism.

When the socialist government of Mário Soares was sworn in in July 1976, it became clear that political stabilisation had begun, though it also became evident that any immediate advances towards the publicly defined national goal of socialism were going to become very problematic indeed. The inflationary policies of democratic socialism and its redistributional efforts are often electorally very costly, as seen in the rise in popularity of the parties of the centre and centre-right in Portugal, not to speak of the constraints put on the economy and the governments' fiscal and other policies by international bodies such as the IMF. After the early nationalisation of the banks, a partial (though immensely significant) agrarian reform and other similar measures, it became apparent that the socialist aspects of Portugal's constitution were simply not being implemented. The defeat of the socialists at the hands of the conservative Democratic Alliance at the end of 1979 put them out of the misery of having to rule in a manner quite contrary to their stated ideology. However, by then, incipient deradicalisation of the party had already set in, and a more pragmatic attitude had developed.

In the creation of a liberal democracy in Portugal, the socialists' achievement was considerable: they consolidated a party in the midst of an almost complete political void; they managed to govern despite the permanent confrontational opposition of the communist-dominated trade-union Inter-sindical, and to start a trade-union movement of their own; income redistribution (in the years between 1974 and the beginning of austerity measures in 1977) and the pluralistic institutionalisation of political conflict were very largely their achievement; and their campaign against the official military tutelage of the polity bore fruit in 1982 when it was formally abolished.

Spain

The Socialist Workers' Party (PSOE) had been a major casualty of the Civil War and the subsequent repression, so that for a long time it ceased to exist as an organised force save for the PSOE in exile. However, despite continued repression, socialist groups developed under Francoism and fought against it. Some of them became well-defined political parties alongside the PSOE itself – notably the Socialist Movement of Catalonia and later the Popular Socialist Party – but then a complicated process of convergence led them to merge with the PSOE during the last years of the regime and the early stages of democracy.[7] The old but now considerably rejuvenated PSOE (its foundation goes back to 1879 and its roots are even older) became practically the sole force within democratic socialism. The first years of the constitutional monarchy established after Franco's death saw the steady rise of the PSOE as a vast, powerful opposition party. There was a corresponding decline of small left-wing, revolutionary parties; only the minority Andalusian Socialist Party held its own for a while. As for the communists, their evolution into a moderate Eurocommunist Party seemed to transform them into yet another small social-democratic party, though the strength of the traditional Leninist factions within it belied this perception.

Unlike its fraternal parties in Greece and Portugal, the PSOE was through consultation directly involved from the start of the transition process in Spain. Indeed, its co-operation as well as that of the communists was vital for the success of the transition, for it helped to legitimate it and make it possible. The role of left-wing opposition (jointly at first with the PCE and other smaller groups) befell the PSOE at the beginning especially as, in stark opposition to Portugal though in a manner not altogether different from that of Greece, the first democratic government had to be right of centre if the armed forces and the most conservative elements of the dismantled regime were to tolerate liberal democracy. The acceptance by socialists of this political system meant their immediate exclusion from power, though the possibility of a socialist government in Spain was opened even by a constitutional and electoral system designed to favour, in principle, conservative forces.

The sequence of extra-parliamentary bargains and general compromises with the established powers – as in the socialists' early co-operation with the king and the transition government of Adolfo Suárez, followed by a 'social compact' (Moncloa Agreement of 1977) about wage claims and labour peace and, later by a deal for the control of regional devolution after the failed coup of February 1981 – proved the socialists' capacity for a 'responsible' conduct of public affairs, sustained by the statesmanlike style of their leaders, Felipe González and Alfonso Guerra. Fortunately for them, it did not create major problems for their failure to follow a socialist line. The widespread popular feeling was that socialism was simply not possible in the country at least for as long as the army and other ultra-conservative *de facto* powers were there to impose their veto. In Spain, the downfall of dictatorship had brought popular joy, but in no case did it generate a stage of intense euphoria linked to revolutionary promises. Very widespread popular awareness of the constraints of the political situation led to a rapid decline of the smaller radical parties, although the realisation that those constraints could also smother some of the radical hopes of many democrats gave rise to much political *desencanto*, or disenchantment leading to apathy. This seemed to recede later, when a socialist electoral victory appeared possible in 1982. In fact, such a victory when it came was hailed by the socialists as the end of *desencanto* itself; but other observers were not so sure.

In general, however, the respective socialist parties achieved early prominence in the new Mediterranean democracies without sufficient definition or even legitimation of their ideological identities. While over time there has been a clear shift of the fulcrum of secular radicalism towards the left, there has nevertheless – at least in the eyes of orthodox Marxists in southern Europe – been a poverty of the Marxist tradition in the region. (By contrast, the scope and originality of Spanish anarchism and anarcho-syndicalism cannot be overlooked). From the early 1960s onwards, the theoretically somewhat unsophisticated socialist movements and parties of Spain, Greece and Portugal began to acquaint themselves with Marxism. But the question for the entire region is whether Marxism arrived too late to sink really deep roots in the left. In some quarters, such as the rebellious university student body, Marxism became a nearly universal, albeit thin, subculture. It provided a certain coalescence to the democratic movement, and it caused a profound unease in the ruling circles of the several authoritarian regimes as well as among the traditional and professional middle classes. By contrast, in the everyday struggles of the workers' movement, revolutionary Marxism was not always considered immediately relevant – 'conditions were not rife' – save as a means for collective identification, even though for some it did provide a rallying focus for revolutionary or quasi-revolutionary action.

The tendency was to see the circumscribed revolutionary efforts of the time as mere adventures. Furthermore, coinciding with the incipient development of the so-called 'consumer' economy in the 1960s, there occurred the rise of new forms of radicalism which represented a challenge to the political formulas and strategies proposed by the 'official' left on the basis of its received and highly derivative Marxist wisdom. This ensuing conflict, as for instance reflected in the theoretical struggles inside the Spanish Communist Party, involved diverging interpretations of the dynamics of the societies concerned. There has therefore been a problem of competing ideologies to which the established political forces of the traditional left reacted slowly and not always easily, suggesting a grave case of cultural indifference. Alongside or outside the mainstream, bicephalous socialist-communist left, southern European radicalism accordingly continued to force on that mainstream left a constant redefinition of its position. Consequently, the view that nearly all political movements and parties in southern Europe define themselves essentially in relation to communism is simplistic, for in this region the constant flow of secular radicalism, with its challenge to the established social order, is also a significant force in the configuration of the political left.

This background on the transitional nature of socialist ideology in the new Mediterranean democracies helps one to understand both these parties' flexibility in adapting to the circumstances of the 1970s as well as their roles once they acquired power, as was soon to happen.

SOCIALISM IN THE WORLD OF CORPORATE LIBERALISM

Any analysis of the socialist parties' roles, strategies and performance must take into account the overall environment in which they sought to further democratic consolidation. At some risk of oversimplification, it could be said that Greece, Spain and Portugal joined a world in which liberal democracy had already undergone significant modification. This liberal democratic world was only relatively pluralistic, for it had already developed some way into becoming 'corporatised'. This expression refers to the tendency in contemporary western societies to develop a powerful network of organisations, relatively autonomous from each other and each representing one set of collective interests. These collective interest organisations – or 'corporations', for short – include trade unions, government agencies, employers associations, professional institutes and several other groupings. They are related in different ways to the political parties and the traditional institutions of parliamentary democracy.

In so far as these Mediterranean countries are still 'backward', they are in some ways the *least* corporatist societies in western Europe; although, by the same token, they are also those societies most subject to the power of traditional corporations (such as the Church or interventionist armies) and particularly influenced by traditional networks of clientelism. However, the trends towards further corporatism and bureaucratisation in this region are important enough to warrant special attention to socialism in this context. After all, socialism has a very intimate affinity with the development of the welfare state, and the welfare state itself has become the political framework of 'pluralistic' corporatism. Likewise, socialist parties have an equally intimate though ambivalent relationship with the trade unions; and their *de facto* power as negotiators and compromisers in the struggle for the distribution of income among salaried employees under advanced capitalism is another essential component of western 'corporatism'.[8] In short, the socialist parties have come to power in the new Mediterranean democracies in a situation which includes four different levels of structuration in interest politics:

1. A parliamentary-political sphere incorporating a multi-party system, which reflects the prevailing patterns of social inequality and class cleavages, and which is not altogether dissimilar to that found elsewhere in western Europe.
2. A neo-corporatist structure also reflecting developments elsewhere in the advanced capitalist world, where interest representation of trade unions, employers' organisations and state and para-state institutions play an important role in determining the nature of political reality and the distribution of power and influence throughout society.
3. Traditional cleavages such as religion/secularism and traditionalism/radicalism, which are far more specific to the region.
4. Clientelistic and personalistic power networks, regionalistic and ethnic nationalistic identities, and other forms of political structuration which are, again, quite specific to the Mediterranean region.

It is within this frame of reference that we can consider, once again, each of the national cases separately.

Portugal

Participation in provisional governments during the immediate post-revolutionary period and two years in office as an elected party (1976–8) culminated in a grave crisis of confidence in the socialists on the part of the electorate (débâcles in trade union [1977] and local government [1978] elections). This might have been related to Soares' willingness, with his firm pragmatism and refusal to strike any alliance with the communists, to form coalitions with the right when faced with ministerial defections from his own ranks. Nevertheless, a remarkable recovery ensued. By 25 April 1983 the PS again became the predominant party in the country, with 36 per cent of the votes cast and 101 deputies in the assembly. That allowed it to lead a coalition government in conjunction with the social-democrats (Mota Pinto's party, with 76 deputies). The opposition was made up, basically, of Alvaro Cunhal's 44 communist deputies and another 30 on the right.

In order to form this coalition, the Portuguese socialists had to abandon the Marxist, collectivist and – to a lesser extent – *étatist* leanings, to which an important section of their party adhered. Its left had always been weak (despite momentary appearances), but it now became weaker still. Though Soares can be said to be a monetarist only *malgré lui*, his government has been forced to apply the most drastic austerity programme to be implemented by any western socialist leader, practically in the very style which has become the hallmark of the Thatcher government in Britain. The difference with Portugal is that in its case conditions were imposed by the IMF in May and June 1983, so that the government could obtain desperately needed loans. Lisbon thus embarked on a series of brutal public expenditure cuts, which soon became felt in a country whose standard of living was the lowest in western Europe, and which had at least 400,000 unemployed in a population of only 9 million people by 1983. (A figure of 700,000 unemployed in the near future has been given as a real possibility by sympathetic observers, given the austerity measures undertaken.)

The options of the 'central bloc' (PS-PSD) which now rules Portugal appear to lie strictly in the area of further modernisation, as the prime minister himself has repeatedly stated. According to Soares, socialism can and must be reached through social reform and not through public appropriation of the means of production.[9] In his opinion, however, further reforms cannot be wholly initiated until at least 1985, assuming that the financial bankruptcy of the country is overcome by that date. Meanwhile, the country is landed with such white elephants as the massive industrial plant complex at Sines in the Alentejo (built before the democratic coup) and for which the government would like to attract foreign investment. Yet, this has not been forthcoming in part due to the stringent labour laws introduced in the heat of revolutionary zeal, which restrict the right to hire and fire. The socialist-social democratic government is now pledged to revise the laws, roughly in the same manner vainly attempted by the last conservative administration during its four years in office from 1979 to 1983.[10]

Modernisation as a programme (instead of socialisation) cannot entirely be seen as a *volte-face* in Portugal. From the start, the first priority of the party was to take radical measures in the direction of the first rather than the second process. Decolonisation, basic social reforms, consolidation of pluralist democracy (in tune with the guidelines of the Socialist International) and a firm refusal of a large permanent role for the MFA as military overseers of the polity were its first achievements. They set the tune for things to come, for the further demilitarisation of the Portuguese state continues. The formal dissolution of the MFA 'revolutionary council' can be seen in that context. Another step would be General Eanes' removal from his post as president by a future victory of Mário Soares himself at the next presidential elections. Should this event take place, it would go beyond the merely anecdotal significance some attach to the profound hostility which exists between the two men. From the standpoint of the political structure, the 'civilianisation' of the state means that Portugal is converging still further towards the model of other western liberal democracies. Until recently, Portugal was the only country where the military surveillance of the state and the constitution was institutionalised. Only the 'progressive' nature of that surveillance blurred its long-run implications or made it easily forgivable in the eyes of many democratic observers both at home and abroad. Yet, the presence of this specific element of Mediterranean corporatism – the military as a relatively autonomous body within the state, and therefore freely intervening in the affairs of civil society – has still not been entirely removed in Portugal. The tasks of internal consolidation of the PS are almost as daunting as those of carrying out vast reform policies in a very difficult economic environment.

Greece

Of all the Socialist parties under review, PASOK is the one that least fits a possible Mediterranean 'model'. During its first two years in power, it was the party that appeared to behave least or less obviously in a 'non-socialist' way, perhaps with the exception of the Portuguese socialists during the tumultuous 'revolutionary' phase of the transition period.

Both populism and charismatic leadership account for the particular appeal of PASOK, distinctly more so than with the other two socialist parties. Yet, this reliance (indeed, over-reliance) on the figure of Andreas Papandreou has had important consequences for the policy course of the party in power. The weakness of the party's structure in controlling the leadership certainly accounts for Papandreou's great independence in making decisions and also in changing direction. For instance, there has been a certain scaling down of the original radical and traditionally socialist aims. Thus, the 1983 Law for the Socialization of Public Enterprises made strikes very difficult in that sector. (Strikes must now be voted upon and 51 per cent of the votes cast must be in favour for a strike to be declared official.) This has been interpreted as a measure against communists and other activists, but it also puts a brake on the freedom to strike most unambiguously, under the well-rehearsed pretext that by striking against publicly owned enterprises the employees first and foremost harm themselves. Apart from widespread protests, even sympathisers of PASOK are not sure about this law's consitutionality. In another field, the government's efforts to create a really 'socialist sector' of the economy has been sluggish: in the absence of the necessary investments (capital is simply not available) the so-called self-managed enterprises occupy a small and marginal place in the economy.

PASOK and Andreas Papandreou interpreted their own electoral slogan, *Allaghi* (change), as a promise of institutional modernisation opening the way to a transition to socialism. Certainly, the immediate aim has been the reorganisation of the state, the administration and the law: regionalisation has been attempted in one of Europe's most centralised states; public health and medical services are to be improved; the educational and university system is to be reformed; divorce procedures have been eased and antiquated dowries abolished. One of the most outstanding and delicate operations has been (and still is) that of the modernisation of the army. Efforts have been made to 'nationalise' it entirely, in a country where it had been notoriously prone to external influences and even infiltration by foreign personnel, so much so that Greece had practically become a British and, later, an American satellite in this respect. Paradoxically, the policy of military 'nationalisation' together with the pursuit of a substantial degree of independence in foreign policy has meant that Greece under PASOK spends 7 per cent of its GNP on defence, a higher figure than that of any other European country. This is, in turn, linked to the independent stance taken by Greece *vis-à-vis* the joint decisions which EEC and NATO member states are supposed to make. Naturally, supporters of the government tend to see such independence as part of its socialist policies, while socialists in the other Mediterranean countries often fail to see the connection between the two.

Greece's drive towards socialism through reform is exceptional in that it is based on an explicit recognition of the backwardness of the country's social structure. Thus, the political targets singled out by PASOK's leader smack of the traditional imagery of radical socialism. Well into his third year of office, Papandreou points his accusing finger at the banks, *Finanzkapitalismus* and the industrial oligarchy as the enemies to tame. Likewise, in an interesting statement for someone normally advocating vastly interventionist policies, he said that the five-year plan in operation aimed at 'socialising' economic and political life rather than nationalising it. The plan aims at reducing the role and scope of the state, above all in a public sector which, in Papandreou's own words, accounts for 50 per cent of the GNP. An essential part of PASOK's policies, he added, was to pursue 'moral targets' alongside the more institutional ones. For instance, the government intended to end the interference of corrupt middlemen in the economy.[11] Observers of the 'Greek experiment' point at the practical difficulties created by continued inflation (at 20 per cent in 1983), unemployment (at least 10 per cent), widespread and heavy business bankruptcies, a dried-up revenue from migrant workers abroad, falling foreign exchange earnings and declining exports. However, very much in contrast with the socialists in power in France, at least the popularity of PASOK has not suffered any substantial erosion because of its own bold policies. Leaning on often emotional mobilisation, PASOK has counted in its earlier years of power on a large reservoir of popular confidence. In this, it has clearly been aided by its identification with patriotic issues over Cyprus, the Aegean disputes with Turkey and Greece's role as a Balkan nation. Other parties elsewhere in the south could not always count on ideological reinforcements of comparable strength when carrying out the less romantic tasks of a socialist programme of efficient and rapid modernisation, in the absence of a real socialist transformation.

Spain

Whereas PASOK's promise of *Allaghi* was explicitly presented as preliminary to a swift passage to socialism, for the PSOE – which used an identical slogan *(Cambio)* in its victorious 1982 campaign – the promise of socialism was only implicit. Further modernisation and democratic consolidation were its twin stated aims. In many ways, the government programmes of the Spanish socialists were much closer to those of the Italian socialists and republicans than to those of the early Portuguese PS or PASOK.

Even under the dictatorship, while the PSOE was reconstructing its clandestine party machinery, its claims were moderate. Agrarian reform, for instance, then still a serious issue in Spain's vast Andalusian lands, was not included in its agenda[12]. This could be attributed, of course, to the all-important, urgent task of first restoring democracy to the country. Later, the need to tread carefully and not to antagonise the coup-prone section of the army, as well as to achieve respectability among a people long indoctrinated about the evils of socialism and communism, acted as brakes upon any undue manifestation of extremism. The modest expectations of the electorate itself, fully aware of the dangers from the extreme right, helped the orderly development of the PSOE into the vast, majority party into which it had grown by 1982.

It would be wrong to see a moderation which was essentially based on caution as reflecting the complete nature of the PSOE. The Spanish party is an old and complex one. Its revolutionary and working-class credentials are considerable. Its historical strength among revolutionary workers – such as the Asturian coal miners – runs deep. Yet, there is another very important strand within the Spanish PSOE, an equally old and profoundly liberal one, closely related to certain intellectual, educational and secular traditions of academic and republican circles.[13] Save during periods of great strain, both strands have coexisted and even blended in the party. The advent of liberal democracy and the rise of all-round moderation have brought to the fore the more liberal line, especially after the defeat of the party's Marxist wing at the hands of the leadership during the 1979 Congress. Despite its transformation into a *de facto* social-democratic party, this very young political organisation (according to the age of most of its members) is acutely conscious of its historical prowess in war or exile, as well as of its past militancy and fundamentalism whether in opposition or in government. This awareness has been put to good use in the party's successful efforts to confine and contain the communists in their attempt to become Spain's genuine left. The Spanish communists' own extreme moderation, however, has no doubt facilitated the PSOE's consolidation of its hegemony, for the radically inclined sectors of the working class or the middle strata have had nowhere else to turn for their political expression. However, this does not complete the picture: in the first years of democracy all revolutionary and ultra-left parties (and there were several beyond the socialist or communist sphere) have suffered serious setbacks and even dissolution. The demise of the ultra-left nearly everywhere (the most conspicuous exception is to be found within the Basque separatist movement) reflects a massive shift in the popular mood in the late 1970s and early 1980s. In turn, this relates to changes in lower-class economic, political and ideological expectations not without parallel elsewhere throughout western Europe. In many senses, then, the PSOE's moderation together with its almost unabated popularity are expressions of very widespread popular feelings.

The reformism of the PSOE, like that of the other Mediterranean parties, is based once more on the all-pervading idea of modernisation. In the Spanish case, the *leitmotiv* is that the socialist government's task is to embark on a series of reforms that an enlightened conservative or centre party ought to have carried out long ago. The purpose of this line is to defuse antagonism from the opposition and from conservative public opinion but, given the sorry state of many public institutions in Spain, the argument rings true. Thus, the PSOE government has accelerated the process of legal reform already initiated by an earlier legislature with the introduction of divorce and civil marriage; it has even (very cautiously) tackled abortion. Educational reform, and especially university reform, had found immense obstacles under previous constitutional administrations: with its parliamentary majority, the socialist government has succeeded in setting this in motion. In some other fields, such as decentralisation and regionalisation – perhaps reflecting its own centralist traditions and its recent willingness to yield to centralist forces – it has acted in a more devious way. More spectacularly, its minister of defence, Narcís Serra, has managed to engage in a far-reaching reform of the armed forces which, if successful, would not only make them much more efficient for their allotted military task, but also far more obedient to the civilian authorities than they have been so far.

This style of modernisation can be seen in the socialists' policies. On the one hand, these are directed towards the improvement of the taxation system, traditionally scandalously favourable to the rich, the control of inflation and the introduction of a series of measures to combat unemployment. This may, however, come into conflict with the 'industrial reconversion' policies initiated by Miguel Boyer, the minister of general economic co-ordination. Unproductive or uneconomic plants (such as certain iron and steel works) are being closed down. On the other hand, the government wishes its economic policies to be inspired by honesty and efficiency: the expropriation by the state of a vast holding company, whose financial situation was highly irregular, exemplified this approach. Though a section of the conservative opposition accused the government of doctrinaire hostility towards the holding company (whose connections with the right-wing Catholic secular order, the Opus Dei, were evident), the fact was that its assets were not nationalised. They were put back on the market and offered to private bidders as if to show that the socialists had no intention to nationalise at all costs. The same 'neutrality' could be detected in the agrarian reforms being introduced by the socialist-controlled regional government of Andalusia, directed much more towards criteria of productivity and efficiency and skirting age-old demands for collective land ownership or popular management of the *haciendas*.[14]

There seems to be, therefore, a conscious effort on the part of the PSOE leadership to avoid costly 'experiments' in the manner of the French socialists. Spain's economy, they say, could ill afford them. They have embarked instead on a mildly Keynesian path, so as to alleviate the ills of the chronic maldistribution of resources and unemployment. Meanwhile, in the relatively brief period of one (or possibly two) mandates, they expect to have sufficiently modernised Spain's public and political life, so that it fully catches up not only with the rest of western Europe but, more significantly, with many developments of its own society, whose demographic, economic, class and urban transformation largely preceded the advent of liberal democracy.

While in each national example there have been intrinsic or special reasons for the adoption of moderate strategies by the various socialist parties, it could generally be said that the structural environment of growing corporatism has acted as a fundamental constraint on radical policies. On the other hand, in the Portuguese and Spanish cases, the socialists sought to reduce the influence of traditional corporations (specifically the military) in their own cautious way; although, in the Greek case, there were emerging signs that the party once in power might well be affected by traditional patterns of clientelism. Futhermore, in explaining the shift from radicalism to moderation obvious mention should be made of the dictates of the economic recession, for while programmes of structural change invariably require heavy governmental expenditure those entailing civil modernisation are usually much less costly.

CONCLUSION

Under liberal democracy, moderation is nearly always the price of power. The socialist parties and movements of southern Europe have won their victories and achieved the tolerance of their once intransigent foes by dint of deradicalisation.

One possible inference from the shift to moderation, which in varying measures has been detected practically everywhere, is that southern European socialism has ceased to be 'principled'. At its mildest, it has become identified only with the freedoms of liberalism and with a vague sense of social justice. Prime Minister Mário Soares of Portugal seemed to understand it in those very terms when, asked about his definition of socialism late in 1983, he said that it was 'before anything else social justice and freedom, the participation of the citizens in the life of the state and society, and in the enterprises; [Socialism] means decentralisation and industrial co-determination; it is a régime that must deepen democracy . . . as well as increase solidarity'.[15] Save for a reference to government 'plans' (with its implied *étatisme*), the statement could be subscribed to by any welfare state liberal or moderate social democrat anywhere. More optimistically, the southern move towards reformism could be understood as a preliminary step, that socialists have been forced to take within the framework of their societies, which will surely open the way eventually to the real task of evolving toward socialism. Of these two interpretations, the first appears as a correct description of what has happened, and the second as a correct description of what many supporters of socialism would still like to be the case.

The recognition that moderation and modernising reformism are really the chief tasks so far undertaken by the southern European socialists could easily lead to the conclusion that we are witnessing in that region the fulfilment of a process which democratic socialism achieved long ago in northern Europe. It is as though, once advanced industrial capitalism and its attendant socio-structural changes had finally arrived in the south, their political dictates had to follow suit and join the characteristic all-European brand of welfare state, corporatist, liberal democracy. The political ecology of reformist socialism would then follow the economic ecology of advanced capitalism. One long cycle in the economic, political and ideological development in one area would, in due course, be followed by a parallel change in another. This is perhaps too neat to be true, and certainly too unfair to the aims, intentions and ideals of the southern European socialists.

A less sceptical interpretation of the marked shift from structural change to genuine modernisation may be in order. Anyone who is familiar with the characteristics and problems of Mediterranean societies must also be aware of the formidable task that real modernisation poses to any authorities and political movements attempting to implement it over a relatively brief period of time. The slightest acquaintance with the fiscal problems of the southern states and the limits of their economic structures will certainly explain the constraints of governments in the implementation of socialist measures. Faced with these constraints, radical critics may say, socialists have opted for a mere displacement of structural changes towards moralism (i.e. towards administrative reform), the introduction of fairer legislation on matters of family law, sexual equality, workers' rights and a struggle against corruption in public life. But this argument is itself misplaced because the consolidation of human and civil rights is no mean thing anywhere, and it has no order of priority in terms of democratic socialism: it is coterminous with it.

A more serious argument would be that which hinges on the question of the integration of the working classes within the system of liberal democracy, in which process socialism (in its social-democratic, reformist guise) has acted as the agent. Yet, in the analysis of the southern European situation, it has to be pointed out that the class structures of the region have changed almost beyond recognition over the decades following 1945. Initial increases in the industrial proletariat and working classes and spectacular decreases in the rural populations were followed later by a decline in the unskilled workers' sector, a growth of the highly skilled working class and corresponding development of urban middle class strata, paralleled by occupational diversification and the steady spread of salaried employment throughout the population. The cleavages and antagonisms on which socialism had once based its 'anti-system' position have either disappeared, undergone mitigation or been considerably blurred. Inequality itself, of course, has not 'diminished', but its forms and implications have changed. The picture that arises is in part similar to that found elsewhere in the west, with the question of the emerging forms of inequality, domination and social control under the new conditions of corporate liberalism.

Once the present phase of left-wing political ascendancy is eventually over, observers will no doubt detect further flaws in the socialists' performance, but there are achievements, however, and possibly the near future will witness further successes in the task of reform and improvement of public life. Yet it is likely that the least conspicuous achievements will be the more lasting ones in the life of the southern European countries. They include, on the one hand, the growth of political sophistication and civic culture and, on the other, the completion of democratic consolidation. Thus, by virtue of the socialist successes, for instance, Greeks, Portuguese and Spaniards have learnt to distinguish between democratic socialism and its totalitarian version. Then, of course, the transition to democracy in the region could not have been wholly completed until the traditionally excluded socialists had reached power peacefully and had been allowed to govern in an orderly and constitutional manner. Once in power, the socialists have been carrying out the necessary reforms that other forces were unable or unwilling to introduce.

From democratic transition to constitutional consolidation: that is at least what socialism has meant. Never before had socialists managed to take over the highest offices of the state in Greece, Portugal and Spain. This was the final and necessary stage that the new Mediterranean democracies had to reach in their long and arduous path towards regime transition and inner concord.

ACKNOWLEDGEMENTS

Despite its limited scope, this essay owes much to the help and advice provided by friends and colleagues. It was written, in the first place, at the simultaneous though unrelated instigation of Nicos Mouzelis (LSE) and Geoffrey Pridham (Bristol University). The results of the first draft were presented to a Conference on 'Greek Socialism in Comparative Perspective' at the London School of Economics, November 1983. Material and data on Portugal were provided by Manuel Villaverde Cabral (Institute of Social Research, Lisbon). Chryssi Vitsilakis (Centre for Mediterranean Studies, Athens) allowed me to interview her at length on PASOK's contemporary and future likely policies. Jacqueline Rees (University of Bradford) provided me with much information on the region and timely critical comment. Norma Bowes assisted in editing and typing under considerable strain. I would like to express my gratitude to all.

NOTES

1. For the distinction between 'government' and 'opposition' socialism, see A Pelinka, *Social Democratic Parties in Europe* (New York, Praeger, 1983).
2. Northern European radicalism is not as exceptional as this paragraph may imply, if one takes account of the radicalisation of the British Labour Party and some aspects of Swedish socialism, e.g. its attitudes towards world peace and international human rights.
3. For a general comparative study of the social structures, economies and polities of these countries, see S. Giner, 'Political economy, legitimation and the state in Southern Europe', *British Journal of Sociology* (June 1982), pp.172–99.
4. A.W. Salomone, *Italy in the Giolittian Era* (Philadelphia: University of Pennsylvania Press, 1960), p.42.
5. G. Galli, *Storia del socialismo italiano* (Bari: Laterza, 1980), *passim*.
6. For my discussion of Portugal's socialist party, I have relied considerably on an unpublished paper by Maria José Stock and Bern Rother, 'O décimo aniversário do PS (1973–1983): trajectòria de um partido'. As the authors point out, there is still not available any substantial study of the PS since 1974.
7. See E. Díaz, *Socialismo en España: el Partido y el Estado,* (Madrid: Mezquita, 1982); J.F. Tezanos, *Sociología del socialismo español* (Madrid: Tecnos, 1983).
8. For my own use of this term, see S. Giner and E. Sevilla, 'From Corporatism to Corporatism: the Political Transition in Spain', in A. Williams (ed.), *Southern Europe Transformed,* (London, 1984). It is always used by me as a *dimension* for understanding macro-sociological developments; there is no such thing as a corporate society, only degrees of corporatism.
9. Speech by Mario Soares of 10 July 1978, see *Portugal Socialista,* August 1978, pp.23–5.
10. *The Times,* special report on Portugal, 14.7.83.
11. *The Times,* 1.12.83.
12. E. Sevilla and J. Taberner, 'Reforma agraria a regañadientes', *Diario 16,* 17.11.83.
13. E. Díaz, op. cit., pp. 7–40.
14. *Financial Times,* 23.11.83, special survey of Andalusia.
15. Mário Soares, interview in *El Pais,* 14.11.83.

The International Context of Democratic Transition

Alfred Tovias

INTRODUCTION

Many scholars have stressed that the failure of the Second Spanish Republic was largely due to internatonal factors and events not under the control of those who had succeeded initially in performing a peaceful transition from the dictatorship of Primo de Rivera (1923–9) to the republic in 1931. Economic historians have produced clear-cut evidence of the tremendous impact that the world economic crisis had on the Spanish economy, with some years of delay in relation not only to the USA (where it had already started in 1929) but also in relation to other European countries (where it hit by early 1931), notably in Germany where the Depression was crucially instrumental in the collapse of the Weimar Republic.

One could say, so the argument goes, that 'double bad luck' contributed considerably to the end of the Second Spanish Republic. As from 1932, Spain had to confront the inevitable adjustment to a deteriorated world economic situation at a time when domestically the public was expecting economic miracles from the republic.Three or four years later, with a domestic economic crisis still present, political, diplomatic and military developments abroad (e.g. the rise to power of the Popular Front in France, or the invasion of Ethiopia by Italy) were to have an immediate impact on the Spanish domestic political scene. But by that time the experiment was already doomed, for international economic factors played a larger role than international political developments in the failure of the Second Republic.

Up to what point can we draw an historical parallel with the democratic transition that has taken place in Spain, Greece and Portugal since the mid 1970s in a period of economic crisis? If the 'bad luck' theory is right what functioned differently this time, given the relative success of the present democratic experiments? Or if the differences between the two settings are not striking, is the theory therefore irrelevant? In that event, should one resort to an alternative theory?

The focus of this chapter is on international factors with relevant linkages to domestic developments. The discussion follows a chronological approach by periods, and for two reasons the economic calendar is preferred to the diplomatic one: first, because the 'bad luck' thesis mentioned above favours the economic explanation; second, because the three countries being considered fall clearly under the western sphere of influence and have not been subject to any serious east/west competition for their loyalty. Four periods have marked economic developments in the western world:

1. 1945–73: Reconstruction and boom of the western economies.
2. 1973–9: Economic crisis and partial adjustment to the first oil shock.
3. 1979–82: Economic crisis and adjustment to the second oil shock.
4. 1982–?: Recovery?

Diplomatic factors will also be taken into consideration, especially as the Middle East during this period became a theatre of increasing confrontation, although they constitute a secondary dimension to the economic explanation.

THE PRE-1973 PERIOD: A STORY OF BOOM AND DIPLOMATIC STABILITY

That the general economic prosperity of the west in the 1960s had a beneficial impact on these three countries is indisputable. In the 1960s and up to 1973, Spain, Portugal and Greece enjoyed higher rates of growth than the Six or the Nine. While in the latter GDP increased in volume on average by an annual rate of 4 to 5 per cent, in the three southern European countries annual growth rates revolved around the 6 to 8 per cent mark.[1] It is commonly agreed that the tourism boom, combined with the absorption by other OECD countries of cheap labour from southern Europe and a boom of direct investment into that area, had a tremendous influence on the balance of payments and the growth rates of the three countries.

The three dictatorships followed this change, but were not responsible for it although, to be sure, they facilitated growth by opening up their economies. In the case of Spain (1959), the government was almost forced to do it to prevent a collapse of the economy and with it possibly of the regime. The OECD boom undoubtedly contributed to the survival of the Spanish and Greek dictatorships. Portugal is a *sui generis* case, in that it still behaved as a colonial power with the economy largely directed towards the colonies. However, as V. Curzon has shown,[2] Portugal was the main beneficiary of EFTA's creation, suggesting that the country was not so closed in the 1960s, as sometimes said, to western economic influence.

Democratic Europe did not counteract actively any of the adaptive policies implemented by the dictatorships. To be sure, some of their opponents in the Benelux countries tried to limit the degree of the EEC's economic co-operation with Franco's Spain by rejecting Spain's economic integration into the EEC beyond the partial preferential agreement formula.[3] There was also the 'freeze' imposed on the EEC association agreement with Greece at the time of the military junta. However, in the two cases, this resistance was economically unimportant. In other words, the liberalisation of the three economies proceeded essentially with the acquiescence of all the OECD countries, and not only of the USA. It is still an open question whether this acquiescence occurred for self-interest reasons or was part of a plan for bringing those three countries to a higher level of economic development, thereby allowing for a smooth transition to a western-type democracy. In the opinion of this author, the first explanation seems the more convincing, for there was no evidence of a debate in Europe or in the USA on the latter theme in the 1960s.

Turning briefly to the strategic front up to the mid-1970s, NATO's southern flank seemed unchallenged. Portugal, Greece and Turkey were fully-fledged members of the Alliance and Spain had been firmly attached to the west by a bilateral agreement with the USA since 1953. US bases in Greece and Turkey controlled the sea lanes in the Aegean, and covered the eastern Mediterranean and the Middle East. Even though by the end of the 1960s and beginning of the

1970s the US Sixth Fleet began to be challenged by the Soviet Eskadra, the stategic implications of this had so far not been far-reaching, since the Suez Canal remained closed.

ECONOMIC AND STRATEGIC CONSEQUENCES OF THE FIRST OIL SHOCK FOR THE THREE COUNTRIES

From the end of 1973, the rapid increase in the price of oil was to have two devastating consequences for the economic situation of the three countries. A direct one came clearly from the fact that Greece, Portugal and Spain were among the most energy-dependent countries in the OECD. According to the International Energy Agency (IEA), Spain's oil imports accounted in 1980 for about 68 per cent of her total primary energy consumption. In 1978, the import of oil represented 28 per cent of total Spanish purchases abroad. The increased oil bill became an economic nightmare precisely for countries which had based their industrialisation strategies on abundant and cheap energy. Indirectly, they were also affected because the OECD entered a recessionary period, which was bound to hit economies that had been opened beforehand precisely in the direction of the OECD countries.

Strategically speaking, the 1973 oil crisis implied that the stakes were higher in the Mediterranean, both for western Europe and for the USA. Security of access to oil has consequently become a first-rank preoccupation, not only because unpredictable states like Algeria and Libya are important oil producers but also as much of Middle East oil moves across the Mediterranean, altogether implying that the prosperity of western Europe could easily be challenged by any aggressive attitude on the part of Mediterranean neighbours.[4] Very soon after October 1973, three governments at least (those of the USA, the UK and West Germany) realised the importance of maintaining pro-western stability in southern Europe at a time when economically this had become more difficult to achieve.

Domestic developments in the Iberian peninsula reinforced this concern. December 1973 saw the assassination in Spain of Admiral Carrero Blanco, who had been appointed by Franco to guarantee the survival of the régime after his own death, and this together with a worsening of the Basque problem created a new uncertainty. Portugal was embroiled in a colonial war which was taking a heavy toll on its economy. It began to be realised that economic prosperity could not be ensured by the current state of affairs under the two dictatorships. Backing them could now possibly provoke strong counter-reactions. Thoughts turned to the question of how to facilitate an orderly transition to democracy, not leaving any void that could be exploited by the Soviet Union. Economically, the danger seemed limited in the short run as far as Spain was concerned, for that country could take foreign loans and try to make the most of its traditionally pro-Arab policies.

In Portugal, however, events developed more quickly than expected. The economy began to decline rapidly after the revolution of April 1974, both because of the repatriation of hundreds of thousands of people from the lost colonies and also because of the world-wide economic crisis. Since Portugal was much poorer and had a lower growth record than Spain or Greece, its credit-worthiness was therefore much less. Beginning in 1974, Portugal's balance of payments, normally in surplus, moved into deficit. The GDP growth rate increased by only 1.1 per cent in 1974 and declined by 4.3 per cent in 1975. Economic destabilisation led to political destabilisation, and there was an attempted leftist coup at the end of 1975. At this stage, West Germany and the EEC backed by the US intervened. In October 1975, the Nine decided to accord extraordinary financial aid of about $200 million from the European Investment Bank and to open discussions for the improvement of the 1972 Portuguese-Community trade agreement. Later on, the loan was increased.[5] The leftist coup did not succeed, but the authorities, still unsure and facing national elections in the spring of 1976, decided to reflate. Given the low level of confidence of foreign borrowers in the ability of the new Portuguese government arising from the 1976 elections to handle the political and economic situation, there followed a second foreign exchange crisis. This time (June 1977) 14 countries decided to act under the leadership of the IMF and provided Portugal with $750 million over 18 months. Germany and the USA provided two-thirds of the total. The results were spectacular, and the balance of payments deficit was eliminated by 1979.[6]

In the case of Greece, the role of the western powers was somewhat different. The dictatorship had collapsed in July 1974 not for economic reasons but because of its foreign and defence policy failures, notably over Cyprus. In other words, the military in power failed in their own field of specialisation, and they suffered accordingly a loss of prestige.[7] The USA and NATO were rightly or wrongly seen as having supported the dictatorship, and as having condoned Turkey's invasion of Cyprus. In protest, Greece under civilian leadership withdrew from the integrated military command of NATO.[8] At the same time, the Greek lobby put pressure on the US president to take some action against Turkey (early in 1975 an arms embargo against Turkey was imposed), while the Turkish government began to speak of considering new stategic options. Thus, in the course of one year the cohesion of the entire southern flank of NATO was called into question, a situation that was to last for five years. Turkey and Greece have always been viewed as being strategically linked, something reinforced by the fact that they are geographically isolated from the rest of NATO. That is, in the case of an attack from their north, each depends on the other for support. By the same token, conflict among the two leads automatically to a cumulative deterioration of the whole southern flank's strategic position.

Not surprisingly, this problem in relation to NATO affected Greek interest in joining the European Community. Prime Minister Karamanlis could point out domestically that the EEC's commission and council of ministers had taken consistently tough positions towards the preceding military junta, such as with the 'freeze' of the 1961 Association Treaty. For both diplomatic and domestic political reasons (in the latter case a wish to buttress the new democratic regime), Karamanlis soon presented Greece's application for EEC membership in June 1975. Only the EEC commission expressed some concern over this, not only in reference to the economic consequences of Greek membership but above all because of its impact on relations with Turkey.[9] Some Greeks even wanted to assign a strategic value to membership. 'Turkey

11

will think twice before attacking an EEC country,' was a Greek statement that frightened the commission, maybe because it was not accustomed to considering strategic questions. After all, the first enlargement had not entailed this kind of consideration. The commission's hesitations were, however, pushed aside in 1976 by the council of ministers, which chose to take a calculated risk given the position of Turkey. The reasoning was the following: politically, the Community had to give a clear yes to Greece and then take care of Turkey's interests by providing further economic help, while delaying the negotiations with Greece as long as possible.

Returning to Spain, Franco's death in November 1975 opened the way for the transition, and this was backed with no hesitation by the west, including the USA. Economic adjustment to the oil shock and the western economic crisis was postponed, as with Greece, because Spain's economy was much healthier than Portugal's. Her reserves were higher, as well as her international credit-worthiness. At the same time, however, regionalist claims, non-existent in the case of Greece or Portugal, had a potentially destabilising influence especially as it could irritate an army that was more inward- than outward-looking. The Spanish army has always been extremely sensitive to any matter affecting the 'unity' of the country. A related question was whether or not the postponement of economic adjustment was necessary in order to ensure a smooth transition to democracy and hence make a military coup less likely even though there was no pattern of direct army involvement in economic and social affairs, as in Portugal. In fact, the postponement of the search for a solution to the economic problems until late in 1977 (Moncloa Pact),[10] four years after the first oil shock, was to have negative consequences. When the second oil shock broke in early 1979, the stabilisation plan had not had time to produce all the desired effects.

For both Portugal and Spain, establishing new EEC links appeared to be a second-rate priority in the first two years of their transitions. To be sure, both countries could not ignore Greece's own application for membership,[11] and this by itself precluded too long a waiting period for dealing with the issue. But neither was there urgency, as in Greece's case, on foreign policy grounds. For the new Iberian democracies, such foreign policy considerations could for the moment be shelved.

Then, at the end of 1975, the scene changed in Portugal. The Socialist Party, which had up to 1974 been anti-EEC, now saw Portugal's membership of the Community as a way of preventing a second leftist coup attempt. The socialist parties in power in Germany and the UK came to the same analysis: while, economically speaking, Portugal was not ready for membership (something stressed particularly by France), EEC membership now appeared as a political necessity. Pre-accession, as suggested by the EEC Commission, was no solution, because the important thing according to Soares was to enter the Community soon and then undergo a long transition period. In this respect, the situation was similar to Greece's. After all, so the argument went, the EEC should be able to absorb the two countries, given the small size of their economies. In other words, the price to be paid by the Community was considered small compared to the overall potential risks from leaving them out, especially in the light of the events of 1975 in Portugal and the 1977 Greek elections. The Portuguese Communist Party consistently drew 15 to 20 per cent of the popular vote, while PASOK obtained in 1977 over 25 per cent of votes in the Greek national elections. Both parties were anti-western, in so far as they postulated withdrawal from NATO, the withdrawal of US bases and non-entry into the EEC.

The context was different in the case of Spain, because her greater economic size meant substantial economic adjustment problems for the Nine after her entry. Moreover, the political costs of leaving Spain out appeared less, for there was at least no danger of destabilisation from the political left, as in Greece or Portugal. The only possible reason for pushing Spain's entry to the EEC was the chance of preventing a rightist coup, but very soon in the debate the way it appeared to some was that there was a certain political risk in having Spain in the Community, precisely because with her size a successful coup could endanger the Community itself in all kinds of ways (by 'infection', by 'paralysis', etc.). After the attempted coup in Spain in February 1981, this pessimistic line of thinking became more outspoken by stressing that Spain must first get her political house in order and then join the Community, not the other way round. It was partly for the same reason that Greece and Portugal persistently tried to show that their case was totally different, for they were trying to enter the Community before Spain and so avoid being part of a general package deal.

Given the Community's basic apathy towards Spain's candidature almost from the beginning, one wonders why the Spanish governments and parties decided to push so hard for entry, as from 1977. Was it because of distrust towards the other ally, the USA, as was the case with Greece? No. Was it to overcome geographical isolation and exclusive military, financial or economic dependence on a major power? Not really. What seems closer to the truth is that the factor of having been absent from world affairs for some time played a role in Spanish post-Franco political thinking. Entry into the EEC could be regarded as part of a general activation of Spain's foreign policy in all directions. It expressed the will to see Spain present in the world and a return to an ambitious diplomatic tradition.[12] A long list of diplomatic initiatives taken between 1976 and 1979 demonstrated this point. During that short period, Spain entered the Council of Europe, re-established diplomatic relations with the USSR after more than 40 years, participated in the Non-Aligned Summit at Havana, became a member of the UN Security Council, won the candidacy for organising in Madrid the Third Session of the European Security Conference (CSCE) to start in 1980, and became an observer at the Organisation of American States and the Andean Pact and a member of the Inter-American Development Bank.

Spanish membership of the EEC was favoured for at least three other major reasons at that time. First, it was perceived as a way of consolidating a recently born democracy. At the very least, membership should give the new Spanish regime an aura of international respectability, in contrast with the image of Franco's Spain. Second, there was the idea of participating in what was perceived in Spain as the 'European adventure' from which she had been separated since its inception. Spaniards have tended to think rather idealistically in terms of the original movement for European unity, without taking sufficient account of the complex and somewhat disappointing reality of the Community. As in Portugal, general ignorance of the actual character of the EEC was widespread.[13] Third, many informed circles have stressed the net economic gains from accession to the EEC. Here they touched on more solid ground. According to recent research by this author,[14] it appears that membership would offer an historical opportunity to develop the great agricultural potential of Spain, thus also achieving a better domestic regional balance. Industrially, integration would imply a redeployment of the Spanish industrial base along the same lines as in other EEC countries as a result of accession; i.e. the development of intra-industry trade with other Community countries as partners. Such a redeployment would make the most of the fact that, being a 'border country' in relation to the EEC, Spain could succeed in the rapid assimilation and improvement of foreign technologies. Membership, however, means adjustment with its inherent costs, but Spain seems well placed in relation to the rest of Europe, given the relative youth of her population, something which facilitates horizontal mobility.[15]

The case of Spain showed how much – as with the other two countries – European, strategic and domestic political considerations were closely linked. This was no surprise in view of international concern over the Mediterranean following the first oil shock of 1973, which had predictably disruptive and potentially destabilising effects on the three countries because their economies were very vulnerable to precisely this kind of development. However, this very concern on the part of western countries expressed through financial assistance and a readiness to involve Greece, Spain and Portugal as partners in European integration was important in mitigating the effects of this event during these crucial formative years of the new democracies.

ECONOMIC AND STRATEGIC IMPLICATIONS OF THE SECOND OIL SHOCK FOR SOUTHERN EUROPE

The revolution in Iran in early 1979 induced a new quantum-jump in the oil price, aggravating the plight of Spain, Portugal and Greece, both directly (by. a deterioration in terms of trade) and indirectly (by contracting external demand originating in OECD countries). The oil price reached new heights at the end of 1980, when hostilities between Iraq and Iran opened, leading to a further drop in the supply of oil.

In contrast with the first oil crisis, a postponement this time of economic adjustment to the new situation was much more difficult to achieve. The international financial situation was tighter and many newly industrialising countries, including the three in question, had been accumulating debt since 1973. The deterioration in the economic situation of the three countries was therefore unavoidable, and became a reality sooner rather then later. For example, the non-agricultural annual GDP growth rate in Spain, which was still 4 per cent in the 1974–5 period and 2.2 per cent between 1976 and 1979, dropped to zero per cent on average for the period 1979–81.

From a strategic viewpoint, the fall of the Shah (1979), the crisis in Afghanistan (1979) and the Iran-Iraq war (1980) enhanced the importance of Turkey for the West. Of course, after the first oil shock, Greece, Portugal and

Spain had also acquired greater strategic importance than before because of their position in relation to the Mediterranean and the Middle East. However, Turkey ranked that much higher because of its position between the Soviet Union and the Gulf. This change in the Graeco-Turkish strategic balance had a predictable impact on domestic developments in Greece. The government of George Rallis was confronted by an opposition led by PASOK, which asserted that the new developments would be to the detriment of Greece. Moreover, the domestic situation in Turkey during 1979–80 was so chaotic, PASOK argued, that a diversionary attack on Greece was not to be discounted.

Although the pro-western military coup in Turkey in the autumn of 1980 reduced these fears somewhat in Greece (as in the rest of NATO), it was too late for Rallis to redress a domestic situation aggravated by the economic crisis, which ensued after the second oil price shock.[16] EEC membership from January 1981 could not help to solve the Greek economic dilemma. On the contrary, soon after entry imports from the Community increased at a higher rate than exports to it, expanding an already large trade deficit. As expected, PASOK won the parliamentary elections in the autumn of 1981. At first, it looked as if the new government was going to make radical changes in foreign policy, such as withdrawal from EEC and NATO or the closing down of the US bases. PASOK stressed that membership in the Community would obstruct any socialist experiment in the domestic economy. Very soon, however, the government accepted that it was not so much the Community as the domestic economic situation which precluded for the moment any large-scale expansionary programmes. Politically also, Papandreou knew that a referendum on possible withdrawal from the Community could only be initiated by the pro-EEC prime minister Karamanlis according to the constitution. In that situation, it seemed better to stay in the community while maintaining publicly that Greece needed to renegotiate her entry terms, given the economic situation. This strategy worked, for in early 1983 the EEC commission proposed to grant an extra £1.6 billion to Greece and to delay tariff cuts on EEC imports, which were originally scheduled to take place up to 1985.[17]

In relation to NATO, tension grew after PASOK's accession to power in the autumn of 1981. The preceding Rallis government had decided a year before to rejoin NATO's integrated military command, justifying this by saying that only thus could Greece obtain modern equipment and prevent an attack from Turkey. Turkey's new military government had not used its veto against Greece's request, which undoubtedly ameliorated the political atmosphere between the two countries. On becoming prime minister, Papandreou hence found a less conflictive situation than before; although more recently Greece has refused to participate in NATO manoeuvres that would not include some procedures implicitly recognising Greece's sovereignty over disputed areas in the Aegean Sea.[18] Finally, in the summer of 1983, a new agreement was reached between the USA and Greece which foresaw the closure of the four US bases over a period of 17 months starting by 1989. Clearly, the strategy of Papandreou's government is partly angled to satisfying as much as possible the electorate of the Greek left as a whole by displaying some radicalism in foreign affairs. This is related to the need to obtain from the trade unions (which are controlled by the two left parties) some wage restraint and a general moderation over economic and social issues, not to mention electoral competition from the communists. The government knows that it cannot substantially improve the economic situation, whereas there is some room for manoeuvre in foreign affairs.

While the impact of the second oil shock had for Greece both economic and strategic consequences, the economic effects dominated the scene in Portugal. The crisis in western Europe led to increased unemployment among Portuguese foreign workers there and an immediate fall in their remittances sent home. EEC protectionism against labour-intensive products reached new heights and hit Portugal's textile sector heavily. These balance of payments difficulties were compounded by the lack of confidence of foreign investors in the Portuguese economy (including foreign workers). This situation does much to explain the instability of governments in the following years. For instance, in 1983, Mário Soares and his Socialist Party – expelled from office in 1978 – were returned by the electorate to extricate the country from a confidence and financial crisis. The foreign debt had reached more than $14 billion. Soares seemed eager to enter the EEC as soon as possible in order to solve some of Portugal's financial problems. According to his statements in the past, the EEC should replace the IMF in its banker's role, but whether the Community would be prepared to meet this expectation is another matter. In the very short run, the only ready help Portugal can acquire is from the IMF.[19] In October 1983, its board had to approve formally an 18-month standby agreement to lend Portugal $480 million, accompanied by $250 million in special drawing rights. In turn, this package should permit the raising of a further $300 million in syndicated loans. But the package deal involves the cutting of the balance of payments from a record $3.2 billion in 1982 to $1.25 billion in 1984. The medicine is hard to swallow, which probably explains why Soares and his government think that other lenders (e.g. the EEC) might be less rigorous or more generous.

One can draw some parallel between Spain's situation and Portugal's after the second oil shock. The new oil crisis produced a total halt in Spain's economic growth. Unemployment increased rapidly (from a rate of 8.5 per cent in early 1979 to 15.4 per cent in the last quarter of 1981, according to OECD figures), reaching one of the highest levels in the OECD. This threatened the position of the Suarez government, already under pressure from the Basque terrorist ETA. The situation seemed somewhat analogous to that in Turkey, although violence had not yet reached the same levels. Western acceptance of the military takeover in Turkey was taken by a minority in the Spanish army as a sign, together with Reagan's accession to the US presidency, that the moment was appropriate for a similar attempt in Spain. As in Turkey, their primary stated intention was to 'open a parenthesis' in the transition to democracy rather than a simple return to dictatorship, motivated by the desire to stop the devolution process and eliminate terrorism. The economy was of no immediate concern. In other words, those initiating the February 1981 coup knew well that they must count on civilians to redress the economy if they wanted to succeed. Independently of the fact that the coup did not succeed ultimately because of the King's firm refusal to support this attempt, the speculation of the putschists on possible US backing revealed a poor evaluation of the situation, for Turkey after 1979 (and possibly even before) was of much higher importance for NATO than Spain in the east-west strategic context. Moreover, the danger of an anti-western coup or revolution (whether pro-Soviet or Islamic) was not present in Spain.

Democracy was saved, but this event led both government and opposition parties to some clearer thinking over what now appeared to be the most direct threat to the perpetuation of Spanish democracy: the fact that the army was basically the same as the one which had emerged from the Civil War. The solution might come from the country's role in NATO. Entry into the integrated military structure of the Atlantic Alliance would be likely to reorientate the army's attention to external matters rather than domestic politics. Moreover, joint manoeuvres with other more technologically advanced armies and international contacts between army professionals would modify the attitude of isolation among Spanish army personnel, and hence reduce the scope for domestic political misunderstanding and the perpetuation of fantasies. Also, the required modernisation of equipment and improvements in military technology would help to keep the army busy. This thesis was supported by the fact that those officers with more democratic leanings were also the most pro-NATO, not only for the reasons mentioned above but also because it was in their interest to agree with the principle accepted in NATO, but not in their own army, that promotion should depend on ability and not on seniority. Other arguments had been aired before the February 1981 coup to justify Spain's accession to NATO,[20] but they did not weigh much in the sudden position adopted by the governing UCD. For more than the five years it had been in power, the UCD had always stressed the lack of urgency in deciding on this issue.

The Socialist Party (PSOE), the main opposition party at the time, had opposed NATO entry for many different reasons. The party insisted that the army's temptations could be solved by a redeployment of its forces to the periphery of the national territory to guard the borders of the country instead of maintaining an important military presence around the capital, as in Franco's time. Some arguments put against NATO entry have since proved to be unfounded, such as the fear of 'provoking the other block' or of 'harming Spain's relations with the Arabs or the non-aligned world'. Also, the allegedly unbearable economic costs of membership seem to have been exaggerated, if one compares what other middle-sized countries in western Europe are spending on defence. Finally, it is difficult to argue that being a NATO member means 'an increased risk of nuclear destruction to the Spanish people', given that the four US bases in Spain in any case place Spain in the eyes of the potential enemy in the same category as many other NATO countries. From 1981, some circles in the PSOE began to agree with the UCD's arguments mentioned above, in particular that the most pro-NATO army circles are also those closer to the spirit of the constitution. Accordingly, the party's opposition to NATO was replaced by a less intransigent position stressing that Spain had been outside NATO for more than thirty years and that it could continue with this situation; i.e. keeping a bilateral agreement with the USA but without NATO membership.

This more moderate position opened the way for the next step, for should Spain enter NATO against the will of the party (something that happened in June 1982) it could remain absolved of the responsibility of that decision while asserting that 'one thing is not to get into NATO, another is to opt out'. It has since been widely accepted in the circles of the PSOE government elected in 1982 *a posteriori* that the UCD argument about NATO constituting a common cause for the government and the democratic sectors of the army is fully valid. However, party pressure is sufficiently strong to make Felipe Gonzalez settle for an intermediary position, of freezing Spain's integration in NATO's military command, while remaining in the Atlantic Alliance until a referendum on the issue in 1985. Paradoxically, such a solution does not contribute to tackling the army problem.

In conclusion, the second oil shock once again had disruptive effects on the three countries, for the same reason as before, all the more so as this time international financial circumstances were tighter. Furthermore, the diplomatic and strategic situation surrounding the Mediterranean had grown more uncertain. However, this perilous environment ultimately sharpened the sense of commitment among political élites in the three countries to the new democratic regimes and their determination to make a success of them. This was demonstrated by the way in which domestic partisan differences over the issues of NATO and EEC membership receded when this broader question came to the fore.

THE OIL GLUT AND THE OECD'S ECONOMIC RECOVERY AND THEIR POSSIBLE EFFECTS ON DEMOCRATIC CONSOLIDATION IN SOUTHERN EUROPE

The first, and even more so the second, oil shock have had a permanent impact on consumer and investment behaviour in the OECD area. The effects of oil saving and improved efficiency in its use have begun to be felt since the end of 1981. Compounded by the impact of the economic recession on oil demand, an oil glut developed because of the failure of OPEC to adjust its price to the new international economic situation. After more than a year, OPEC was finally obliged to reduce the price of oil from $34 to $29 a barrel. Consequently, the oil bill of the three countries being examined has been very much affected by these developments since 1981, relieving some of the pressure on their balance of payments.

A second favourable economic development has been the recovery in the OECD, following that in the USA. According to EEC figures,[21] the Ten's industrial production rose 0.7 per cent in the first quarter of 1983 in relation to the last quarter of 1982, compared with the rates in the third and fourth quarters in 1982 of –1.8 and –1.7 respectively. Moreover, the rate of unemployment has stabilised at 10.7 per cent in the second quarter of 1983, after having increased continuously since 1979, with a decline beginning in the summer of 1983. According to the IMF, the rate of growth of production in industrialised countries should reach 1.5 per cent in 1983 in relation to the preceding year, while increasing to 3 per cent in the second quarter of 1983 in relation to the first. This last rate should be maintained throughout 1984.

Such developments are expected to have a substantial and positive impact on the exports of Spain, Portugal and Greece. In other words, economic constraints should hinder domestic politics in these three countries less than before, and give some breathing space to the three new socialist governments, which were voted into power *inter alia* for economic reasons.

There are, however, two caveats to this more optimistic scenario. First, the possibility of yet another oil crisis, given the permanent turmoil in the Middle East, cannot be excluded. Second, a world-wide debt crisis calling into question the present economic recovery is another possibility. A financial crisis in one of the three countries is a risk assessed to be small by the experts. The gravest problem is with Portugal, which in volume terms would be manageable at the international level. Spain would be another matter, but the basic situation there is much healthier.[22]There would, however, be a link between a third oil shock and the international financial situation. A new increase in energy prices would create enormous problems for the three countries for they would have difficulties in raising another time round the funds needed to pay for the increased oil bill, given the fear prevailing in banking circles of a repetition of the last decade when outside funds were used many times to finance current consumption or long-term public investment (like motor roads).

CONCLUSION

The international economic context has certainly not facilitated democratic consolidation in Greece, Spain and Portugal, although it may be said to have contributed to the acceleration of the transition from dictatorship to democracy (in particular in Spain). This was both because of international and European support for the new democratic systems as well as a strong commitment in the three countries to their success. In particular, the possibility offered by the international financial community to these countries to postpone their adjustment to the first oil shock may have been decisive, bearing in mind that such an alternative was totally unavailable, for instance, to the Spanish Republic in the 1930s.

As to the diplomatic situation, there is little doubt that détente in the 1970s eased the transition to and consolidation of democracy. This was notably the case with Greece, for her geostrategic location in relation to the Middle East, the Soviet Union and especially Turkey could have played havoc with any peaceful transition to democracy, had the general environment been one of cold war. Even after the end of détente at the end of that decade, when in any case the new Greek democracy was already established, the changed international setting did not act to the detriment of domestic stability. This was basically because almost simultaneously a military regime acquired power in Turkey, and in order to gain western acceptance it cooled down relations with its neighbour, so contributing to the stabilisation of the whole area.

In short, the international context which from the mid-1970s seemed generally at first sight to be unfavourable to the delicate process of establishing new democracies nevertheless contained various features which made any repetition of history of half a century ago very unlikely. These features were the following:

1. An international economic system fundamentally different from that of the 1930s, with its strong awareness of, and institutional networks for, stabilising the interdependence of national economies.
2. The new strategic importance of the Mediterranean in this period, reinforcing the commitment of other West European countries to democratic stability in Greece, Spain and Portugal.
3. While foreign and domestic policy considerations were closely interlinked in the three cases, these countries were not subject to the kind of international interference deriving from rivalry between hostile political systems, as was notoriously so with Spain in the 1930s.
4. The existence of integrative international organisations like the EEC and NATO which provided some external outlet for domestic political tensions, particularly so far as the political ambitions of the military were concerned.
5. The fact that public discontent with the performance of the economy tended to be channelled within the new democracies, in the sense that it operated against particular governments in office rather than against the political systems as such.
6. The absence of any credible alternative to the democratic model, as discussed by Di Palma in his chapter, was strengthened by the influence on these new democracies of the West European states.

Hence, the lack of any real historical parallel with the 1930s allows one to conclude that the 'bad luck' theory has been vindicated, for during the last decade democratic forces in the three countries have been able to count on a sounder international environment compared with the earlier period in order to move relatively peacefully from dictatorship to democracy.

NOTES

1. See OECD, *Main Economic Indicators*, Paris, OECD, various issues; and *World Bank Atlas*, Washington, various issues.
2. See V. Curzon, *The Essentials of Economic Integration*, (London: Macmillan (for the Trade Policy Research Centre), 1974).
3. See A. Tovias, *Tariff Preferences in Mediterranean Diplomacy* (London: Macmillan (for the Trade Policy Research Centre), 1977), p. 71.
4. J. W. Schneider (ed.), *From Nine to Twelve: Europe's Destiny* (Alphen, Sijthoff and Noordhoff, 1980), p. 121.
5. See N. Van Praag, 'European Political Co-operation and the Southern Periphery' in *The Mediterranean Challenge: I* (Brighton, Sussex: European Papers No. 2, 1978), p. 78.
6. One can find the same kind of western response in the case of Turkey.
7. The failure was much more significant than the one of the Spanish army in the Sahara at the end of 1975, since the Sahara was not in the backyard of Spain, as Cyprus and Turkey are in relation to Greece. Turkey is omnipresent in Greeks' minds.
8. G. Minet *et al., Spain, Greece and Community Politics* (Brighton, Sussex: European Research Centre, 1981), p. 112.
9. Ibid., pp. 100–3, and pp. 134–5.

10. L. Tsoukalis, *The European Community and its Mediterranean Enlargement* (London: G. Allen and Unwin, 1981), p. 83.
11. Greece applied for membership in the EEC in June 1975, while Portugal and Spain applied respectively in March and in June 1977.
12. See G. Minet *et al., op. cit.*, p. 4.
13. On this point, see Tsoukalis, op. cit., pp. 115–21.
14. A. Tovias, 'The Effects of the Second Enlargement of the European Community upon Israel's Economy' in E. Gutmann (ed.), *Israel and the Second Enlargement of the European Community: Political and Economic Aspects* (Jerusalem: The Hebrew University, 1984).
15. On this and related subjects, see J. Aguirre *et al., España Año Cero* (Madrid: Espasa-Calpe, 1982) and J. Donges *et al., The Second Enlargement of the European Community* (Tübingen; JCB Mohr (Paul Siebeck), 1982).
16. The GDP (evaluated at 1975 prices and exchange rates) decreased by 0.6 per cent in 1981 (OECD, *Main Economic Indicators*, April 1983). The crisis was particularly felt in the first five months of 1981, when output of manufacturing industries fell by 3.2 per cent (*Quarterly Economic Review of Greece*, 4th Quarter 1981, The Economist Intelligence Unit).
17. *The Economist*, 2 April 1983 and 23 July 1983.
18. On the Aegean dispute, see G. Rosenthal, *The Mediterranean Basin, Its Political Economy and Changing International Relations* (London: Butterworths Scientific, 1982).
19. *International Herald Tribune*, 3 October 1983, p. 7.
20. For example, the idea that Gibraltar could became a NATO base once Spain is in and therefore blur the issue of sovereignty; or that in the event of an attack on the Canary Islands, Ceuta or Melilla by some African country, Spain could count on NATO's help. The latter is an unproven assumption, since the Alliance covers Europe and not Africa, while Gibraltar has never been so high in the Spanish agenda after 1975 as to make of it a reason to enter NATO.
21. Commission of the European Communities, *The European Economy*, Supplement A, No. 8–9 (August-September 1983).
22. G. de la Dehesa, 'Perspectivas a medio plazo del endeudamiento exterior de España', Paper presented at the VIIth IEA Congress, Madrid, September 1983, p. 19.

Government Performance:
An Issue and Three Cases in Search of Theory

Giuseppe Di Palma

> A people who were not in conflict about some rather fundamental matters would have little need to devise democracy's elaborate rules for conflict resolution.
>
> Dankwart Rustow[1]

This essay is not a full account of the relative performance of the new democratic governments of southern Europe. Since the proper evaluation of performance and its correlates – especially when it comes to new democracies – seems to me to be still very much at issue, this essay is rather a critical exploration of this question with examples drawn from the region.

Is there something especially difficult about government performance in new democracies, something debilitating in their newness? To support this view there is as a minimum the double notion that new democracies are born with a legitimacy problem and that effective performance is closely connected with legitimacy. Democracy – so goes the argument – is an inherently incohesive system of government; it is a system of compromise, a set of rules for mediating plural and competing interests, to which a country takes poorly after the inevitable trauma of authoritarian or totalitarian demise. For one thing, resentment against democracy builds among those leaders and supporters of the old regime who have lost benefits, power or more, as a consequence of its demise. For another, there are many who do not subscribe to democracy as a system of government, irrespective of personal costs or benefits. These principled opponents are to be found not only among the loyalists of the past regime but also among those who fought it hoping to replace it with their own brand of totalitarianism/authoritarianism. But democracy cannot rely on force and repression alone to resist its opponents without imperilling its authenticity. In fact the use of force, even when needed to save democracy, may end up by alienating whatever democratic support there exists. How then can a new democracy consolidate itself if it can only rely on competitive means – means that its opponents shun and its practitioners plainly cannot practise? Immobilism and indecisiveness in a vast area of crucial policy issues seem natural outcomes of this predicament, feeding in turn on to illegitimacy.

Given the predicament, the successful redemocratisation of West Germany (or for that matter postwar Japan) and the widely acclaimed effectiveness of their governments have been seen as fully exceptional cases, in which the decisive but exogenous factors that tilted the scale in favour of democracy are taken to be prolonged Allied occupation and carefully staged political reconstruction under close supervision by the occupying powers. At the same time, the clearest examples, and somehow the rule, when it comes to the plight of new democracies have been taken to be Italy and France; two countries that rebuilt democracy with little if any foreign supervision and little if any restraint upon domestic centrifugal forces. Thus, not for anything, Italy is still regarded as Europe's permanently sick democracy, and in France the Fourth Republic lasted only thirteen years.

Without fully discounting this line of analysis and its bearing on the particular cases, I propose a second look. Exactly because, I will argue, transferring allegiance, support and loyalty to a new regime is largely a matter of calculus and interest, it is not inescapably true that new democracies suffer from a problem of legitimacy – on the contrary. And though in a new and untried democracy, born naturally through and into conflict, problems of government performance *seem* aplenty, neither is it necessarily true that any such problem hides one of legitimacy and/or will feed negatively on to legitimacy – even if we understand the latter as a fact of calculus and interest. In a competitive democracy, new or old, government performance is always at issue. But whether the issue is or becomes unmanageable, leaving governments without space for choice and manoeuvre, depends on how the problem of legitimacy has been resolved to begin with. All of which, I will also argue, points to a sturdier view of new democracies overall; though, within this view, significant differences exist between the three southern European cases at hand – Spain, Portugal and Greece.

Dankwart Rustow wrote in 1970 that, for the historical record, democracies have been born nearly always as nothing more than a compromise. The compromise brought together forces who were or could be engaged in an otherwise inconclusive struggle for regime supremacy, and served therefore to terminate or forestall political confrontation. Rustow's remarks have two interesting and promising implications for new democracies – especially those which, like ours, return for the second time to democracy after a dictatorial interlude. First, 'genuine' democrats need not pre-exist democracy, and in point of fact they rarely do so in any substantial numbers. Second, being a means for reconciliation, the democratic compromise need not be more than a second best for the parties that negotiate it.[2] In other words, the rules of the democratic game are more a matter of instrumental agreement worked out among competing leaderships and institutions, *which accept to remain competitive within the new agreement*, than one of pre-existing popular or elite consensus on fundamentals. This much is forcefully implied in the quote from Rustow with which I open this paper. Therefore the transfer of allegiance from dictatorship to democracy, though always difficult, does not require exceptionally favourable circumstances, and the viability of a new democracy rests ultimately in making the transfer, if at all possible, attractive, convenient or compelling. It is to what make the transfer finally attractive, convenient or compelling though initially difficult that I now turn my attention.

TRANSFERRING ALLEGIANCE TO DEMOCRACY

I will leave out of my analysis those rare and intellectually less absorbing cases in which the transfer of allegiance is made almost inescapable by objective circumstances;[3] I will instead concentrate on those cases in which calculus, choice and leadership prove more decisive, as well as challenging and difficult. I suggest two sources of challenge.

In the first place, short of a holocaust brought upon the dictatorship by its own wars, it is unlikely that its crisis is so total as to leave a perfect vacuum of interests, organisations and allegiances in which a new democracy can safely step. Even if a dictatorship were to be overthrown by a revolt of its domestic enemies and nothing else – an unlikely occurrence, since either the dictatorship has a monopoly of force or it is already coming apart internally – it is most improbable that armed victory can cancel and reverse in one stroke the legacy that the dictatorship has left in the institutions and in the minds of people. The job begins, rather than ending, with armed victory. This is the more true if – as in our countries – to be overthrown is in fact an authoritarian rather than a totalitarian dictatorship; that is, a dictatorship that does not exercise command through newfangled and ruthless institutions of its own but makes do by penetrating and co-opting the existing structures and institutions (armies, bureaucracies, regular courts, conservative economic interests . . .). And it is even truer if the authoritarian regime, instead of falling in one piece at the hand of its enemies, falls apart because of internal exhaustion. Indeed, this seems to me the way in which authoritarian regimes go down most of the time: without having done anything so irreparably wrong to doom themselves unequivocally, they become, by the nature of their closed system, sluggish, inefficient, unable to adjust to changing times, irrelevant; or by liberalising they trigger higher expectations; or they substantially alter the place that some of their organised constituencies (most dangerously, the army) occupy in the regime; or worst of all, they show inability to accommodate the crisis of confidence that typically accompanies the death or incapacitation of the first dictator. It is in response to any combination of these circumstances that forces that are part of the coalitions supporting or running a dictatorship may come to consider it as finally expendable and disposable and may be tempted to secede.[4] Whether it is a matter of values and beliefs or one of self-interest, allegiance to dictatorship is not eternal and locked in. In all these cases of dictatorial crises, from revolution to secession, the challenge for the democratic forces is largely similar: since old interests have not disappeared into thin air, but may also be tempted to transfer allegiance, how can a new democracy accommodate them in the new compromise while removing those structures, through which the interests operated, that are incompatible with political democracy?

The challenge just described accurately depicts the predicament of our three southern European countries. Though there are interesting differences between them as to the precise status of the challenge – differences which will be of relevance later – what is important to stress at this point is the underlying commonality. In none of the countries did the transition make a clean slate of the past, except in its specific institutional forms. In all cases therefore the question of democratic legitimacy hinged on the treatment of the authoritarian past.

But this is only the first challenge. The second challenge does not come from inside the authoritarian regime. In countries like ours, which experienced a liberal or outright democratic period before the dictatorship, it comes from the fact that the various social and political forces called to set up the institutions of the reborn democracy tend to draw different lessons from the failure of the first competitive experiment. Of major importance is the fact that the left, even when recognising its own mistakes at the time (sectarianism, internal dissension, excessive self-confidence) puts less emphasis than the moderate and conservative forces on the past excesses of unbridled parliamentarism. Rather, it tends to blame the old parliamentary system for having been socially backward, elitist, insufficiently democratic, wavering in the face of the authoritarian threat, or even hiding and abetting already existing authoritarian practices. Therefore a new democracy that wants to aid the conversion of the authoritarian right is compelled, because of this, to be especially sensitive to the left's concerns as well – lest it appear to be a democracy as narrow as the old. For example, measures that could be taken to rationalise political democracy by rationalising the party system, parliamentarism, the electoral process, executive powers and management of class conflict may be regarded by the left as tampering with its freedom of action in particular. The challenge to democratic leadership stemming from the concerns of the left is the more significant as, short of the catastrophic obliteration of totalitarianism that brings disgrace upon *any* extremism and advises moderation instead, any other resumption of democracy is likely to witness the emergence in full of a potentially extremist or 'maximalist' left.

The double challenge which I just described indicates that all sorts of coalitions of dissent from dictatorship take shape during the transition. They involve the traditional enemies of the dictatorship, themselves minimally divided on whether their aspirations are democratic, uncertain or clearly non-democratic. They also involve forces seceding from the dictatorship yet (since secession is not necessarily toward democracy) similarly divided on their aspirations. The point is to transform these essentially negative, uncertain, shifting and even conflicting coalitions into one coalition of consent for democracy. Though the transformation is by no means a sure thing, democracy has some trump cards to play.

The best trump card is actually what we often consider to be democracy's weakness. It is exactly because democracy is a system of compromise, it is exactly because of its openness and open-endedness, because its game is never final, because nobody loses once and for all and on all arenas, that under certain circumstances the democratic game may finally appear attractive, convenient or compelling even to its detractors – be they loyalists or enemies of the old dictatorship. In other words, a coalition of consent for democracy can rely upon and draw strength from a moderate compromise: a compromise that attracts as wide a spectrum of opponents as well as former loyalists of the dictatorship, leaving out if necessary only a few weakened dissenters.

MATERIAL AND REGULATORY-INSTITUTIONAL BASES OF THE TRANSFER

Naturally, however, this type of compromise must rest in turn – and can in fact rest by the nature of democracy – on material bases. There are basically three such bases, three also being the key constituencies whose consent to democracy must be secured:

1. Since we are talking of capitalist democracies, there must be collective consent to the reproduction of capital. Though the matter seems obvious, this requires less obviously avoiding policies of democratic reconstruction designed to hamper significantly capital's capacity to accumulate and invest or, worse, designed to punish capitalists collectively for their real or alleged class role in the advent and running of the dictatorship.[5]
2. Similarly, most of the state institutions that served the authoritarian regime (army, bureaucracy) are meant to serve democracy as well. Therefore, in order to secure such service, their internal self-rule may have to be preserved. Otherwise said, in the transition to democracy policies should be avoided that can be construed as retroactive punishment of the state institutions' personnel *as a class*, rather than as necessary removal of legal features added by the dictatorship or as well-meant reforms. And reforms should come to terms with the preservation of internal self-rule and the institutions' involvement in those reforms.
3. Crucial to this first part of the compromise is the consent of the left. But how to secure its consent, and possibly even its participation in promoting the compromise? The answer is that the left in turn must be secured ample space for democratic action in the party, electoral, parliamentary and labour arenas. Sooner or later, in other words, it must feel in the legitimate position to weigh publicly and contractually in the stimulation, allocation and social uses of privately produced wealth. I should add that this strategy of co-optation of the left, if successfully executed, may even attract to the democratic game a left that is potentially extremist by label or advocacy if not by deeds.

Though I have referred to the three parameters of the compromise as material, to convey readily the idea that there must be tangible incentives, it should be clear that the compromise is not about a fixed distribution of corporate spoils: it does not and cannot guarantee ahead of time exactly how often, how much and when each actor will win or lose. The point is of importance to understand what constitutes democratic legitimacy and how it relates to democracy's authoritative performance. To be sure, each of the three social and state formations aspires to a corporate voice, resources and rewards of its own. And these aspirations the democratic compromise recognises. Still, within the parameters just described the compromise is really about a competitive political market. More precisely, it is about what Adam Przeworski calls uncertainty[6]– the shared uncertainty of political outcomes that naturally results from a competitive market with multiple arenas, in which politico/institutional and societal positions of relevance for outcomes are deployed in dispersed and countervailing fashion. In other words, the compromise is not about results but about a set of rules of the game: norms, procedures and institutions whose operation will probabilistically and therefore only uncertainly effect a fair balance of winning and losing. This is all that democracy can at best offer those who enter the compromise. Conflict, as Rustow's opening quote implies, will remain – except on the rules themselves. But this is an important point. If rule agreement is reached, its institutional nature and the very knowledge that each institution will impinge on outcomes only partially and probabilistically mean that the agreement, by allowing substantial leeway on actual performance to come, has a span of endurance. It means that democratic legitimacy does not rest on a specific set of policies, on delivery, on performance, but rests precisely (and more safely) on rule agreement.[7]

To be sure, the agreement is instrumental, a means to an end; and political actors, even when they consent to sharing losses and victories and are reassured that the sum-total of the game is positive, will try to bend both means and ends in their favour. Therefore, agreement on rules will be implicitly tested against performance and may at times require renegotiation if, for reasons having to do with the rules' actual performance or their changing environment, performance falls eventually outside a tolerable range of expected outcomes. In sum, it would be wrong to think that political actors who manage to reach and maintain rule agreement do it in a peaceful, orderly and undramatic manner. On the contrary, hammering out the agreement and keeping it in place will naturally be accompanied by confrontation, tension and animosity – a target of which is performance itself.

Yet a crisis of legitimacy stemming from the latter remains an unlikely occurrence, given the range of performance which rule agreement tolerates. Thinking of the corporate interests and aspirations of the main social and state formations discussed above, it can be said that as long as the rules of the democratic game seem designed to protect mutually those interests and aspirations, each formation will still be capable of adapting to variance in performance that – either by policy choice or exogenous circumstances – affects the formation negatively. Also, a democratic government that can rely on rule agreement will feel more comfortable about pursuing partisan majority policies over the possible objections of the opposition and about exercising in effect its 'market supremacy', without fearing that it violates mutually expected outcomes. In simple terms, government performance will gain from rule agreement.

TRANSFERRING ALLEGIANCE IN THE EUROPEAN HISTORICAL AND INSTITUTIONAL CONTEXT

If we bear in mind all the above, we should be able to keep the drama that marks every democratic transition and consolidation – irrespective, in my view, of final accomplishments – separate from those accomplishments. But have we always been so capable? In assessing the events of Greece, Portugal and Spain we seem to have been victims, especially in the first and more uncertain phase of their transitions, of dire historical memories and cultural-geographical preconceptions. In at least two of the cases, and in some way all of them, I will argue that we have given excessive substance to drama, for those dire historical memories seem actually to have worked to deny their own prophecy. We have hence attributed problems of performance that have other causes to a crisis of legitimacy, exaggerated such problems or made them too close a harbinger of such crisis.

Certainly, a scenario in which drama and substance do coincide is not at all unthinkable. It is a scenario that speaks against the three-pronged democratic compromise I outlined above. It has been presented in paradigmatic form by Guillermo O'Donnell with Latin America and the crisis of bureaucratic authoritarianism as referents, but I can cast it as well in terms of the southern European *problématique* of the seventies.[8] The point however is that – as I will show in a moment – the scenario is not necessary. The scenario starts, as O'Donnell sets it up, with the full revival of civil society in its old as well as new economic, social and cultural components. The new components – which find expression through *movimientos de base, groupuscules, asociaciones vecinales* and similar – are themselves the product of the new culture of demands and autonomous participation of the seventies and are therefore not limited to aspiring democracies. However, by combining with the inevitable post-dictatorial escalation of long-suppressed labour and economic demands by workers and various sectors of the middle classes, they can mobilise strata of society ranging from the latter to previously unorganised and marginal urban poor. A climate of apparent disorder, unruliness and anarchy will ensue, triggering actual fears among sectors of the bourgeoisie and the state. If we combine the new mobilisation, the fears and the general economic weakness of the region (whether southern Europe or Latin America) especially visible in the seventies, it is not difficult to forecast inflation, unemployment, state deficits, disinvestments, flights of capital and balance of payment problems.

This, however, is as far as the scenario will inescapably travel. Whether it will escalate into an economic crisis of major proportions, continues O'Donnell, and into a crisis of legitimacy, I would add, depends on something else. It depends above all on the role of the politically organised left and its relation with civil society. A left that is maximalist in its economic and political demands, bent perhaps on purging the elements of the old regime, and perhaps even in control of the transition, will end up by threatening capital's capacity for reproduction as well as the state's need for order and self-rule. Being as uncertain as they are historically about their strength and hegemony, and being therefore not alien from repression, sectors of the regional bourgeoisie or more so of the state will likely react with *contragolpismo,* thus bringing the initial steps of the scenario to their 'logical' conclusions.

But another type of left can also be envisioned. A left that understands the threat of *contragolpismo,* and can also afford to act with greater caution without imperilling, or thinking of imperilling its future role; a left that can subscribe to the following words by a member of the executive committee of the Spanish Socialist Party: 'Democracy and its consolidation come first, before our political programs ... because the Spanish right has shown that it can live very well under both authoritarian and democratic regimes, while the left can only survive within a democratic framework.'[9] A left, in sum, that understands how the right is perfectly capable of living in a democracy, but will not do so without institutional guarantees and cannot otherwise be easily routed. This does not require that the initiative for a democratic compromise should come from the left (it can as well come from the right), but it does require that the compromise rest largely on the participation – because of attraction, convenience or compulsion – of the left.

In view of the quote above, my claim that such a left (and a similarly accommodating right) have evolved in southern Europe will not come as a surprise to the reader. Indeed, the generalisations I have been presenting originate in a reflection on the southern European redemocratisations of the seventies. They best fit the Spanish case. They are not far removed from the Greek one. And they will only need some firm amendments when we come to Portugal.[10]

The question I am now ready to address is why the social and state formations of these three countries came to accept the democratic compromise. With individual amendments to be introduced when necessary, the answer applies as well to all European cases of redemocratisation following the Second World War. It begins by recognising something special in the European experience of redemocratisation. What is special is that, in replacing fascist or pseudo-fascist dictatorships, European countries could count on reviving or recycling for democracy a series of political and state institutions with a long historical tradition of their own – longer in fact than the life-span of any particular regime and predating dictatorship. Some of these institutions (political parties, unions and lay organisations of the Church) may have gone underground under the dictatorship; yet they never disappeared. Others may have served the dictatorship (bureaucracies, armies, judiciaries, business associations); yet they never became coterminous with it, never defined or were defined by it, and were possibly shunted aside by new and specifically totalitarian institutions (single parties, corporatist syndicates, special tribunals, party militias, secret police). It is true that in some cases (the army in Spain) the state apparatus or parts of it installed and ran the dictatorship. But what is important to remember is that in such cases the dictatorship emphasised depoliticisation and demobilisation, while the state apparatus still presented itself as the historical and impartial guarantor of domestic law and order. All of which confirms the fact that in Europe the state apparatus has always been concerned (not always successfully) with protecting its impersonal, non-political, legal-professional status. Exactly the type of status which democracy can also guarantee.

This institutional weight of the past (and a past that had been liberal and even democratic) has been in my opinion at least necessary in making European returns to competitive politics successful. In the first place, it helped state institutions placed at the service of dictatorship to secede, as a first step toward reaffirming their legal-professional autonomy within the state. In the second place, of all possible outcomes of the crisis the institutional weight of the past favoured democracy *tout court*, over another dictatorship or some 'guided' democracy. One consistent aspect of the various crises of dictatorship in Europe has been the prompt re-emergence of political parties and party allegiances, even after decades of interruption of competitive politics. But this re-emergence has been possible exactly and only because each of the two key European social formations – the bourgeoisie and the working class – had party traditions to return to and with which to vie within the crisis. In turn, once and because these traditions were revived, it made much less difference what the 'natural and instinctive' regime affinities of those social formations might have been. What became instead of paramount importance was the preservation and consolidation of the party-political space of each social formation, in a political arena that proved immediately to be highly competitive.

Thus, once the crisis of a European dictatorship was under way, the country's institutions and social formations, each with their own coveted spheres of autonomy and social presence, were sooner or later compelled toward coexistence. They were compelled by the very weight of their diversity and co-presence, and so as to avoid the prospect of a dragged-out and inconclusive fight. That is why they ended up by accepting exactly the three-pronged moderate institutional compromise which is at the heart of democracy. In addition, the international economic context of stagflation, industrial adjustment and global re-equilibration within which the transition of the seventies occurred also spurred those compromises by giving them a specific content, compelling in its own terms. It decisively tilted the compromises toward a self-imposed deferral of labour's economic demands – without however ruling out (quite on the contrary) governments of the left in the near future.

THE CASE OF SOUTHERN EUROPE

I have presented democracy as a method, an institutional set-up for conducting a competitive game which, exactly because it is competitive, is not called to secure any specific set of policies. Thinking of democracy otherwise, and trying in fact to define and achieve democracy exclusively by radical policies that are 'socially advanced and popularly orientated' either backfires or leads to forms of guided or organic democracy that differ little in methods from the authoritarian regime they replace. Conflict involving these two antagonistic conceptions of democracy, between and within the army and the political parties is what made the first steps of Portuguese democracy so perilous, at least when compared with the other two countries. In view of the model of European transitions presented above, there are no simple explanations for the conflict, but the role of the army is of special importance. To begin with, the fall of the dictatorship came through an easy and bloodless army coup inside a wavering and backward regime, militarily in serious trouble. Mistaken for a popular revolution, the coup created a feeling of dangerous elation among the victors as to the radical transformations that the revolution, guided by an organised army, should and could legitimately bring about in the apparent vacuum of power and interests suddenly left by the dictatorship. Further, opposition to what appeared to be taking quickly the features of a guided democracy came not only from the civilian parties but from within the rebellious army itself; something which made the initial resolution of the conflict less a matter of negotiations and more one of showdowns. It could be said that all three minimum ingredients for a democratic compromise were violated at the time – including the third one, given the constraints imposed by the military-civilian extreme left on the democratically orientated and dominant Socialist Party. Nevertheless even in Portugal a gradual rerouting of the transition toward a workable democratic compromise has been possible. It took the victory of the electoral over the guidance principle in 1975–6, the eventual emergence (of all things) of a dominant centre-right government coalition in 1979, and the recent repeal of the guidance features contained in the 1976 constitution, with the preservation at the same time of some of the social reforms that give space to a democratic left.

By comparison with Portugal, the return to democracy in Spain was instead characterised by a much greater attention to the problem of easing the transfer of allegiance and accommodating vastly different constituencies. The example of Spain in this regard is almost paradigmatic, in view of the fact that the death of Franco left a regime otherwise entrenched, mildly liberalised in politics and with an expanded economy purposely integrated into that of western Europe. Since that death was not the kind of event that necessitates dictatorial collapse, any pressure for significant change could have lead, as anticipated at the time, to a showdown and a bitter outcome no matter what. But perhaps the secret of Spain's success, and what puts into question the conventional view that allegiances cannot be transferred, is the very fact that the transition to democracy was initiated and lead throughout by legitimate heirs of the dictator. This, plus the fact that this leadership made it a point of skilfully using the constititional means offered by the dictatorship itself to achieve the explicit aim of full electoral competition, forestalled, co-opted and even transformed two likely sources of dissent: dissent from the unrepented nostalgics of the dictator, and dissent from those opponents of the same who were entitled to suspect a transition guided of all by *los de siempre*. The success of this strategy has allowed what I have elsewhere called a mutual 'backward and forward' legitimation easing the convergence of allegiances on the new democracy.[11] But, to repeat, the very fact that past and present co-existed in the transition demanded the respect of the three minimum components of the democratic compromise: a capitalist economy and economic culture, the rehabilitation of the old state institutions, and a social democratic political culture likely to govern in the foreseeable future.

The Greek transition to democracy presented some features in its early stages that, without in any way approaching in seriousness those of Portugal, raised some questions about the evolution of the democratic compromise in that country. However, those questions have not withstood the test of time. The original picture was mixed. For a variety of reasons which I examined elsewhere, [12] and which placed the nostalgic right (and the left) in a weaker position at the transition, prime minister Karamanlis was able to implement on his own a plan to authenticate and extend the new democratic order that is without precedent in modern Greek history (rejection of the monarchy by overwhelming popular vote, trial of junta leaders but not of the army, freedom of action for the communist parties ...). At the same time, however, though the Greek transition did not show the conflict between opposite transitional strategies so typical of Portugal in 1974–5, it did not adopt Spain's explicit *politica de consenso* either. Instead, the same conditions that allowed a swift authentication of the democratic order also allowed Karamanlis to leave the left opposition, in particular PASOK, out of the constitutional process and to implement a 'gaullist' constitution whose aim appeared to be the perpetuation of his party's rule. In effect, not only has that monopoly over time proven quite ephemeral; more important, PASOK'S successful response to the constrictions of the gaullist model has not been one of progressive polarisation and centrifugation but one of convergence toward the centre in images and appeals. In pursuing convergence, PASOK never raised any question about the enduring appropriateness of Karamanlis' constitutional set-up,[13] never repudiated as lenient the already firm conditions under which the nostalgic right and compromised state institutions had been allowed to partake of the democratic compromise, and considerably diluted its much touted and strident Third World socialism.[14]

ON THE FINAL QUESTION OF PERFORMANCE

There is now the problem, to return to the theme of this paper, of fitting this sturdier picture of southern European democracies with the palpable evidence of poor performance, especially in the economic sphere, not just of Portugal – as one might expect from the above – but of all three countries. But is it really a problem? So far I have mainly argued forward, from legitimacy to performance. I will now argue in reverse, starting from performance.

In the first place, it is incorrect to equate economic performance specifically with government performance. Economic performance refers generically to how well the economy of a country is doing, its actual health. Indeed, its typical indicators (especially in analyses of southern Europe) are in the form of aggregate statistics – rate of inflation and unemployment, balance of payments, budgetary outlays and deficits, GNP, money supplies, investments, prime rates .... In sum, the evidence really points to what in policy analysis are called outcomes. And policy analysis reveals that outcomes have no clear connection with what analysts mean by government performance, i.e. policies instituted by governments with a given intent in mind. A recent assessment of comparative policy studies sums up the case as follows:

> Often budgetary outlays and assumed performance variables, such as income, education or health levels were used as the dependent variables. Not only were such variables relatively crude indicators of the concepts of policy process and outcomes, but their use involved a chain of casual inferences of questionable merit. As the growing literature on policy implementation suggests, it is often difficult to assume that budgetary expenditures reflect changes in policy, that such expenditures then are actually turned into effectively implemented programs, and that these programs in turn achieve the expected results. Each link in this chain ought to be examined before we conclude that a regime has failed or succeeded in reallocating resources and in affecting income, health or education levels.[15]

In sum, while policies have consequences that deserve study, starting from outcomes leaves the matter unanswered. Yet most of the studies of policy performance abroad, in particular the studies of our three new democracies, are narrowly focused on the outcomes of a yet unchartered implementation process.[16]

In the second place, if we cannot equate economic performance with government performance specifically, much less can we infer that problems of performance stem from the fact that the governments we are dealing with are democratic and new. Indeed, even if we were to take for proven that poor performance reflects a problem of governance, it does not follow that the problem is connected with democraticity and newness. For one thing, problems of governance in the economic sphere (assuming that they are such) are nowadays shared by almost all western societies, some of them (Latin America) not at all democratic. For another, though it is true that the question of economic performance is particularly acute in our countries, we cannot overlook the fact that what is specific to these countries is not only the novelty of their democratic governments but also the fact that these governments have inherited particularly weak economies, further weakened by readjustments in the international economic order. Could the old authoritarian governments or more consolidated democracies have done better? Alternatively, though the problems of governance may be general, could the reasons be specific to each type of regime? I am not ruling out any of these possibilities, but at the level at which performance has been studied in our countries we are not equipped to test them.

It may be true that democratic government performance cannot be assessed by objective means-end criteria of the type implicit above, but rather by criteria of public expectations – performance thus being in the eyes of the beholder. But this still would not make our countries a clear case of poor performance, closely connected with regime legitimacy. We can readily recognise that when it comes to public reactions to governance it does not always matter whether or not specific governments are actually responsible for economic outcomes. I have already implied that, as part of the natural drama of new democracies all sorts of accusations can be laid down against their governments and their policies. They come not only from residual nostalgics but also from disappointed democrats of all shades, as well as from oppositions drumming up electoral support and not at all alien in the process from charging the government with mismanagement of the transition. Greece, Portugal, and Spain are certainly no exception to the pattern. Given the particular temper of the seventies, what has been consistently at issue in the accusations of the opposition has been economic performance – whether the betrayal by the Spanish *Centro Democratico* of its early social democratic promises, or the economic chaos brought about in Portugal by the policies of nationalisation and agrarian reform adopted by the military/left coalitions, or the unwillingness of the Greek *Nea Democratia* to free the economy of the country from the spiral of dependency.

However, if we choose the criterion of public expectations we obviously cannot equate each and all policy dissatisfaction with poor performance. Since it is in the nature of a competitive democracy that some interests lose some of the time, every democratic government by that criterion would perform 'poorly'.[17] Hence we must recognise that, despite overt political language often to the contrary, what is at issue is broader and more difficult to assess than concrete demand satisfaction. Government decisions emerge out of a process of aggregation, elimination, reformulation, deferment, give-and-take and the conflict that often surrounds the process is not only about which demands should be entertained, which decisions should be made, which deferred, but also about how the process should be conducted, what role the contestants in and out of government should have, what symbolic or tangible side rewards the losers should reap.[18] In other words, the outcome of the process – decisions – will not be evaluated by the affected parties in the light of immediate demand satisfaction alone but in the light of a more distant and aleatory, as well as more encompassing calculus of reciprocal and prospective gains and losses. Within this calculus the criterion of individual demand satisfaction becomes a criterion of mutual decisional equity. And since equity can only be safeguarded (and only probabilistically) by a set of agreed-upon decisional rules, this discussion takes us back to my earlier discussion of the democratic compromise and the rules of the game.

There, I wrote that the presence of rule agreement allows governments a degree of decisional leeway and choice, without fearing violation of the democratic compromise. I now propose more precisely that if we assess democratic government performance in the light of public opinion and societal interests – a sensible criterion in view of the fact that democratic performance seems to be very much in the eyes of the beholder – then the least elusive and most generalisable if indirect way of assessing whether performance is satisfactory/equitable and therefore generally free of conflict-generated political constraints is to see whether or not there exists agreement on the rule for democratic decision among those actors who could otherwise stalemate governance.

I have already argued that, with the partial exception of Portugal, our three countries have developed rule agreement in the transition. We can now point to evidence that the agreement endures past the transition. One democratic decisional rule, in fact the classical one as well as the simplest, but also the one that a difficult democracy can least afford, is the rule of alternating majorities. Clear-cut changes in government have recently occurred in all three countries – in 1981 in Greece, in 1982 in Spain, and in 1979 and 1983 in Portugal. The historical importance of these changes is double. Other contributors to this issue rightly stress the historical novelty of socialist governments, and in all three countries contemporaneously. I would like to stress another aspect: major government changes of the type that have taken place in our countries are a good test of whether rule agreement and the democratic compromise that the rules are supposed to sustain are really holding up. Despite the electoral rhetoric and the fact that the oppositions have not been averse to accusing previous governments of mismanaging the transition, the victory of the oppositions has not set in motion a process of reciprocal delegitimation, a coming apart of original agreements and therefore a crisis of regime legitimacy. Nor has the coming into power of socialist governments led to a flurry of radical policies. On the contrary, early rhetoric notwithstanding (the case of Papandreou's PASOK being by far the most glaring), the basic policies of the socialist governments, especially in the economic sphere, are above all remarkable for the fact of differing only incrementally and sectorally from those of their predecessors.

One way of looking at this convergence is to say that the reality of the domestic and international economies of the seventies has undercut the socialists' room for manoeuvre, and since the socialists do not seem to be appreciably better at curing the economy, this speaks poorly for the viability of our young democracies. I prefer to remind the reader that the fact that alternating governments are not bent on undoing each other's work is exactly what makes the rule of alternance acceptable – and the advantage is the greater in view of the poor or poorly understood fit between government policies and economic outcomes anyway. Otherwise, alternance could threaten the expectations that are built in the democratic compromise. It may be true that the capitalist reality of the seventies has locked our countries in a conservative version of the compromise, and one may wish a more innovative democratic model for the future of these countries. But though such conservative compromise and the limited room for manoeuvre it leaves may feed *desencanto* with democracy, the political risks of forcing a substantial alteration in the terms of the compromise may be considerable, while the policy results may be ironically meagre or downright perverse.

Awareness of these risks may be another reason why the socialist governments of southern Europe have chosen to distinguish themselves less for their economic policies and more for their stand on moral, civic and symbolic issues, as well as on foreign and international affairs. But here as well much is a matter of image more than policies. Moral and civic issues have been historically employed by the southern European left as an avenue for social regeneration and for striking at collective class, religious and institutional enemies. The reforms of the leftist governments during the Second Spanish Republic are just one example. But the socialist governments of the eighties seem decidedly more guarded on these matters. Much of the moralisation has not taken the form of policies, but remains at the level of expressive gestures. As well, governments have avoided using civic reforms for the purpose of frontally attacking specific groups and institutions – usually connected with the old regime.

Similarly, it is at least an overstatement to say that foreign and international affairs have been used as an area for socialist distinctiveness. In Greece the greater international assertiveness of Papandreou's government – again more often a matter of gestures and declarations than one of actual policies – has actually found sympathetic ears among more conservative groups and state institutions, and can also be seen as a strategy of consensus and party legitimation within the democratic framework. In Portugal foreign and international affairs do not seem, in fact, to be among the most salient government concerns. Only in Spain do they seem to be more divisive, but only by comparison with the other two countries – and at any rate, always in a context within which the socialist government does not distinguish itself for programmatic determination. Again, here too the limited margins for manoeuvre by domestic governments may well reflect the international constraints of the day. But the unwillingness of socialist governments to challenge those constraints in ways that can be resented domestically represents also a choice, and one of significance in the maintenance of a smooth rule of alternance.

CONCLUSIONS

There is no denying that the young democracies of southern Europe were born and will continue to function in an era in which problem solving is very much in demand. There is also no reason to believe that they are behaving any differently at problem solving than other western societies i.e. poorly. Nor is it surprising that their governments, being new and untried, as well as saddled with particularly weak economies and the re-emergence of demanding civil societies, are being held responsible, correctly or incorrectly, for failures at problem solving. The thrust of my paper has been a cautionary one. Before drawing dire inferences we should reflect on a point made by Dankwart Rustow: the democratic game, once the initial momentum is set, rewards those who play it; and even those who come to play it out of *force majeure* rather than conviction may find their decision more palatable once they begin to live with it.[19] The fact that the game is competitive, rough, conflictive and even a source of *desencanto* does not subtract from the fact that it is shared. It takes more to dislodge agreement once it is set. Even in Portugal, where the search for agreement has been protracted and difficult, it appears that the threshold has finally been past.

Besides, when it comes to transitions, crises and the like the very fact that loyalties are a relative matter also means that they are not likely to be transferred or simply withheld unless some other game is available. But a return to an authoritarian game, only years after it has shown itself unable to satisfy its own supporters, seems a remote possibility.

Of course, we may be wrong and events may overtake us. Crises and transitions are set in motion and evolve by a concatenation of events; the probable effect of each one on the next escapes social scientists at this stage of their arts. But this is not the point. The point is more simply to recognise the type of events and circumstances that are more likely to set the stage for a crisis (without determining its evolution). Since they must have something to do with the dislodging of rule agreement, I venture to say that the type of policy problems our new democracies suffer from do not, even in the context of newness, quite fit the bill.

NOTES

1. Dankwart Rustow, 'Transitions to Democracy,' *Comparative Politics*, Vol. 2, No.3 (April 1970), p.362.
2. Ibid., p.357.
3. I am thinking of cases such as the fall of Nazism, and possibly Imperial Japan. Nazism's total defeat in a war designed to secure the thousand-year Reich could not but leave an utter organisational and power vacuum, a final sense of apocalyptic and self-induced failure, and an ingrained fear of any new totalitarian experiment. Without overlooking the very important role played by Allied and German leadership in guiding and rationalising democratic reconstruction, it could thus be said that – once West Germany had been made geopolitically safe from the Soviet Union – choice and leadership in the transition overdetermined the final result. In West Germany there was no question of allegiance to anything other than democracy.

4. See the ample observations on these points in Philippe Schmitter, 'Speculations about the Prospective Demise of Authoritarian Regimes and its Possible Consequences,' paper presented at the Conference on the Prospects for Democracy: Transitions from Authoritarian Rule. Woodrow Wilson Center, Washington, DC, 1980.

5. For the record, I do not believe that the bourgeoisie as a *class* can play a significant role in the advent and survival of dictatorship – at least not in the highly institutionalised party and state context of Europe.

6. Adam Przeworski, 'Some Problems in the Study of the Transition to Democracy,' paper presented at the Conference on the Prospects of Democracy, op. cit.

7. A more exhaustive discussion of the points made in this paragraph is contained in Giuseppe Di Palma, 'Party Government and Democratic Reproducibility: The Dilemma of New Democracies,' in Francis Castles (ed.), *The Future of Party Government: Problems and Concepts* (The Hague: De Greuter, 1984).

8. Guillermo O'Donnell, 'Nota Para el Estudio de Procesos de Democratization Politica a Partir del Estado Burocratico-Autoritario,' paper presented at the Conference on the Prospects of Democracy, op.cit.

9. Interview by author reported in Donald Share, 'Two Transitions: Democratization and the Evolution of the Spanish Socialist Left,' paper presented at the Annual Meeting of the American Political Science Association, Chicago, September 1983, p.12.

10. The view I will present is a somewhat sturdier view of those transitions – the Portuguese in particular – than the one I presented in 'Founding Coalitions in Southern Europe: Legitimacy and Hegemony,' *Government and Opposition*, Vol.15, No.2 (Spring 1980), pp.162–89.

11. Ibid., p.170.

12. Ibid., pp.175–8, 187.

13. At the same time, not unlike in Portugal, the president of the republic, despite the gaullist potentials of the office, has come to play a role as guarantor of constitutional equilibria and collective interests. With Karamanlis as president and Papandreou as prime minister, this has made possible what George Mavrogordatos calls a 'charismatic tandem'. George Mavrogordatos, 'Rise of the Green Sun', Centre of Contemporary Greek Studies, King's College, London, Occasional Paper 1, 1983, p.20.

14. An exhaustive and revealing analysis of PASOK's electoral convergence and why the party should be considered a centrist rather than a socialist party is contained in ibid. Of special interest are opinion data showing that the distribution of PASOK's supporters on the left-right scale is typical of a centrist party. A comparison with Giacomo Sani's identical data for Italy and Spain reveals a curve strikingly similar to that of Italy's Christian Democracy and smaller secular parties. See Giacomo Sani, 'Partiti e atteggiamenti di massa in Spagna e Italia,' *Rivista Italiana di Scienza Politica*, Vol.11, No.2, (August 1981), pp.235–79.

15. Thomas John Bossert, 'Can We Return to the Regime for Comparative Policy Analysis? or, the State and Health Policies in Central America,' *Comparative Politics*, Vol. 15, No.4 (July 1983), p.420.

16. This focus on outcomes has a reason. An extensive survey of available policy analyses reveals that almost all of them, even when authored by accredited scholars, are journalistic in style – appearing in such publications as *The Economist* and *Current History*.

17. In a formal analysis of decisional rules in democratic institutions Douglas Rae shows that more democratic institutions do not necessarily produce greater satisfaction with decisions. Douglas Rae, 'Political Democracy as a Property of Political Institutions,' *American Political Science Review*, Vol. 65, No.1 (March 1971) pp.111–29.

18. The sentence is paraphrased from my *Surviving without Governing: The Italian Parties in Parliament*, Berkeley: University of California Press, 1977, p.19. For a more extended treatment of the criterion of expectations and how it affects the evaluation of performance see ibid., pp.15–24.

19. Rustow, op.cit., p.358.

ABSTRACTS

Comparative Perspectives on the New Mediterranean Democracies:
A Model of Regime Transition?
Geoffrey Pridham

The transition to democracy in Spain, Greece and Portugal is an obvious subject for systematic comparison because of the parallel and similar development in these countries. Furthermore, the argument for considering them as a Mediterranean case-study in regime transition is strengthened by the combined approaches of comparative politics and area studies. This argument is examined with respect to both general comparative approaches and relevant theories of democratic transition. The author comes to the conclusion that in the relative sense it is indeed viable to speak of a 'Mediterranean model' of liberal democracy; this is notably evident in the uppermost question here of regime stability, relative socio-economic backwardness and the fact that political cultures have not yet been 're-made' to accord with and support the new democratic institutions. There can, however, be no absolute case for such a model, and in fact in an institutional sense these new democracies are in many respects similar to other liberal democracies in western Europe. It is held that these three cases of new democracies have essentially passed through their periods of transition and are moving towards democratic consolidation. In short, if there are 'many roads to democracy' then the three countries under review together provide one of them.

Spain's Evolutionary Pathway from Dictatorship to Democracy
Kenneth Medhurst

Spain's distinctive transition from dictatorship to liberal democracy is viewed as a still uncompleted process. The following aspects of this evolutionary transition are highlighted: the nature of Franco's dictatorship together with the political and socio-economic changes that made his regime unviable; the political options at the time of his death with an emphasis on the emergence of Suárez's government which, with monarchical support, presided over the transition process launched from within the existing state apparatus and entailing a dismantling of the dictatorship's characteristic institutions; the adoption of a new constitution with attention to those factors promoting co-operation between government and opposition and to the electorate's responses to change. Finally, more recent experience is assessed in order to evaluate liberal democracy's prospects. Emphasis is placed on a certain de-radicalisation of the polity, potentially de-stabilising violence and military institutions with a continuing if diminished veto power.

Transition to, and Consolidation of, Democratic Politics in Greece, 1974–83:
A Tentative Assessment
P. Nikiforos Diamandouros

Attention focuses on the strategies employed by the Greek civilian leadership in its attempt to effect a smooth transition to, and a lasting consolidation of, democratic politics in Greece, following the collapse of the colonels' authoritarian regime in 1974. It also seeks to relate the Greek case to the various theoretical debates concerning transition to, and consolidation of, democratic politics particularly in southern Europe and the southern cone of Latin America. The nature of consolidation in Greece and the confining conditions which affect it are specifically discussed.

Continuity and Change in Portuguese Politics: Ten Years after the Revolution of 25 April 1974
Thomas C. Bruneau

The regime founded with the Constitution of 1976 in Portugal is fundamentally different from the regimes preceding it. While continuing as a liberal democratic system, however, the regime is changing due to political instability arising not from modifications in voting, but rather the fragility of the main political parties. This instability has led to constitutional revision resulting in a format which is more parliamentary than presidential in the division of powers. However, due to the very political instability (at the party level) and the continuity in popular attitudes, the president still asserts substantial influence. Unity is currently being stressed in the context of severe economic crisis, and the party system is likely to change.

Spain: Parties and the Party System in the Transition
Mario Caciagli

Social and historical as well as institutional factors have contributed in post-Franco Spain to the formation of the party system. Other specific factors have contributed, which are dependent on the modality of the passage from authoritarism to democracy: the change managed from above and the 'reforma pactada' have conditioned the parties' capacity for solid political and organisational development. Aspects of political life in the following years (politics of 'consenso' and isolation of the political élite, demobilisation and 'desencanto') have accentuated this initial situation.

The rapid and profound changes in the choices of Spanish voters from the first elections of 1977 until the cataclysm of 1982 confirm the instability of the relationship between the parties and the electorate, and do not allow us to single out a definite model for the party system, which remains a fluctuating one. With the predominance of the PSOE, the most serious problem remains the political weakness and organisational confusion of the bourgeosie.

This analysis looks at the continuity/ discontinuity of the party system with regard to the past; the continuity in the electoral influence zones; the rejection of politics and the parties during the years 1978–80; the relationship between parties and cleavages (nationalism, classes, religion); and the typologies of the party system discussed among the political scientists.

Political Parties in Post-Junta Greece: A Case of 'Bureaucratic Clientelism'?
Christos Lyrintzis

The party system that emerged in Greece after seven years of dictatorial rule exhibited considerable similarites but also important differences in comparison to that of the period prior to the military junta. The extent and nature of these differences and similarities are examined by looking at the main political parties constituting the post 1974 party system. It is argued that although significant attempts have been made to renew and reorganise Greek political parties, traditional elements tend to persist in the new party system, notably with 'bureaucratic clientelism' as the modern form of the old clientelistic practices. Despite the smooth institutional transition from authoritarian to democratic rule in Greece, the transition from the old pattern of parties to modern well-structured political formations effectively integrating the various social forces into politics is far from being completed.

Social Cleavages and Electoral Performance: The Social Basis of Portuguese Political Parties, 1976–83
J.R. Lewis and A.M. Williams

In the ten years since the end of the Salazar regime, there has been a succession of governments and electoral coalitions in Portugal. Yet, at the same time, the social bases of electoral support have been established remarkably quickly given the infancy of democratic institutions. A study of the electoral geography of the 1976, 1980 and 1983 general elections therefore provides important insights into political developments in the country. Particular attention is paid to the relationships between the Social Democratic Party and the Socialist Party, located in the still fluid centre of the electoral spectrum. A further dimension is added to interpretation of political change, if the remarkable social and regional reverses of electoral support in the presidential elections are considered. Overall, the picture presented is one of emerging patterns of continuity, but at the same time containing serious factors of instability in what is still a new party system.

Southern European Socialism in Transition
Salvador Giner

In the early 1980s, the electoral successes of all the socialist parties in southern Europe led to the formation of socialist governments (France, Greece, Spain) or to government coalitions presided over by socialists (Italy, Portugal). This essay concentrates on socialism in the three newer liberal democracies, looking at the common features, problems and strategies of Spanish, Greek and Portuguese socialism. It examines the role played by socialists both in the various transitions to democracy and in its consolidation. The main theme in the discussion is provided by the socialist 'transition' itself, from radicalism to moderation. It investigates the shift from programmatic structural change (collectivism and revolutionary egalitarianism) towards a moral reform of public life and democratisation and modernisation in both the state and civil society. It places this in the perspective of the new political and economic arrangements of the West – which could cautiously and metaphorically be termed 'neo-corporatist' – and sees in their constraints important reasons for that shift. It concludes, however, with an emphasis on the fact that 'modernisation' and change in the once-hostile attitudes on the part of socialists towards the public realm and to politics in the South is no mean achievement.

The International Context of Democratic Transition
Alfred Tovias

As in the Spain of the 1930s, the transition and consolidation of democracy in the three southern European countries under focus have taken place in a period of world economic crisis, which indirectly threatened the experiment. However, a series of features in the international political economy (like the availability of large financial backing from international, governmental and non-governmental institutions or the existence of European integration schemes) made any repetition of history very unlikely. Moreover, there is little doubt that 'detente' in the 1970s, implying a diplomatic context entirely different from the one forty years before, eased the transition to and the consolidation of democracy.

Government Performance: An Issue and Three Cases in Search of Theory
Guiseppe Di Palma

Theories that link government performance to legitimacy in new democracies are questionable and excessively pessimistic on two grounds. First, since transferring loyalties to a new democracy is a matter of calculus and interests, and since new democracies are in the position to make that calculus appealing, it is not necessarily true that new democracies suffer from a problem of illegitimacy. Second, though in new democracies, born naturally through and into conflict, problems of government performance *seem* aplenty, it is not necessarily true that any such problem hides or feeds one of legitimacy. In fact, there are also questions about the quality of the evidence that is used to assess government performance. These points are exemplified by reference to the new democracies of southern Europe.

Index